95

15

BROWN OUT

BRIAN BELTON

BROWN OUT

A SEARCH FOR THE TRUTH

AN EXTRAORDINARY AND FASCINATING INSIGHT INTO THE FORMER WEST HAM CHAIRMAN TERENCE BROWN

First published in hardback in Great Britain 2008
by Pennant Books

British Library Cataloguing-in-Publication Data:
A catalogue record for this book is available from
The British Library

ISBN 978-1-906015-11-4

Design & Typeset by Envy Design Ltd

Printed and bound in Great Britain by William Clowes Ltd, Beccles, Suffolk

Pictures reproduced with kind permission of Action Images.

Pennant Books
A division of Pennant Publishing Ltd
PO Box 5675
London W1A 3FB
www.pennantbooks.com

Brown Out *is a search for truth.*

The honesty of Mary Wolfe has both inspired and educated me.
I dedicate this book to her, my Principal.

Acknowledgements

I am indebted to Terence and Jean Brown for their help in writing this book. Their help in terms of accuracy about Terry's time on the West Ham board were something more than invaluable.

I would also like to thank West Ham's first black player, the late John Charles, who once told me, 'They make their devils and this makes their heroes and everyone just follows like sheep. Baaa! Question that and they'll do their best to make you out a devil or a fool or a liar. Of course, that's when you really know you've found the truth!'

CONTENTS

BROWN OUT

PROLOGUE

A friend who is far away is sometimes much nearer than one who is at hand. Is not the mountain far more awe-inspiring and more clearly visible to one passing through the valley than to those who inhabit the mountain?

KAHLIL GIBRAN

May 2006. I'm sitting alone in my front room 275 miles north of the Boleyn Ground, hoping my one-year-old son doesn't wake for a couple of hours. My pregnant wife has thoughtfully taken my other two children out and, as the teams line up and 'Bubbles' echoes around the Millennium Stadium, I feel a tingle down the back of my neck.

A very different situation from when an eight-year old me sat alone in the living room of a maisonette in Dagenham and watched Brooking stoop to head home the winning goal, or five years before that when I stood outside the Black Lion pub in Plaistow, just a 10-minute wander through the back streets of Newham from Upton Park, to watch the Cup come home.

I may have experienced profound changes in my life and undergone a significant personal (and physical) journey, but there is one constant – West Ham United. It never was an option for me to do anything but support the claret and blue. My family continues to follow the trials and tribulations of the mighty Irons despite the fact that we are now distributed across the UK, from Fife to Essex via County Durham. Brian Belton's books are testament to this fact: once a Hammer always a Hammer. Brian delves into the rich social history of the East End of London, the place of my birth and the home of generations of my family, his books charting the symbiotic relationship between club, area and people.

There aren't many Dexters left within the M25 now but I will always be proud to be a Cockney and, in my mind at least, that means supporting West Ham United. I may not be the greatest West Ham fan in the world, but there remains a part of me that is forever a Hammer. It is this pride, these strong values, this passion that runs through the history of the club and the history of my family's support of the team. It doesn't matter where I am or what I'm doing, my past and my future will always be connected to West Ham United and I'll always be proud to be a Hammer.

Enjoy this book and continue to blow bubbles wherever you may be!

Stuart Dexter – husband, son, father, East Londoner, youth worker, friend, Hammer

FOREWORD

I'm dreaming dreams,
I'm scheming schemes,
I'm building castles high.
They're born anew,
Their days are few,
Just like a sweet butterfly.
And as the daylight is dawning,
They come again in the morning …

Sometimes the best way to demystify a miracle, especially when it has hardened into a mystery, is to take a fresh look at it through the eyes of an unbeliever. So, when I was offered the chance to write the Foreword for Brian's Belton's new book on Terence Brown, I immediately sought advice from the 'the girls' – my two daughters, Nadine and Ella – just as I did when I scribbled my first piece for *Over Land and Sea*. Needless to say, the feedback was positive as here I am scribbling what I think will do justice to a book that only Belton could have thought of and written.

The timing is perfect as the dust is beginning to settle on a period of history that every supporter of West Ham United will no doubt be turning over in their minds. It has been a turbulent time in the history of this club, but, contrary to what many Hammers are expecting regarding the so-called 'Icelandic Revolution', I am of the opinion that we missed a big opportunity. The so-called miracle of seeing the back end of

BROWN OUT

Terence Brown has now hardened into a 'mystery'. Terry Brown 'instinctively' knew it was time to sell up and get out, just as he 'instinctively' knew that the time was right to step into the 'hot' seat in May 1992.

Terence Brown's ascendancy as chairman of the Boleyn Castle coincided with Rupert Murdoch's BSkyB Television monopoly and the founding of the Premier League. In a certain sense, it could not have been otherwise, as Terence Brown had an 'eye' for a deal. He was to become a player (although a very tiny one) in a global football market. The globalisation of football capital has, as is now absolutely clear to everyone, facilitated off-the-field activities that have become more complex and less controllable. The transfer market is notoriously complicated, where informal chats, anonymous tip-offs and secret meetings, and the trafficking of young players have become part of the process of securing deals. Having experienced the Redknapp transfer years, where the Boleyn Castle was transformed into a revolving door as far as the ins and outs of players were concerned, Terence Brown has found himself dealing with the likes of Kia Joorabchian and his ilk.

Once events were set in motion between Terence Brown, Paul Aldridge and Kia Joorabchian's Media Sports Investments group (MSI Holdings), all kinds of rumours and myths began to unfold. At that time, very few people knew about so-called third-party agreements – although Terence and Aldridge did – but arrangements of this type, which have been very common in South America and Africa, have become part of the English game in recent years.

One of the suggestions was that West Ham United might become the East End version of a feeder club under MSI and their offshore faceless backers, until the Icelandic biscuit man and his Landsbanki backers stepped in. My family in Argentina and Brazil were telling me all about Mr Joorabchian and his business dealings when Carlos Tevez and Javier Mascherano arrived at the Boleyn.

For example, Joorabchian's relationship with Julio the 'Don' Grondona, President of the Argentine Football Association and a Loyal Lieutenant of FIFA's Sepp Blatter, was on every 'serious' commentator's lips as was his business dealings at Corinthians Football Club. Nothing moves in Argentina without the 'Don' knowing about it and, of course, that includes giving the 'nod' for a deal to go through or not. Joorabchian's astute business eye would sweep over the football landscape, littered as it is with insolvent clubs and pick off the brightest young talent, naturally paying their families, who are from poor working-class backgrounds, a pittance. In short, the great majority of them could almost be viewed as 21st-century serfs. Business hawks or, if you like, head hunters buy shares in the 'economic rights' of young players, often paying initially for the players' training or accommodation; then these fixers become entitled to all or a big chunk of any transfer fee if the players do well and are 'sold' on to a bigger club.

Pinhas 'Pini' Zahavi, the Israeli 'super-agent', learned this trade in South America. In fact, his close associate Gustavo Mascardi, an Argentinean, knows the Argentine and South American football market inside out. For some years now, Zahavi has been acting as an 'adviser' to Global Soccer Agencies, the company with a half-share in Mascherano. Zahavi helped broker the deal that brought the two players to West Ham. Pini Zahavi was no stranger to Terence Brown; he had dealt with the agent during the sale of Rio Ferdinand to Leeds United. Gustavo Mascardi was behind the Juan Pablo Angel transfer to Aston Villa. If you followed that 'tale', you will no doubt know that a great part of the money for the transfer fee ended up in bank accounts all over the world including Bogotá and, predictably, Switzerland.

Everyone seemed to have their fingers in the proverbial football pie at Corinthians, the club of the great Brazilian maestro Socrates. There was the exiled Russian Mr Berezovsky, now in permanent exile in London, as well as his close business partner from Tbilisi, Georgia, Badri Patarkatsishvili, the chairman of Dynamo Tbilisi Football Club. Badri had been 'touted' at the time, as the 'real' man behind the West Ham negotiations. On 12 July 2007, a Brazilian judge issued arrest warrants for Berezovsky and Joorabchian, as well as a number of other British and Brazilian suspects, in connection with an investigation against the MSI, which are accused of money laundering. Joorabchian resigned as secretary. Berezovsky was thought to be the main financial backer of MSI. Since Berezovsky, Kia Joorabchian and a certain Noyan Bedru were not in Brazil at the time, the warrants for their arrest were forwarded to Interpol. Berezovsky dismissed the Brazilian investigation as a part of the Kremlin's 'politicised campaign' against him.

It all began so idealistically under the so-called tutelage of Tony Blair and Alistair 'the best ever all-round spinner' Campbell. When the Labour government came to power in 1997, we were all told that football had to clean up its act. Grotesque amounts of money are being made to the detriment of the fans, we were advised. The game of football has been at the centre of British cultural life for well over a hundred years. Football fans are at the heart of the game and are being 'ripped off' and it has to be 'stopped'. The game must be given 'back' to the fans where it has historically belonged.

But, for all the huffing and puffing of the Blair/Campbell offensive partnership, nothing, *absolutely nothing*, of substance has been achieved regarding the control of the sickening amounts of money that are being made through the Premier League to the detriment of the grass roots. In fact, it has gone in the opposite direction. The so-called 'Independent Football Commission', launched by the Blair government all 'guns blazing', and which was hailed as the panacea for our game, has disappeared. Every thoughtful lover of football senses that there is something fundamentally rotten at the heart of the sport and what we are all living through will have to change. Whether it is through the direct involvement of the fans or through the internal implosion of the whole enterprise, something *will* happen because it cannot continue in this way. A very astute observer of life once said: 'All that is human turns to dust.' Belton's book will open the door to the mystery that was Terence Brown.

John Ballantyne – *Over Land and Sea*, West Ham fanzine, est. 1989

INTRODUCTION

Who are you going to believe, me or your own eyes?
GROUCHO MARX

This book is the story of a complex time and an enigmatic man. He came into an institution steeped in tradition that was based partly on myth but founded on a distinctive local culture that he himself rose out of. The story of his experience blended with the organisation he led is, some might say, a tale of intricate manoeuvring and at times confusing complexity. However, for me, an historian of sport in general, and football and one East London incarnation of the game in particular, what follows is a study of power, intrigue, politics and the place of a peculiarly culturally clad sporting entity in the era of global financial dealing that no controlling body has been able as yet to fully understand or come close to managing.

At this time, the economics of football might be translated metaphorically as a reincarnation of Dodge City. It has its Wyatt Earp and Doc Holliday figures, brave yet necessarily flawed enforcers that just about manage to hold back the excesses of the milieu that are enacted by individuals often portrayed as figures synonymous with the Clantons and McLaurys, taking full advantage of the situation that teeters on the cusp of chaos. At times, it is hard to tell the difference between sheriff and outlaw as the dealing, ducking and diving fragments into a multidimensional drama that gets played out on the event horizon of an economic black hole.

Hence, the days of the 'local football club' have long gone. As you take your seat in your stadium of choice, you have been sucked into the ergosphere of an international financial maelstrom. The modern chairman looks out on this prospect. The reward is to milk the stars; the danger is tumbling into the singularity and the certain destruction which will follow.

THE ANONYMOUS CHAIR

During his time with West Ham United, Terence 'Terry' Brown showed himself to be much more than a 'what you see is what you get' chairman in the mould of, say, Wigan's Dave Whelan. Nor has he been the sort of 'Jack the lad' entertainer boardroom figure that the likes of Simon Jordon evoke. Indeed, when he has been involved in one type of get-together or another with his fellow chairmen, he has tended to observe the resulting crashing of egos with a measured contempt.

For most of his time as a board member at Upton Park, Brown has remained a shadowy figure, not prone to courting publicity or fame. He became a public figure only after accusations about mismanagement of the club obliged him to respond openly.

Brown rarely gives interviews and few pictures of him exist. He has confessed to purposely fostering a relatively inconspicuous role as chairman, in comparison to his counterparts at other clubs. During his sojourn as the Hammers head honcho, Brown never felt that his relative anonymity was a problem, considering that job was being done by the club website, which provided information on a daily basis. But he struggled with persuading the tabloid press to comment on any good news or sensible arguments when West Ham put forward explanations of the board's position, especially in times when the club's financial situation looked less than healthy.

When questioned about the growing profile of football chairmen, Terry recalled Jimmy Greaves writing in the *Sun*, 'There was a time when you couldn't even name a football-club chairman let alone recognise them in the street. They were grey-suited men who drank white wine in the bowels of the main stand and watched unrecognised from the best seats. They let the manager and players get on with the game and take the limelight their efforts warrant. However, nowadays, there is an egotistical breed of chairmen who think they know it all.'

When Terry became a member of the West Ham board, there was an unwritten policy that the chairman did what he could to stay in the background; this demonstrated an understanding that the players were the stars of the club, but it also avoided any potential criticism. Few cared or really knew what the board did, so up to the 1960s any dissatisfaction was vented on the players; thereafter, when most managers began to take on responsibility from their boards for the selection of teams, they too became open to censure.

Brown always believed that the board remaining relatively anonymous was the best way of doing things. Around the start of 2004, he had wanted to adopt a higher profile because of the need to explain to fans the causes of and strategy that would be used to address the problems the club was facing, both on and off the pitch, but he did not see that as contradicting the practice of the chairman staying out of the limelight.

In common with most of the West Ham directors of his era and before, it continues to be very difficult to find anything about

BROWN OUT

Brown's background before football. This might make a deal of sense from his personal perspective, but among the rank and file of supporters it can also raise suspicions, especially those of us brought up in an East End culture that can often interpret secrecy as having something to hide. Brown's detachment certainly had its cost among the players, some of whom nicknamed him 'Mr Dead' – a character on the *Harry Enfield Television Show* – as Brown had the habit of wearing a very serious demeanour when he ventured into the dressing room. However, it must be said, others have seen Terry as a sort of father figure, who has guided and helped them from their earliest days. I have often seen him in the pouring rain stand and watch the youngest West Ham teams play out the most dour of games. It is hard to think of a more consistent and faithful Hammers spectator, right across the club's age range, than Terry Brown.

BROWN THE FAN

Brown has more than once talked of how he is basically a West Ham fan and, unlike many of his peers, this is more than rhetoric. A few hours after the last game of the 1992/93 season, a 2–0 win against Cambridge United, which guaranteed the Irons promotion to the Premiership, Brown asked the groundsman to leave the floodlights on for a few hours so he and his younger brother, Ken, could have an improvised kickabout behind closed doors with a few friends on the sacred Boleyn Ground.

The Browns were defeated 5–3, and Terry cites his wife Jean's poor goalkeeping as the main cause of the loss. But, as Jean is just five feet tall and was obliged to play her part in high heels, which caused her to be a tad slow coming off her line, combined with the fact that Billy Bonds, then manager of the club, later let Brown know that he would have turned out for his side if he had known of the game, it would seem that Terry's team selection might also have been questionable.

This is something most of us who have known and loved West Ham all our lives would have done given half a chance. It is the activity of someone who feels the hum of Hammers belonging and wants to be part of whatever that is.

The West Ham Museum was, for a time, a source of personal pride for Terry. He has been an avid collector of Hammers memorabilia for many years and I have had the privilege of a personal view of much of it. His most treasured possession is the 1923 FA Cup Final ball that he loaned to the museum. Second on his list of prized items is the 1923 semi-final ball from the match at Stamford Bridge against Derby County, which the Irons won 5–2. Both footballs are signed by the respective teams. Terry also has an England cap awarded to Len Goulden for the international match in 1938 against the Rest of Europe. Brown has told of how the club have a vast amount of memorabilia which was not displayed in the museum and he had hoped one day that these items might be exhibited in the Dr Martens Stand. However, the museum, that was an expensive novelty for the pockets of the fans, lodged in one room at the back of the club shop, proved to be a failure and closed a few seasons ago.

When Brown, Cearns and Warner, the 'old guard' of the West Ham board, left the club, the scale models of the Thames Ironworks ships that had adorned the interior of the Dr Martens Stand were banished with them, and the impressive sight of the HMS *Warrior* no longer imposes itself on the lobby of the main entrance to the Upton Park hotel and administration complex but, as a quarter-of-a-million-pound artefact, lies deteriorating in storage, banished by the current regime as a reminder of the past.

In the 16 years prior to his resignation as club chairman,

Brown missed just one home and one away game. After the 'Chicken Run' was rebuilt and transformed into the new East Stand, Terry and Jean took up places there. Later, of course, the Browns used the Boleyn Executive Lounge and then the Academy Suite, before finally concluding a lifelong tour of the stadium by moving into the directors' box. Brown has always thought that, when he finished his time on the board, he would return to the East Stand, making the proviso that it would be if he was allowed in by the existing incumbents, which in the near future doesn't seem very likely.

Terry met Jean at a party to celebrate West Ham's 1964 FA Cup success. Like many supporters, he didn't have a ticket for Wembley (but I did!) and wasn't a season-ticket holder at that time; however, he attended a celebration party at the Tate & Lyle Social Club in Silvertown. He has few memories of that evening as Jean takes up the horizon of his memories of that particular 'do'.

The mid-1960s was a time of transformation for the Hammers. The successes of 1964 and 1965 and, of course, the World Cup win in 1966 shaped Brown's mature view of the club he has supported from boyhood. Qualifying for Europe between 1964 and 1966 was enormously important and, for Brown, along with most other supporters of his generation, this provided a powerful feeling that West Ham United represented the area and people of which it is part. At the same time, the era created what the club would become over the remainder of the 20th century. However, by the first years of the new millennium, that symbiosis would be severely tested and its future threatened.

It is hard to translate today the enormous impact the Hammers glory years had on the Docklands district. Today it would be like winning the Premiership and Champions League in successive seasons. Hence, for Brown, qualifying for European competition in 1999 and 2006 couldn't compare to that magic time in terms of the Hammers' potential to make an impact on an international level, although he naturally enjoyed both the qualification and the games the Hammers played.

Before the end of the 'swinging' decade, Terry had a season ticket for the West Stand at Upton Park. Those with season tickets were (and to some extent still are) a sort of preliminary shareholder at any club. In the 1960s and 1970s, becoming one of this elite was a mark of a closer bond with the club; no longer a foot soldier, bustling on the terraces, the season-ticket holder, along with a guaranteed seat and segregated social facilities, gained political and organisational clout as an embryonic investor in the future (albeit maybe just one season) of the Hammers. As such, this part in Brown's life might be recognised as the beginning of his movement up the Upton Park food chain.

TO THE BOARD

At the point when Brown joined the West Ham board, they were an odd, seemingly eccentric group relative to those one might expect to find populating the dens of modern commerce. No one appeared to put much in in the way of financial support. As had been the case for much of the club's history, the Cearns family held sway. Barclays bank manager Martin Cearns had recently 'inherited' the role of chairman from his dad Len, who had been a director at Upton Park since 1948. Len was elected vice-chairman soon after the death of his father, W. J., in 1950, and succeeded Reg Pratt as chairman in May 1979. So Martin was the fourth generation from the Cearns family to be involved with the West Ham board. Martin's uncles, Will and Brian, were also board members.

The rest of the 'team' was made up of a few businessmen and

members of the Hills family whose forebear Arnold is recognised as the founder of the club that was first incarnated as Thames Ironworks in 1895. Senior among the Hills 'clan' in the last part of the 20th century was Charles Warner, the cousin of Arnold Hills's grandson Patrick.

During Brown's first days as a director (and well before), Cearns the elder was known as 'Mr Len' around Upton Park. A bit like a local squire, although he was a property contractor by profession, he was shown deference by nearly everybody in the employ of the Hammers. Most fans my age and younger saw him as a removed headmaster figure. Len and the Cearns tribe certainly were not objects of hate, but they had something of an artificial aristocratic air about them which set them apart.

Of course, there are always some supporters who are proud of the club's tradition of carrying the likes of the Cearns and Hills families spluttering into the modern world, but to many their perceived pretensions and pomposity were as archaic and foreign as feudalism.

The 'West Ham way' seemed to be the mystic ideology that held this group together. To me, every time that phrase was uttered it brought to mind the 'Lambeth Walk' and, in fact, it was a dance at one point. This credo was supposed to have included employing managers dedicated to producing attractive attacking football, although that was more a rumour than an actuality as the flirtation with Lou Macari demonstrated. Sid King, the Hammers' first manager, was a pragmatist first and foremost, and the teams that his successor Charlie Paynter produced were known more for their dour physical presence than anything else. Ted Fenton was no more than a figurehead, and the work of players John Bond, Ken Brown, Malcolm Allison and Noel Cantwell really produced the successful teams of the late 1950s and early/mid-1960s that Ron Greenwood inherited. Greenwood was always acknowledged as a great coach, but was never a 'man manager' and, after the end of the 'Allison effect' in 1965, really did not achieve very much at Upton Park. This wasn't surprising, given that significant members of his squad often turned up for training or even matches the worse for drink from the night before, a cultural trait of the Hammers that Ron seemed to have no means of addressing. John Lyall, a hard-man defender in his playing days, did create sides that punched well above their weight, and is probably the best manager West Ham has ever had, but he was effectively betrayed in terms of the 'West Ham way' and was replaced by Macari, who hardly had time to make any impact at all. Billy Bonds led by example and did well, but Bonzo was brought in more to appease angry fans still smarting from the dismissal of Lyall than to promote the 'West Ham way'. His position was usurped by Harry Redknapp with board member Peter Storrie playing a background role. 'H' did provide entertainment, but a lot of the time it was more reminiscent of a Fred Karno's circus than Real Madrid.

However, the 'West Ham way' did have some credence in the club's ability to produce young talent, but, certainly over the years, this has had more to do with the talent and dedication of Academy director Tony Carr and coach Jimmy Frith and the interest of Brown than with any West Ham manager.

BUSINESS IS BUSINESS

Professional football is a business; professional clubs are companies, they sell shares and so have shareholders. While we the fans know this *intellectually*, I'm not sure we have ever accepted this in our hearts. We see football as belonging to us and spiritually it does. But the material aspects of the game are 'owned'. Belonging is an ephemeral desire, a wishful feeling that is expressed and realised by collectives. Ownership is founded on economic theory and law and has its carnal incarnation in documentation (contracts, bonds, etc.). Brown made around £31m by selling his stake (7,392,000 shares) in West Ham United, Charles Warner (4,252,000 shares) £17.9m and Martin Cearns (1,844,000 shares) £7.76m. The price of a season ticket with an unrestricted view in Upton Park's Upper East Stand was at that time £620.

Like any shareholder, Brown and his colleagues had the right to sell to the highest bidder, including foreigner investors, who bring in new finance, but, as this book will demonstrate, this is very different to the kind of financial bedrock provided by the likes of the Cearns family. This 'brave new world' is, in fact, a 'world apart', not a place that Terry was equipped to thrive in and he knew it. He hinted at this in the winter of 2006 when he wrote, 'I am pleased with many things that I have achieved but in my heart of hearts I knew that it would be impossible for me to take us on to the next level as everyone craved. Football has changed beyond recognition from when I first became chairman. In those days, local businessmen who were fans ran their local clubs. That is not the situation now. Today top clubs are run by international businessmen with funding coming from across the globe.'

Just as the Cearns family made way for Brown to take on the aggressive football economics of the 1980s and 1990s, so Brown has been pushed aside by a form of commerce in which he really has no place.

From the beginnings of professional football in Britain, the football market has taken little account of the game's history, or the emotional ties that fans have to the clubs they support. But until quite recently it was in the interests of those involved in that market to look as if they *did* treasure the essential soul of the sport. Many, like Terry Brown, certainly did have affection for the team they were involved with, but the bottom line was, and had to be, business. Put simply: no business, no club – or at least not a club that people in their tens of thousands would want to put their hands in their pockets to pay to watch.

But the belief still continues that the soul of football has to be protected from naked financial speculation and this has, in part, given rise to the movement which has seen supporters' trusts formed at many English clubs.

The government has given its support to the trusts, and over three years the former Sports Minister Richard Caborn oversaw increased funding of £1.8m to Supporters Direct, which championed fan involvement in the running of clubs. But the government has done little, and probably can do little more, to enable supporters to purchase the kind of stakes in clubs that would give them any meaningful influence.

Indeed, the whole notion of 'fan ownership' is becoming less and less achievable as the commercial success of the Premier League continues to price clubs out of any market entry within the reach of fans.

Shareholders United, aka the Manchester United Supporters Trust, boasted 32,000 members at the height of the protests against the Glazer takeover at Old Trafford, but were unable to stop the £1 billion buyout. Like the Icelandic coup at Upton Park, this was financed by way of hedge funds. The dealings hauled a great weight of debt on to the decks at United, the future impact of which can only be guessed at, or feared in the light of what happened to Northern Rock late in 2007 and the American 'sub-prime' loan market, which in the long run can only mean that borrowing will be harder/more expensive.

The notion that football clubs are mutual organisations, wherein supporters and directors co-operate for the good of the club, was reinvigorated as a notion as part of the commercialism that engulfed football following the 1992 creation of the Premiership. This drew on football's social heritage. The majority of clubs started out as institutions formed by people keen to organise the game as a beneficial pastime in an era that regarded physical activity as 'character building' and a boon to the good of the Empire and the nation. West Ham, like some others, started with the support of an employer, with a mixture of pious moral objectives and their own fiscal ends in mind (a happy, fit workforce is a loyal, productive workforce).

The Football Association, the body of governance and as such guardian of football's soul and its laws, in the last decade of the 19th century sanctioned clubs becoming limited companies. This gave the clubs protection from personal liability that might accrue from the growing costs of catering for the mass audience football could command.

The consequence of this was that clubs could sell shares to attract finance. But, in order to prevent football from transforming into just another means for investors to make profits, the FA prohibited club directors from giving themselves salaries and restricted the amounts of money that could be paid out in dividends – Rule 34. Ways were found to circumvent these limitations, but, in the main, they worked to stop the worst excesses of commercialism impinging on the game. However, with Saturday crowds amounting to millions by the 1920s and 1930s and players being paid a pittance under the low ceiling of the maximum wage, someone must have been doing all right out of the game.

In 1983, Tottenham Hotspur became the first club to float on the stock market, which changed everything. A holding company was formed by the Spurs board and this allowed them to evade the FA's rules, a situation which went unchallenged by the FA.

As the urge to 'follow the Spurs' grew exponentially, the Football Supporters Federation (FSF) stood by and watched impotently. No one argued for the retention and strict application of the spirit of Rule 34, the protective gift of the game's founding fathers. Hence, we plunged into uncharted oceans of multi-billion-pound television contracts and the creation of the accretion disc that vacuumed in players (good and bad) from every corner of the planet.

Meanwhile, the FSF threw itself behind the government's Football Task Force (FTF) that in 1999 made the case for better regulation to allow football to exploit its commercial potential more effectively, but at the same time the FTF didn't want it to betray the game's roots or values. If ever there was a contradiction in aims, that was it. The proposal was Rule 34 turned on its Victorian head.

Either through a purposeful effort to divert or kill off action or just blithering naivety, the FSF championed supporters taking on significant stakes in clubs and restrictions on the price of tickets, and called for a 'fit-and-proper-person test' to be applied to football-club directors and for the FA to make sure that future takeovers of clubs would be in their best long-term interests.

The FA, the Premier and Football Leagues dismissed all of this (of course), saying that regulation of the commercial era was superfluous. The government did not challenge this view. Football shareholders made millions on the stock market but this did not make clubs more stable financially. In fact, it probably made matters worse for many.

Now there really are no restraints on foreign finance coming into the English game, as takeovers become commonplace, and debt increases as everyone looks to Chelsea as a financial model, instead of the madness it encapsulates. Roman Abramovich, the Glazers (who chucked about £660m of borrowed money into Manchester United, a club that had been previously free of debt) and Randy Lerner are welcomed with open arms.

BROWN OUT

All these people have fronted the creation of fragile entities. Look north to Hearts and their encounter with Vladimir Romanov. Foreign financiers want profit and are not too concerned about how they get it. But overseas owners are a far too easy target. For every Romanov, there's a Bates; nationality doesn't really come into it. All massive finance is now international and hedge funds and offshore banks are not just the tools of non-British speculators. Those who have sold out to foreign owners have been British nationals and they have trotted off and invested their money somewhere else (maybe abroad). However, at least Terry Brown had some connections with West Ham that transcended finance.

Now the game is purely money as far as major shareholders are concerned. This has no colour and no country; it has no restraints and is not held in check by any morality or ethical limitations. All we can do is stand by and watch. Money talks in any language.

Perhaps we can look with hope to Spain. Barcelona and Real Madrid remain clubs founded and run on membership; Barça players wore Unicef on their shirts as they claimed victory in the Champions League while keeping tickets for seats at the Camp Nou within the range of their supporters' pockets. But Spanish football is Asda compared to the Harrods of the English game. The greatest football market by far has its centre in England and the Premiership and, amid the game's biggest ever boom, everything – players, grounds, clubs – has a price. A handful of shareholders who have had stakes in clubs for decades – the likes of Martin Edwards, Doug Ellis, the Cearns family and Brown – benefit, but now, just like the fans, they, too, are being pushed by forces to which they are not equal.

The chronicle of Terry Brown's era of influence at West Ham provides a unique insight into this world and what it really means. It is a universe in which few of us would want to exist.

Brown is remarkable because he sailed those waters. An East End entrepreneur who started his working life as a factory janitor, he knew how to operate with all the killer instinct and Cockney cunning often seen as indicative of the district into which he was born.

CHAPTER 1
CHANGE

All changes, even the most longed for, have their melancholy;
for what we leave behind us is a part of ourselves; we must die to
one life before we can enter another.
ANATOLE FRANCE

Two points but 14 goals behind Aston Villa – who would live on in the Barclays First Division – West Ham finished the 1988/89 season seven points clear of the bottom club Newcastle United. John Lyall, the Hammers manager in the late 1980s, was greying, but he was still a fit man, despite his passion for cigarettes. He had taken his side to a League Cup semi-final in 1989; however, that achievement had been cancelled out by the 5–0 aggregate destruction at the hands of Luton Town.

But the Hammers' relegation – only their third in the club's near-century of history – from the top flight of English football had been more than a season-long saga. The previous term, they had scraped 16th place, yet were separated from 'drop boys' Chelsea by only half-a-dozen goals. However, the mediocre 1986/87 campaign, which saw the Irons lodged in 15th position, should have been ringing alarm bells and appropriate action taken. However, time had run out and the days, weeks, months and years to come were to be marked by a revolution in the way West Ham was run.

This said, there is no way that John Lyall or anyone else could have predicted that Monday, 5 June 1989 would be the start of the transformation in the East End of London. This sudden evolution would see the steady plod of comfortable tradition – which like all custom offered the security of predictability – make way for a brand of razor entrepreneurship that rode on the blisteringly sharp edge of an unforgiving business credo, harnessing West Ham's 94-year inheritance of sentiment, hope, loyalty and identity.

Lyall woke up in his home in the Essex countryside to a beautiful sunny day. Nine days before, he had scheduled a meeting with his chairman for that morning; the telephone call he got while working at West Ham's training ground in Chadwell Heath summoning him to the home of Len Cearns, the West Ham chairman of 10 years standing, would not have been a surprise. John often met with the chairman there.

It wasn't hard for John to fit Cearns into his schedule that summer day in 1989. The players were away on their close-season break. John was planning pre-season training and thinking about a schedule of friendly games with his coaching staff. He was looking forward to the weekend that would mark the start of his only break in a year. He was going to the Norfolk Broads for a week of fishing. John had kept West Ham with the elite of the nation's football for seven seasons, taking the Hammers as high as they had ever been in 1986, just 10 years after he had guided the East Londoners to the final of the European Cup Winners Cup. At that time, he had been in only his second year as team manager, working alongside the club's general manager Ron Greenwood. Lyall had experienced relegation before (West Ham's first for 46 years) and after three campaigns in the old Division Two had led the Irons gloriously back among the big boys as Champions in 1981 (that was only the Hammers' second major Championship victory and the first for 23 years). The same year, he had seen his side unluckily defeated by Liverpool in the League Cup Final, just a year after his underdog Second Division Hammers had beaten the mighty Arsenal in the FA Cup Final.

Lyall arrived at 1 Meadow Way, Chigwell, on the edge of Epping Forest, at the arranged time of 10.30 a.m. The home of Len Cearns and his family since before the Second World War was less than half an hour's drive for Lyall in the club Mercedes from Chadwell Heath. He met with 'Mr Len' in his dining room, which like the rest of the house reflected Cearns's conservative, conventional nature.

The two men sat facing each other over the big family dining table. As was the usual practice when the chairman and the manager met at Meadow Way, the table had papers laid out on it. But Lyall had not been offered the customary handshake or a cup of tea and he sensed that Cearns was tense. John was an astute man and his time with men in the game had made him sensitive to the atmospheres generated by human emotions. The pleasure of glory, the anxiety and apprehension that permeates the pre-match ambience and the fear of the great opponents all had a kind of smell for Lyall; people's eyes betray their souls and John was a man that had made a habit of reading the slightest flickers exuded by human tells. If ever you spoke to John, you felt him – always with a slight smile on his face – reading you.

Cearns was an involved chairman compared to many of his era. He would visit Upton Park once or twice a week and wasn't a man to shirk from giving his opinion to managers. But this always fell short of interference and John never felt that there was anything less than mutual respect between him and his chairman, although they were never friends in any sense.

John's four-year contract was due to end on 30 June and Cearns came straight to the point; the decision had been made by the board (Cearns, his brother Will, son Martin, along with property developer Jack Petchey and solicitor Charles Warner). He told arguably West Ham's most successful manager ever, the man who had been leading the Irons for 15 years and was the First Division's longest-serving manager, 'I'm sorry, John, but the directors have had a meeting, and by a majority decision have decided not to renew your contract. I don't want to go into details. The decision is irreversible.'

I have met John Lyall many times during my life, as a young footballer, a youth worker and a few times as a writer during the period between leaving Upton Park and his untimely passing in April 2006. Along with his charming wife Yvonne, he made me and my family extremely welcome at his farmhouse, situated not too far from Ipswich. John immediately befriended my son Christian as I have seen him win over so many shy lads over the years. None of us has forgotten how one of the Lyall family's 'guard geese' bit my wife Rosy's bum as Yvonne was showing her and my young son around the grounds (Christian was helpless with laughter for days after and still smiles when we talk about it now … oh yeah, so does Rosy).

John was an adorable man, one of those people you could listen to for hours and come away knowing that you had been educated, but also cared about. Over the years, I have interviewed more than a hundred current and former West Ham players and have yet to come across anyone who had a bad word to say about him. This is amazing because those players cover the club's history from the 1920s to the present day and all the time John was at the club. It is a remarkable testimony to the man who for me was and is the Hammers' greatest ever manager. Why? Because he was not just a manager of his players; he was 'our' manager, of all the Hammers. He was genuinely concerned about us and never lost sight of the fact that fans are more than supporters. He knew that they are the lifeblood of the club and, first and foremost, human beings who respond to kindness and respect.

The removal of John Lyall happened a few months before Terry Brown was asked to join the West Ham United board of directors in 1990. Brown accepted the role without any reservations.

At the time Terry was a well-known figure among the higher echelons of the club's culture. He had four seats in the Academy Suite and had been an executive club member since 1982. Terry had served on the testimonial committees for Eddie Chapman (former Hammer and chief executive of the club), Phil Parkes and Tony Gale and had sponsored Billy Bonds's testimonial game. Brown had also arranged testimonial weeks for players at his Sussex Beach Holiday Village. These men were granted this type of reward in recognition of their loyalty to the club. These events boosted the players' funds but also attracted holidaymakers to the resort (near to Earnley, with the sea views of Bracklesham Bay, near 'The Witterings' villages, eight miles from Chichester) that Brown and his brother Ken owned. The Village also sponsored cars for certain players, advertised and sponsored matches. The village hosted 'West Ham United Soccer Weeks' and a Penalty Prize competition. Terry and his brother Ken, alongside three former Upton Park heroes, Tony Gale, Phil Parkes and Alvin Martin, were an unbeaten five-a-side team at the Holiday Village.

As such, the influence of Brown and the regard for his approach to corporate development were being absorbed into West Ham's bloodstream well before he became involved at board level. Perceived as a young, aspiring champion of business, Brown represented a force of modern commerce pulsating and growing within the 'body politic' of the inner courts of the Upton Park presidium.

In 1990, long before the question of supporters' trusts arose, the Hammers board were looking for supporter representation, but this was not going to be drawn from the then current ranks of the North or South Banks or even the famous Chicken Run at the Boleyn Ground. Brown, already established via the authority of his actions and the influence of his business achievements, was seen as a prime candidate for this position together with 41-year-old Peter Storrie, a director of a furniture company, who in his time at Upton Park was to hold a number of posts from managing director and chief executive to (amazingly) director of football before taking up similar roles with Portsmouth, Southend United (where his salary of £120,000 a season raised more than a few eyebrows) and Notts County.

As these 'young bloods' stood on the starting line of power, being brought in by the old guard to enable and facilitate change, Cearns would have needed to show himself equal to the cause to which he had set them. The ending of the Lyall years was the start of a new dynasty led by an ethic that had always been present within the environs of the Boleyn Ground, but which until that moment had been restricted by the perceived need to present at least a veneer of an institutional soul and the restraining power of a community ethos.

A legend had been ousted, one that would still be celebrated long after those who banished him were forgotten.

For the first time in 27 years, West Ham had fired a manager. The last had been Ted Fenton, although Ted's departure was never actually termed a sacking. John's answer to Cearns's statement was typical of the stoical strength of the man: 'Fair enough, Mr Len.'

John never found out who on the board had voted for or against him. He told me that, although he had been at Upton Park for 34 years, having done almost every job in the club (except he'd never been asked to cover a turnstile), he was not shocked by what happened; he was just surprised by the *way* it happened.

Cearns asked Lyall to agree to a press statement that told of the club not wishing to renew his contract. John refused, saying he wanted to be free to say what he thought fit. The chairman told Lyall he was prepared to wait 24 hours before releasing the news. Lyall told him, 'You've made your decision ... I think it should be made public immediately.'

The West Ham chairman then gave his house guest the option to resign. John, a man of great integrity and honesty, and feeling that everyone associated with the club should know the truth, replied, 'No thanks, Mr Len. If I've been dismissed, I've been dismissed.'

Years later, John told me, 'I didn't want to hide the truth. I thought it was important that people knew what happened.'

Lyall knew how everyone in football would see the West Ham board if the whole truth was known. Cearns was, of course, understandably reticent about this. The chairman then told John that the club were happy to organise a second testimonial for him (Lyall had been given a testimonial after he was forced by injury to retire from playing). He turned this down, feeling that the fans had done enough for him; that they owed him nothing. In fact, he felt that he owed *them* for the loyalty they had shown to him over the years.

Later, John did accept an *ex-gratia* payment of around £100,000 plus the Mercedes he had used to drive to his last meeting at Chigwell.

On his return to Chadwell Heath, Lyall told his coaching staff, Mick McGiven, Tony Carr and Billy Bonds (Ronnie Boyce was on holiday), about what had happened. Naturally, they were taken aback by the news. John told me, 'I didn't have any idea that I was going to be fired. I was just thinking about the next season. When I had thought about it at all, I thought that things might go the same way as they did with Ron Greenwood, taking on a job like general manager. I'm not sure I would have wanted that but I would have thought about it. In football, you're always going to be judged on your most recent record, that's the way it is and you accept that, but the board had shown in the way they worked with Ron [Greenwood] that they knew about the value of continuity as far as managing the team was concerned. West Ham had been relegated and so you would expect some response to that.

'Unavoidably, the meeting with the chairman was difficult after he spoke about the board's decision. He was very matter-of-fact, cold, particularly considering I'd been at the club for the best part of 35 years. But that might have been nerves. He was doing his job as the club chairman and I think he believed that what he did was the best thing for the club, although it was a bit strange as it wasn't the usual way West Ham went about that sort of thing.

'Was I upset? I don't know how anyone couldn't be after all that time. But looking back I felt a bit numb. I didn't know how to react really. But, by the time I got back in the car, I had accepted the fact and that, as I couldn't do a thing about it, I had to get on with things. You have to make the most of what you've got in the end and it wasn't too hard to see what advantages there were.

'The aspect of it that stayed with me, what disappointed me in a lasting way, was that the chairman didn't offer even a word of thanks. There was no handshake either. I got up from the chair, then he stood up on the other side of the table and, after walking out of the dining room, I let myself out of the front door. It was nice to get outside.' John smiled and gave a little chuckle.

The statement from the board that followed the meeting between Cearns and Lyall was noteworthy mostly for its brevity:

CHANGE

'West Ham United FC directors have decided not to offer John Lyall a new contract as club manager at the end of his present contract which expires on 30 June. The directors would like to thank John Lyall for his long and loyal service to the club. Ron Boyce and Mick McGiven will formally take charge of the players and management until a new manager is appointed. The vacant position will be advertised.'

Taking this together with the nature of the meeting between chairman and manager, there is a strong suggestion that the board were seeking to make a point about what they wanted the club to be and how they were going to act in future. Although the club made a profit close to £1.5m in 1988/89 despite relegation, a line in the sand had been drawn that seemed to be saying something quite definite about what was perhaps seen as 'functioning in a businesslike way'. That sentiment and not issues about loyalty – which may have been paid lip service in the past – was going to be the guiding principle of West Ham United in the future. Lyall might be seen to have been used as an example of a new attitude that would dictate policy at Upton Park from then on.

When I asked John about this, he reflected, 'Mr Len and Mr Will and their late brother, Brian, were good professional friends to me and what happened did feel out of character with them and the club. I think it would be fair to say that something had changed or that the board seemed to want to do things differently to the way things had been done in the past. What caused that, I don't know. But things don't come from nowhere or, when something happens, it has a cause … it's anybody's guess. Of course, knowing about all that wouldn't make any difference to my situation so it wasn't on my list of things to think about, although, looking back, it probably did mark a change in the way things were done at West Ham. But perhaps that was for the best in the long run.'

Lyall was among the most loved people in football. His dismissal stunned players, fans and backroom staff. Player Tony Gale likened John's departure to a 'death in the family'.

Like many of those who have been associated with West Ham for several years, Lyall thought of Upton Park and the club as 'his', but pretty quickly he decided to look to the future, basically because there are no other options in life. 'When something happens, it happens. I don't see this as fatalistic; I see it as a kind of optimism. One door closes, another usually opens, certainly if you push hard enough.'

He smiled. 'I think that you've just got to live for today and tomorrow. Yesterday can't be taken away from you. I don't need to talk about it to anyone; they were great times. You just have to say, well, I was just grateful for what I had. I'm not a religious man, but do unto others.

'When I left West Ham, I had well over a thousand letters. It would have made a marvellous book. I can't believe there's that many good people about. I don't think you'd get that now. The club was good to me and the fans were good to me and the players were good to me. That means a lot to me. They're the people you've come through.

'Football people are always grateful; they don't want anything. I've offered people work scouting and they've said, "No thanks, I'm all right." I know they need money, but all they want is for you to give them a ring, to ask if they're all right. I still get people ring me once a month after all these years. I think that's terrific. If I was in a position that I could help in any way, I would give them anything. That's more important than anything. It's a great game and it should have great people. It needs great people.

'As a young boy, I was a football fan. I loved football. Then, when I became a player, the players that I was with helped me. Players helped me when I was a coach and when I was a manager. They're your own people. I've still got a lot of great friends at the club. I can't control what happens; that's part of your job. I, at least, had a chance, because some people go into work, they work 30 years at something they hate. I loved my days at West Ham.'

Here John was saying something about what he had seen pass at West Ham; something lost. When I visited him at his home, he told me, 'Football belongs to us all. It doesn't belong to the football people, it belongs to us *all*. West Ham, it's people. Right from the youngest fan to the chairman. That's how it always was for me. It belonged to all of us. I didn't look on it as a religion. But it was people. There were people who stood in the Chicken Run who had made it. They were doing well, in more than good jobs, but you wouldn't have known – that's what I liked about it. Like a friend of mine, a buyer at Moss Bros. Seven million pounds a year! Him and his three mates, all with Rolls-Royces parked in the streets outside the ground, used to get in the Chicken Run …We don't forget. The club wouldn't let you change – you had to do it right; you had to be polite. They set a standard.

'If you're one of those lucky enough to be in it, you're entitled to spend a little bit of time with some of those who support it. You should never be anything other than grateful. People like you got me that lovely view.' John looked out over the wonderful scenery which surrounded his home. Still looking, he said, 'That's what football did for me.'

John's conclusion summed up his feelings about being at Upton Park and his life in general, but maybe it also had something for us all. He continued, 'I was just pleased to play. It's a long race. I can remember sitting at West Ham, doing the wages for Bobby [Moore], Geoff [Hurst] and Martin [Peters]. Then, some years later, I'm their manager. Good people will tell you, "Don't worry about it today – tomorrow's another day." Be grateful and take it in your stride. If you start living for today, it can be a bad day or a good one; the best thing is to ride right through the middle.'

While he was working for Capital Radio, I asked Bobby Moore for his thoughts on the possible reasoning for the dismissal of Lyall, a man he knew well and for whom he had great respect. Bob told me that he thought John was seen by the board as representing the old school of manager – secure, honest and principled, but unable to understand or fully accept the cut and thrust of the modern game and how to respond to younger players (although Bobby didn't agree with this as an accurate assessment of Lyall). However, Moore understood that, when things are not going the way an organisation might want, modern management's focus is to make changes as the first antidote. There is, of course, something to this. Clarity can come from lifting the top off enterprises, exposing issues and flaws that have become (albeit unintentionally) obscured by conventional ways of doing things and/or accepted norms. But, of course, the same procedure can also be incredibly destructive, with the potential for the cure to be more painful than the disease.

Well before the protracted barn dance involving Redknapp, Roeder and Pardew, the last question I ever asked John was about who he thought would make a good West Ham manager. He smiled and said, 'When we used to pick up Alan Curbishley from school in the club van, he asked questions right from the minute he got in and all through training. He never stopped. More than anyone I can remember, Alan was always wanting to learn. As long as I've known him, he's been that way.'

We looked at one another and he was still smiling. That was good enough for me.

One of the great things about spending time with John Lyall over the years was that I became conversant with what West Ham was and also why it existed. It was made by people – people like

CHANGE

John but also the fans – and John understood that. West Ham, perhaps much more than any other football club, is a part of the area it has stood in now for over a century. It has grown out of it as a physical manifestation of loyalty, identity and hope – all highly complex and intimately related human sentiments that one would think of as ephemeral and so not amenable to market forces; investing in football as such was for many years a contradiction in terms. The sacking of John Lyall symbolised the end of this situation. From then on, these deep roots of the claret and blue spirit would be placed in aspic.

But things preserved are usually pretty much lifeless objects. This is a truth John Lyall understood. Those who have bought and sold West Ham might well have traded something called 'West Ham', but that, as you and I know, is not West Ham.

CHAPTER 2
OLD AND NEW

In a bet, there is a fool and a thief.
PROVERB

When Terry Brown took up a position of power at Upton Park in 1990, he had solid credentials as a local man and a supporter of the club. He was born in the West Essex/East London borderlands of Barking, an area that had experienced its fair share of poverty since the demise of the Victorian fishing industry in the area, but it was also a district many aspiring East Enders located to when finances and/or opportunity allowed.

Brown's father and grandfather were both West Ham supporters and were among the 250,000-plus crowd at the 1923 Cup Final against Bolton Wanderers (as was my grandfather), the first Final to be held at Wembley. Terry's father, who in his younger days had boxed professionally and come close to being a championship contender, introduced him to football, more specifically, the Irons, and he made his debut at Upton Park as a three-year-old in the 1946/47 season, the Hammers first peacetime campaign for seven years. West Ham finished 12th in Division Two, having scored 80 goals in 42 games and conceded 76. Frank Neary was the club's leading scorer that term, hitting the back of the net 15 times for the Irons. Over the coming years, Frank would play for Orient, Queens Park Rangers and Millwall.

Terry has no recollection of his first visit to the Boleyn Ground, although he does remember that he wandered off and got lost, so it was probably a reserve-team game. When he was very young, Terry's father would take him mostly to reserve games but he has memories of watching the first team play Tottenham Hotspur in the 1940s.

Brown and son watched their football from what was then the South Bank (now the Bobby Moore Stand). Mrs Brown also came to watch the occasional match, but it wasn't unusual for her to faint in a swaying crowd and that caused her to limit her visits. The stadium was not subject to the same standards as it is now of course; on one occasion, a large piece of rust fell from the roof of the old South Bank and lodged itself firmly in one of the young Brown's eyes; he light-heartedly cited this incident as part of his motivation to rebuild the South Bank. When Brown's uncles joined him and his dad at matches, the whole family would meet in the Chicken Run, which would also be known as the East Stand, an area of the ground that has huge nostalgic resonance for the former Hammers tsar.

HEY, HEY, IN SKIPPED LOU

As a child, Brown told his father that he wanted to become West Ham's chairman and this became his ambition and the job he sought above all others. Looking back, he reflected that his dad, a working-class lorry driver, must have seen this aim as being childish nonsense. But, as Lou Macari replaced John Lyall as the Hammers manager in July 1989, Brown's move into the West Ham boardroom was close at hand.

Although he had spent part of his childhood in East London, Macari, only the sixth man to be manager of the Hammers, was only the second not to have played for the club (the other was Ron Greenwood) and as such he was branded as an 'outsider' from the start. The former Celtic and Manchester United man had taken Swindon Town to the Fourth Division Championship in 1986 and to victory in the play-off final the following year.

Macari was a strange choice for West Ham manager. A well-known disciplinarian whose influences included the great Celtic and Scotland manager Jock Stein, his style and demeanour was out of step with the footballing traditions associated with the Boleyn Ground. That being the case, he quickly found himself dealing with a pack of often contrary and sometimes almost mutinous players. An accomplished if aggressive motivator of men who favoured a long-ball game, Lou was a world away from John Lyall and Ron Greenwood, and of course the coaching staff (Bonds, Boyce and McGiven) he had inherited.

Lou had not been at Upton Park long before the proclivity that his former chairman at Swindon Town, Brian Hillier, had for a flutter became a matter of public note. It was revealed that Brian had placed a bet of £6,500 on the Robins to be defeated by Newcastle in the FA Cup tie at St James' Park in January 1988. He had got odds of 8/13, giving him a return of close to £4,000 (plus his stake) before tax. A copy of a Ladbrokes cheque for Hillier's winnings appeared in the press following Swindon's 5–0 defeat.

Hillier wasted no time in denying all knowledge of the matter but the FA initiated an investigation and announced that they would be getting in touch with Macari who had been the manager of that defeated Swindon side. In due course, the diminutive Scot, who had been a partner in a Swindon bookmakers, took part in a four-hour hearing wherein he claimed that his only part in the whole affair was telephoning a friend who was able to put Hillier in contact with Ladbrokes. After exhaustive scrutiny of Hillier's activities at Swindon, he was eventually sent to prison for three years. Macari was fined £1,000 by a four-man FA commission. For luckless Lou, 'Everyone has been saying that I have come out of this affair well … But, as far as I'm concerned, I've been fined £1,000 for making a single telephone call.'

More allegations concerning illegal payments to players were investigated, but, according to Macari, as all this was going on, the Hammers club secretary Tom Finn told him that the Swindon affair was 'a storm in a teacup'. Finn informed the world, 'It is apparent from the punishment imposed on Mr Macari that his minimal involvement in respect of this matter is accepted by the FA. For the last six weeks, Mr Macari and his family have been subjected to intense media pressure, at times amounting to harassment. Now that this matter is behind him, we trust and hope he will be allowed to return to a normal life and concentrate on his duties as manager of West Ham, commencing with the Littlewoods Cup semi-final at Oldham.'

On 14 February 1990 on Boundary Park's plastic topping, the Irons were routed 6–0. That was the last time Macari's hand rested on the rudder of the Hammers. He didn't appear for the team's journey to Swindon the following Sunday and, at an emergency board meeting, Ronnie Boyce was once more put in temporary charge of the team.

On Monday, 19 February 1990, while waiting for his appeal against his FA fine to be heard, Macari resigned as manager of West Ham. With just over seven months and 38 games under his belt, Lou gained the dubious distinction of becoming West Ham's shortest-serving (non-temporary) manager.

Macari later said that Finn had advised him not to resign because the West Ham board had been ready to support him, but Lou had had enough. Macari's time at Upton Park was short, and, although he personally had little impact on the club's culture, he was responsible for bringing Martin Allen, Ian Bishop,

OLD AND NEW

Ludek Miklosko and Trevor Morley to Upton Park. These men would serve the Irons well in the seasons to come, becoming synonymous with the early 1990s at the Boleyn Ground and the first years of Brown's involvement with the West Ham board.

TERRY THE IRON

Unlike many directors of football clubs, Brown had a good knowledge of the game. The West Ham team that Terry grew up with had its fair share of highly talented players: the likes of goalkeeper Ernie Gregory, who to this day Brown believes should have been capped by England; Scotsman John Dick, a consistent and powerful goalscorer; and Ken Brown (no relation), who was certainly one of the best young defenders in England and eventually won international recognition. Wingers Harry Hooper and Malcolm Musgrove were players in the Hammers mould – skilful, adventurous and energetic. Hooper was one of a long series of players who was sold by the club before he had reached his true potential and, in common with others in that historic sequence, his departure for Wolverhampton Wanderers both angered and disappointed huge numbers of fans. The fact that Hooper's transfer fee allowed the club to buy the freehold of the Boleyn Ground meant little to most supporters including the young Terry Brown. Although the flank man had won under-23 honours, he never received a full cap, but he was selected as a reserve for England's 1954 World Cup squad. Many years later, Hooper told Brown that, as he walked towards Upton Park Underground to take the tube to Kings Cross Station for the Wolverhampton train, he knew he was making a terrible mistake. This confirms what Hooper had told me that he wished he'd never left West Ham.

John Smith's move to North London rivals Tottenham Hotspur was another unfortunate decision on the part of the club. For Brown, Smith was a terrific prospect who had played briefly for a Sunday-morning side, 'The Outcasts', which had split off from Terry's own Sunday-morning team. Brown has occasionally wondered whether Smith might have hindered Bobby Moore's early progress had he remained at the Boleyn Ground. It would probably have impeded Moore's advancement and would almost certainly have prevented West Ham's blond saint becoming the club's youngest ever captain (a record he retained until Alan Pardew made Nigel Reo-Coker skipper of the Irons).

Terry recalled one young player who never really reached his full potential – Johnny Cartwright. Johnny had a big hand in developing the England set-up in the last part of the 20th century, but at West Ham he was an outstanding youth and reserve player who was unable to establish himself in the first team. Brown recollected that John used to play in rubber training boots and thought that perhaps this had affected his progression, although Cartwright himself put his demise down to too much weight-training, which was relatively new to football at the time. However, as a young player, Terry looked to replicate Cartwright's style in his own play and used the same type of boots for a while, although they didn't help him play any better.

Other players who had an impact on the youthful Brown were John Bond and Noel Cantwell, West Ham's defensive partnership that would eventually help the Hammers back into the top flight of English football in 1958. Terry rated this pairing among the best ever that stood in defence of the Irons. That 1957/58 promotion season remains in Brown's mind, particularly the final home match of that campaign against Liverpool, which finished in a 1–1 draw with John Bond scoring for the Hammers. He also has fond memories of the Irons' first Boleyn Ground game in the First Division for 26 years, a midweek match against Wolverhampton Wanderers. Terry was standing behind the goal on the South Bank and was completely in awe of Billy Wright and the whole Wolves team, while wondering if West Ham could stay in the top flight that boasted so many superb sides. But the home team won the game 2–0, thanks to goals by John Dick and John Smith. Years later Terry would stand next to Billy Wright during the one-minute silence in memory of Bobby Moore; the former Wolves and England general cried throughout the entire tribute and beyond.

John Bond was known as 'Muffin' to the West Ham crowd because he had a kick like a mule, although he was never fond of the epithet, but, for Terry, lesser-known player Eddie Lewis, formerly of Manchester United and Preston North End, had an even more potent shot and the fattest legs he has seen in West Ham United shorts. Eddie later became a leading coach in South Africa.

MACARI BREEZER

When Lou Macari failed to turn up for the away game with Swindon, the West Ham directors asked Billy Bonds and Ronnie Boyce to take over for the match at the County Ground. By the weekend following Macari's departure and the game against Blackburn Rovers at Upton Park, Billy Bonds had been confirmed as West Ham's new manager. The appointment was popular with both players and supporters. Tony Gale recalled that the decision was greeted with loud applause in the dressing room.

Over the rest of the season, Bonds guided the club to 10 wins in 17 League games. But it wasn't enough. The Hammers finished the 1989/90 campaign in seventh place, just two points behind play-off qualifiers Sunderland. The Black Cats, who won promotion in the play-offs, had a goal difference of +6, while the Irons had +23, the third best in the League. Only Champions Leeds United and third-placed Newcastle United (who the Irons defeated 5–0 at Upton Park) bettered the East Londoners in the goal-difference stakes.

It is likely to remain a mystery why the West Ham board chose to bring Macari to Upton Park. But former club secretary Eddie Chapman, one of West Ham's longest-serving employees, told me, 'No chairman or director wants to put the club at risk. Yes, Lou Macari was a gamble, but so would anyone have been.' He laughed. 'Brian Clough would have been a gamble!

'I'm pretty sure that they offered him the job for good reasons and that he was who they saw as the best man for the job at the time. Remember, they called Ron Greenwood an outsider at first when he came from Arsenal.

'Macari might have worked out. He kept the same coaches around, Bonds and Boyce. It could have worked. But it didn't, so everyone can say the board was wrong. That's always the way.' He laughed. 'But give them credit; they at least tried to do something. They wanted to bring in new people, with new ideas, even as directors. Change things for the better. They didn't have to do that. They could have just gone on the same way.

'Why did they do it? Because they thought it was something they could do for the best. A lot of the men in the boardroom were sitting where their families had been for generations. Why would they want to do harm to everything their dads and granddads had built? To them, to the likes of me and other people, the club was part of them, like a church or an old school might be for other people.

'When Ted Fenton went and Ron Greenwood came, it was similar. Ted had been Charlie Paynter's boy. Paynter had brought Fenton on from a player. But, when West Ham were promoted, the board thought it had to have someone who brought in some new ideas, new ways. It wasn't Ted's fault. He was a man of his time like most of us. Ron Greenwood was the man with the new ideas at that time and plenty of people said it was the wrong thing to do, that West Ham players had always managed the club and so on; that Phil Woosnam should have been made manager. But you have to say that giving Greenwood the job was probably the right thing. Ted was a good manager, but he would never have had what Greenwood had. Woosnam went to America and took a lot of what he learned from Ron with him. And he did very well!

'John [Lyall] never let anyone down and, yes, he should probably have taken on the same sort of job that Ron Greenwood had when John took the manager's job. But it wouldn't have been the same for someone else to stand in Lyall's shadow as it was for John working with Greenwood around. They were like father and son. Ron had worked with John since he started at West Ham. John would have been glad to see Ron come to training to take a look or offer a bit of advice. I'm fairly sure that might not have been the case with someone else when Lyall popped in to see how things were going. John Lyall was very strong at West Ham. He was a big man to have around. He would never have purposely interfered, I think. But him just being about would have been enough to put some men off. But they wanted something new. They thought it was time to do things differently.'

The hiring of Macari, a personality who was about as far from Lyall and Greenwood as might be imagined, in terms of character and tactical preferences, did seem consistent with an effort on the part of the board to break with traditions and create a new football culture at Upton Park, one premised on pragmatism and building an organisation that could fully exploit the Docklands area's devotion to its football team; they were trying to replace an institution founded on emotive connections with identity with a fully mature organisation locked on the pursuit of a business ethic. However, the introduction of the first non-English manager to the Boleyn Ground was in itself a gamble.

Apart from his time at Swindon, a club that is as similar to West Ham as Wiltshire cheese is to jellied eels, Macari was untested as a manager. After his time in East London, he had a brief spell with Birmingham City and, in 1991, he succeeded Alan Ball at Stoke. He led Stoke to the heady heights of the Autoglass Trophy in 1992 before moving to Celtic where he won nothing in 1993/94. Lou was back with Stoke in 1994 but, after three seasons, had failed to make any kind of mark. His last managerial post was at Huddersfield where he presided over a barren period between 2000 and 2002.

As such, although he was a fine player in his day, history shows Macari to have been at best a mediocre manager, but, even at Celtic at the time, he was unlucky in the clubs that employed him. In retrospect, nothing in the man's past or future provides a reason for his being seen as a better option than John Lyall as West Ham manager. But in 1989 he was 'different' and that may well have been his attraction for the Hammers board. Former Hammer Johnny Byrne told me that Macari was 'shiny and new' and for the West Ham directors he could be seen as the equivalent of the mid-life-crisis bright-red sports car that middle-aged men are sometimes prone to buying.

For John, the board had wanted a break with the past, feeling that continuity had given only limited success. Bringing in a man who, with Celtic and Manchester United, had been associated with success was, in Byrne's view, an attempt to import a sense of ambition to the club that had been missing since the early days of the Lyall reign.

This perspective is thought provoking, and I also think there is much insight in Eddie Chapman's view of events. However, what one can draw from the events surrounding Macari's coming and going hot on Lyall's heels is that there was an effort to establish what was thought to be a more 'businesslike' regime, one that would supplant the 'domestic model' of the 'family club', which may have been seen as defunct in a savage environment wherein merciless competition took no prisoners. This was implemented by the purposeful brand of contemporary commercial action personified by Terry Brown. The 'domestic model' of management is a disastrous set of attitudes, limiting flexibility to grow or contract, all in the name of 'tradition', which can provoke stagnation, something Terry Brown was never going to allow.

CHAPTER 3
THE RISE OF 'H'

*His lack of education is more than compensated for
by his keenly developed moral bankruptcy.*
WOODY ALLEN

Regressing to the domestic model of management, 'Mr Len' (the 'father' of West Ham) turned to one of West Ham's favourite sons to save the board's blushes, and Billy Bonds became West Ham's manager in February 1990. Bonzo was certainly the 'people's manager'; an Upton Park hero, he was hugely respected by everyone associated with the club of which he had been part for a quarter of a century. Bonds had a massive reputation for personal honesty and integrity, and was completely trusted by players and fans alike. The board may have seen Bill as the man to bring calm to the chaotic situation, a 'safe pair of hands'. However, it wasn't clear, even to Bonds, if the board were using him as a stop-gap option, but he later said that he thought that this was probably the case.

At the start of his first full season, Bonds led his men on an undefeated run that started from the opening game at Ayresome Park and continued until their visit to Oakwell on 22 December, a series of 21 games. At the end of that term, the Hammers sat in the runner-up spot in the Barclays Second

Division, just one point behind Champions Oldham and moved into the First Division as a well-disciplined and capable side. But they were unable to acclimatise and relegation followed the very next season. With the coming of the Premiership, West Ham – along with Luton and Notts County – became part of an elite trio of clubs to be relegated *from* Division One *to* Division One.

Following the seeming debacle of the bond scheme in May 1992, Harry Redknapp, having resigned as manager of Bournemouth the previous season, was brought to the Boleyn Ground to assist Bonds. This coincided with Terry Brown's elevation to the post of chairman of the club. From that point, Harry and Terry would become associated with the continuing transition of West Ham United.

In 1967, Redknapp had been Bonds's best man, and the two men, who had together covered the Irons' right wing for many years, had spent many an evening in one another's company at the greyhound track; they shared ownership of Outcast Hunter, a respectable pooch if not an immortal of the traps.

Although Bill never rated H as a first-class coach, Harry's 'one of the boys' attitude was popular among the players and seemed to help in terms of getting ideas over to them. In the 1992/93 term, Bonds and Redknapp took the Irons into the Premiership for the first time, after finishing second in the Barclays League Division One behind Newcastle United. But the subsequent campaign, while preserving the Hammers top-flight status, was not an impressive one. West Ham ended the season in 13th place, 10 points clear of relegation, but Manchester United had won the Premiership a massive 40 points above the East Londoners; even Queens Park Rangers had managed eight points more than the Boleyn boys, finishing in ninth place.

While the board might not have been totally dissatisfied with matters, it was clear that Peter Storrie, in 1994 the chief executive of the club, was far from content. Bonds and Storrie were having problems which came to boiling point before the start of the 1994/95 season. Bonds felt that Tom Finn had been a huge help to him in terms of administrative duties and saw the Hammers club secretary as eminently trustworthy, but he never got on with Storrie. This is not surprising, as the two men were very different characters. Bonds, a South London football man of immense personal honour whose blood ran claret and blue, based his philosophy of life on straightforward veracity. He was still a perfect physical specimen, well built and carrying not an ounce of fat, and he was more than able to better the fitness of most of his players. Storrie was a businessman from Plaistow. Seemingly parochial, Pete budded and blossomed in what was considered the 'better end' of Newham. Although having little background in the game, part of Storrie's role at West Ham was negotiating player contracts. Some might even have associated West Ham's lack of success with his assessments of footballing talent and the allurements that could bring players to Upton Park and motivate them to give their all to the Hammers or to seek to leave the club. Given this, it was almost inevitable that Storrie was always going to attribute the failure of players to the manager's inability to get the best from them. At the same time, it must have been hard for Bonds to accept that Storrie, given his incredibly limited experience of what it takes to play at the highest level, had the insight to make key decisions about player costs and rewards.

ON ME HEAD, TEL

Terry Brown was much more clued up about what it takes to play at a high standard. He and his dad managed to get to more than a few matches and not just at the Boleyn Ground, squeezing in games anywhere in London and often beyond, and, although the Hammers were always his and his family's team, playing was always the priority for the young Brown during the first half of his life. He was a good footballer at school, although in retrospect he saw himself as not being an outstanding talent, but an old school report tells how he was 'rather too absorbed in the study of football to give himself up to the study of English'.

Brown's passion for taking part in the game overcame his desire to watch it and this limited the number of Upton Park games he attended. Apart from a period when he broke a leg as an eight-year-old, most of his weekends were devoted to competition.

Andy Malcolm was another player from Brown's time as a spectator. Malcolm could man-mark anyone. Although in the playground Terry had never fantasised about being any particular player, he looked to replicate the Iron man's skills in his own Sunday-morning youth team, which naturally worked better on some of his opponents than on others. One of the latter was a centre-forward who was so strong that he was almost unplayable at the level Brown was competing in. The striker was Peter Cohen, father of Ben, the England rugby international, and brother of the 1966 World Cup winner George. In an effort to meet this irresistible force, Terry's side chose to leave the centre-half free and assign another player to mark Peter in the way Malcolm might; the tactic, which was at least an attempt to manage the Cohen menace, could not eradicate the onerous threat his presence posed.

Terry graduated to play for Southend United's youth team in the South-East Counties League, but the club had financial problems and were obliged to abandon their youth scheme to save money. The young players were farmed out to their local clubs and Brown was sent to Barking. He was involved in a game against Walthamstow Avenue Reserves, who were perhaps the best amateur side in the London area and one of the finest teams in the country at their level at the time, having won the FA Amateur Cup Final at Wembley twice and drawn

1–1 against Manchester United at Old Trafford in the fourth round of the FA Cup before being beaten 5–2 at Highbury in the replay.

Just as Brown's Barking side made their way on to the pitch, their manager suggested that, as he was so young, Terry should make sure he made his presence felt by the Walthamstow centre-forward, which would ensure that the Avenue striker didn't think he could 'take liberties' with the youngster. Brown did as he was instructed but the crowd were hostile and booed him every time he touched the ball thereafter. That was a new experience for Brown (although it would be a phenomenon he eventually would experience on a regular basis). But Terry was supported throughout the match by the Barking inside-left, who, for Brown, was one of the best players with whom he had played. He remembered thinking what a great coach the man would be.

Not long after this, Terry took his footballing talents to St Albans City. The Friars, like Barking, were an Isthmian League side, so the following season Brown returned with the first team to Barking, hoping to play against the same inside-left who had helped him during the game at Walthamstow. The player did not turn out for that game, but Terry met him for a second time 30 years later when he joined the West Ham United board and recognised Jimmy Frith, who had subsequently become a leading coach in the West Ham Academy.

Jimmy was one of Youth Academy director Tony Carr's most senior coaches and it was no surprise to Brown that all the skills Jim had shown coaching him during that game at Walthamstow Avenue had benefited the young Hammers. Jimmy also coached at Fairbairn House Boys' Club in Canning Town for many years from the 1960s. I was involved in several sessions he organised and, although I never appreciated it at the time, later in life I was to understand that Jim was a great teacher. I became a youth worker at Fairbairn and I watched him coach some of the hardest lads in that toughest of tough areas and wrote a short thesis on his methods for my professional qualification in youth and community work. Jimmy, like Clive Charles, another black Hammer, was more than a coach; he was an educator. He had a way of using football to help kids make the transition to adulthood, take responsibility and deal with the consequences of their actions. Although this is not something I can go into at length in this book, I know that Jim's work at Fairbairn helped save many lives and alleviated a world of pain.

Brown's football career brought him into contact with the professional game from early on. As a kid, many of his Sunday-morning team-mates were on the books of professional clubs. The centre-forward was with Watford and Terry was invited to join him in a full practice match against the Hornets' first team at Vicarage Road. His club were able to move their Sunday-morning match against Walton & Hersham's youth team to the afternoon in order to enable Terry to play at Watford (1958, kids: two games in one day; 2007, Chelsea, etc.: rotation system). The new manager of Watford was Ronnie Burgess, a wing-half and former captain of Spurs and Wales. Ronnie had skippered the great Tottenham Championship-winning sides from 1949 to 1951, when the North Londoners won the old Second and First Divisions in successive seasons. Ronnie can also be credited with discovering Pat Jennings. Burgess played on Brown's side, as did the then 46-year-old Len Goulden, the former Watford manager and West Ham United, Chelsea and England player, who was then a scout for Watford.

Brown usually played at centre-half, but that day took on the right-back role. Ronnie Burgess directed that all goal-kicks should be rolled out to the full-backs who were instructed to overlap down the wing before crossing the ball. Alas, Brown was forced to conclude that Burgess had also told the Watford winger about these tactics as the Hertfordshire club's wide-man closed Terry down with consummate ease. But Ron had the answer and told the young Brown that if he was caught in possession he should simply chip the ball out to the opposite left flank into the path of his own winger; Burgess demonstrated the tactic to the youthful defender during the game, showing him how easy this strategy might be enacted. Unfortunately, Terry's first couple of attempts not only fell 20 yards behind the winger but also went out for throw-ins. Burgess looked at Brown in disbelief rather than anger, seemingly incapable of understanding that hitting long passes was not quite as simple for a young amateur as it was for him. Brown has recalled watching Michael Carrick in the West Ham midfield spray the ball around at a rain-drenched Vicarage Road, making the field look like a small five-a-side pitch; he made the point that when one is asked to do that the pitch seems to grow into a sort of extended Wembley Stadium.

Brown told Len Goulden before the game that his family were West Ham United supporters and that his father was watching from the stand. Terry thought Len felt sorry for him, as during the match he approached him discreetly and said, 'Look, son, whenever you get the ball, just give it to me and get down the right wing as quick as you can.'

This advice seemed to work and Brown's team won 2–1 with Terry's Sunday-morning centre-forward team-mate scoring both goals following crosses from the right.

However, Terry doesn't think he covered himself in glory; his father, who had driven him down to Surrey for the afternoon game in his work van, said nothing until they got home late at night, when he told his wife, 'He's a better centre-half than a right-back.'

BROWN OUT

Brown was disappointed that his dad had failed to make allowances for the quality of the opposition he had faced. But he remembered the game for marking the first time he spoke to a West Ham player, and Len Goulden was one of the Hammers' great stars.

Ronnie Burgess can be counted among the great hotspurs of the first part of the club's history. He passed away in February 2005, two months after his 88th birthday. He outlived Len Goulden who died almost exactly seven years earlier aged 82. Len had played 14 times for England and had been in the side that were obliged to give a Nazi salute before playing against Germany (in reality a combined Austrian and German side) in Berlin's Olympiastadion on 14 May 1938. England defeated the 'master race' 6–3. Len, a Jewish lad from London's East End, scored the final goal of the game in the 80th minute – so much for the theory of 'racial superiority' of the 'Ayrian volk'.

HARRY – THE FOOTBALLING KING OF KINGS PARK DRIVE

According to Redknapp, at about the same time as Bonds and Storrie were heading towards their individual limits of mutual tolerance, Bournemouth were looking to persuade him to make a prodigal return to the halls of management on the South Coast. 'H' claimed that Geoffrey Hayward, who he named in his autobiography as a former Cherries chairman, told him that he was close to reacquiring the Dean Court vestibule of football, but his final move was reliant on Redders making a pilgrimage back down the A35 (Harry's family still lived in Dorset, but he also rented a posh pad in Gidea Park on the East London/West Essex borderland).

The Hayward family had made a significant contribution to AFC Bournemouth throughout its first century. In the early days, Wilf, a local builder, was club secretary. In 1914, the club turned professional and became a limited liability company and Wilf was appointed chairman, overseeing the development of the ground and the club's election to the Football League in 1923. Wilf remained chairman until his death in 1941.

Wilf's eldest son, Reg, joined the board the following year and became chairman in 1947. Like his dad, he stayed in post until his passing in 1960, when Doug, his younger brother, took over as chairman. In 1970, Harold Walker launched his takeover of Bournemouth but later on Doug's son, Peter, became a director and briefly chairman until resigning in 1991.

Geoffrey Hayward was Reg's younger son. Contrary to his tale to Harry, or Redknapp's mistake, he was never chairman of the club but was a director until 1997 and club president until his death in 1999.

According to Redknapp, Geoff told him that he could take any role at the club he wanted – managing director, chairman, manager – but, as tempting as this offer might have been to H, the West Ham board were keen to keep Redknapp in the Hammers fold.

Stories of what happened next have been elaborated endlessly in books and magazines promoting gossip and low-level intrigue. Redknapp and Bonds have each given their view of events several times, and of course crucial elements do not tally (ask any two people separately about an event they shared 15 years ago and you are not going to get a pair of completely congruent narratives). West Ham fans will know the widely accepted report that Bonds was 'stabbed in the back' by Redknapp and would have read Harry's denial that anything of the sort happened. What is for sure is that Billy Bonds MBE, never anything less than a staunchly truthful and upstanding professional, has not spoken to Redknapp since. In the mid-1990s, arguably no one in football knew Harry better than Bonds did, but the West

Ham legend has always chosen to maintain his integrity in the matter, preferring to draw a line under events by claiming to not always be the best judge of character.

Both men agree that in a hotel room in Scotland, while on a pre-season tour prior to the 1994/95 term, Bonds was offered a director of football role at Upton Park by Terry Brown, following the chairman's proposal that Redknapp take over as manager. What is also undisputed is the fact that Bill turned down Brown's offer. Harry's story tells how he had informed Brown about the 'chairman' of Bournemouth's offer, which prompted the West Ham chairman to ask if H wanted to return to the Endsleigh Division Two club because he was looking to manage again. Redknapp claimed to have denied that this was, in fact, the case and that, if he did leave Upton Park, it would be because his home was in the Bournemouth area and the fact that he would be a sort of soccer tsar of Hampshire. Redders reported that Brown's response to this was to offer him the job of manager at the Boleyn Ground and suggest moving Bonds 'upstairs' as director of football. Bonds felt this to be a clear case of being given the 'bums-rush' and decided this was not a game he wanted to be involved in.

However, Terry Brown told me that it was Peter Storrie who had come to him claiming that Harry was leaving the club for Bournemouth and that, if that happened, Bonds would not stay at West Ham. According to Terry, it was this fait accompli that motivated him to offer Bonds the general managership and Harry the role of West Ham manager. He didn't think the club could have coped easily with being hurt by both men leaving the club at the same time.

In retrospect, Terry felt he let Bill down and that both he and Bill were to blame for not sitting down together to discuss Bill's views and whether he would really leave if Harry left to fulfil his ambitions on the shores of the Solent.

Terry knew Bill and Harry were close and accepted the version of events put to him and, with Bill's angry reaction, the situation quickly spun out of control. Both Bill and the club deserved better.

DÉJÀ VU DOWN NEAR POOLE

Redknapp had been in a similar position about a decade earlier. At the start of the 1982/83 season, he had taken up his first major coaching role as assistant manager to David Webb at AFC Bournemouth, half a dozen years after leaving the club as a player. Harry applied for the manager's job when Webb moved to Torquay during the 1983/84 term, but was passed over for Don Megson. Megson was sacked late in 1984 with the Hampshire side close to the bottom of the Third Division, and Redknapp was passed the manager's hat and the big boots of power.

H helped the Cherries avoid relegation and took them to the Third Division title in 1986/87. But, after a couple of seasons as a run-of-the-mill Second Division side, the club flopped back to where they had come from in 1990, having taken the long route to nowhere.

ENTER THE REDDERS

The Monday after a Saturday friendly at Fratton Park, Bonds resigned as West Ham manager and a week or so later Redknapp took over. Before signing his contract, H was advised by West Ham's lawyers to be sure to look at the 'ferocious clauses' disallowing any clandestine payments. These passages motivated Harry to exclaim passionately, 'I don't need to be greedy like George Graham. I don't need to jeopardise my son's life. I couldn't face my son. Money is not my God.'

But money was *quite* important to Harry and he was not shy when expressing his discontent with his £1m-a-year wage packet. He thought the fact that he didn't take home as much as some of his players was 'criminal'. He argued, 'Us bosses could not book a ticket on the gravy train. Suddenly I found I was getting less than my most ordinary player and that can't be right ... Surely my pay should be on a par with my top players?'

Why on earth would Harry expect that? His list of triumphs as a manager hardly merited naming him as a 'rare talent'. (However, to my amazement, he was mooted as a possible England manager on the exit of McClaren late in 2007!)

Years later, Brown was to concede that the club did not manage the events that led to Bonds's resignation well and should have handled it differently. He also accepted that Bonds was correct to have anticipated better treatment by West Ham and confessed that he would have done things another way given a second chance. But Brown did recompense Bonds for the full duration of his three-year contract.

Redknapp was soon to get rid of Ronnie Boyce, another great servant of the club and a hero of the Irons. The next time I saw Ronnie, he was training to be a sheet metal worker which left me totally appalled.

Much speculation has gone on ever since about what some fans have called 'Bondsgate'. There can be little doubt that there was something of a ramshackle Julius Caesar going on at Upton Park in the summer of 1994. The trail of consequences of Harry's mighty tales of being beckoned to the south coast are momentous, but could such stories have been merely a means of bettering his pecuniary position and professional standing at Upton Park? West Ham's 13th placing on the Hammers' return to the English football elite was maybe not good enough for Harry who admitted to being a tad underwhelmed at the time. However, it is difficult to see how a sojourn at the blunt end of Bournemouth Pier in the mid-1990s would have made Redders the potentate of a football Nirvana or, apart from being near to home, improved his life, status or financial prospects.

At the same time, looking at Harry's time with the Cherries begs the question: 'Why would they want him back?' Would he have given back the £100,000 'golden elbow' shoved his way by the club on his departure from Dean Court? Not many Cherries fans were pleased about him getting this in the first place and looked back with a mixture of horror and disgust on the late 1980s, a time when Redknapp was trading players and increasing the club's debt like wildfire. From July 1987 to June 1992, Bournemouth's debt went from £150,000 to £2.6m. In spite of H exibiting the financial extravagance of a lottery winner, drafting a cavalcade of profligate player contracts, the south-coast club were relegated to Division Three in 1990. Debts would rise to £4.4m. In 1992, Redknapp resigned, citing the 'worries and stress' of management as his reason for packing it in. However, although he claimed that he had made the club £848,000 in the transfer market, in fact, in Harry's time Bournemouth's income was nowhere near to matching its costs. The seeming surplus were bare transfer figures totted up and were more than wiped out by the £1m wage bill his deals had generated. Roy Pack, who allegedly called Harry a 'barrow boy', had been a professional with Arsenal and Portsmouth, and he took on the role of financial adviser to Bournemouth. In 1997, he told the *News of the World* that Harry had shown 'a degree of irresponsibility in his actions', and that this had 'developed into the mess we are now desperately trying to resolve. What has happened is almost unbelievable and in a business sense it is ludicrous.'

However, Redknapp arrived at West Ham with an untarnished character, but his style of management would not change, and, in fact, he more or less gave a repeat performance of his time at Bournemouth, while adding a few noughts here and there.

CHERRY AID

Norman Hayward, a distant relative of the Hayward dynasty, was forced out of Dean Court in 1994 in a boardroom power struggle after two years at the helm.

Norman had started his business life selling scrap from his dad's back garden. He built a property business from scratch and ended up buying and restoring Creech Grange, a country house in the Purbecks.

In 2006, he had been locked in a legal dispute with Lloyds Bank that had dragged on for a decade at a cost of millions of pounds. The dispute started early in 1991, when Mr Hayward took over as chairman of AFC Bournemouth. He had agreed to sign a personal guarantee of £650,000 because the club was heavily overdrawn at the bank. In 1994, the bank backed a takeover consortium in the hope that it would bring new capital into the club.

Mr Hayward eventually agreed to sell his shares on the understanding that his personal guarantee would be reduced from £650,000 to £400,000. He also believed that the bank would not be allowed to call on this guarantee until July 1997 at the earliest. But, when the club got into financial problems in July 1996, the bank demanded the full £650,000. Such is the way with borrowed money – situations change.

Just before the beginning of the 1994/95 season, with no manager and a threadbare, raggle-taggle squad, the impoverished Cherries lost their initial seven games, but manager Mel Machin eventually just about saved the side from relegation. Throughout the mid-1990s, financial worries were a constant at Dean Court and late in 1996 the receivers were called in.

But fans rallied and a trust fund was set up. Despite huge support, Bournemouth were a quarter-of-an-hour from disappearing into the mists of football history at one point. However, Trevor Watkins, the club chairman and the person in charge of the Trust Committee, declared that the trust fund was going to bid to take the club over. This produced Europe's first ever community club.

LOSS OF A HERO

Brown's regrets about how the club handled the Billy Bonds/Harry Redknapp situation in August 1994 cannot detract from the sad fact that the much-loved Billy Bonds left West Ham under a cloud when Harry stepped up from being his assistant to become manager. Maybe it was all just a series of mistakes and misunderstandings, but John 'Charlo' Charles (West Ham's first black player), who came through West Ham's Academy system alongside Redknapp, skippering H in West Ham's FA Youth Cup-winning side of 1963, was more sceptical: 'Bonds was brought in to sort everyone out. But West Ham had a tradition of boozers and gamblers and it would have been hard to stop all that overnight. Redknapp could cover for a lot of that and get on with things, but what the fuck does Harry Redknapp know about football? Maybe the board thought Bill would have it all out in the open.' He laughed. 'Maybe that was what it was about.

'Bonds probably knew that and he'd only be in charge for a bit. West Ham did OK under him, got promoted, so how were they going to get rid of him? Then they get relegated and the chance comes along to move him on. Perhaps he knew his days were numbered from the minute Redknapp came back. Anyway, it gave them a way to get him out. What they call it? Damage limitation!' He laughed.

BROWN OUT

Having looked back at that time as a fan, talking to other supporters and reading the different accounts since, it seems unlikely to me that Redknapp would have come back to Upton Park to remain Bill's assistant for very long. That would not have been attractive to Harry, who if nothing else was and is ambitious (some harsher critics might even say greedy). Harry would have returned to the East End with his eyes set firmly on managing his old club. To occupy the seat once graced by Greenwood and Lyall would have been the height of achievement for a man who in his playing days was the Uriah Heep to Bobby Moore's David Copperfield. But as a manager he was more Micawber than Nicholas Nickleby.

Essentially, Billy Bonds was 'old school' West Ham. His values were congruent with Greenwood and Lyall. Redknapp, although at Upton Park from his earliest days, was always a bit on the periphery in a number of ways. He was, in terms of the top-flight-standard footballers he played alongside, a mediocre flanker who was hard-pressed to break into what was, for the most part, an underachieving side. He had come through the Academy route and signed professional terms in 1964. In eight years, he made 170 appearances (21 games a year), scoring eight goals from the wing (less than one goal every eight games). Compare this to Peter Brabrook, the man Harry replaced for a couple of seasons as the Irons number 7, who played from late 1962 to early 1968, netting 43 times in 214 games (nearly 43 games annually over five and a half years, a goal every five games).

For much of his latter years at Upton Park, Clyde Best kept Redknapp out of the side when flankmen, in the aftermath of Alf Ramsey's 'wingless wonders', were very much démodé. But even an ageing and alcohol-marinated Jimmy Greaves, in a claret and blue shirt that hung off him like a shroud, looked a class above Redknapp in his pomp.

THE RISE OF 'H'

Harry came back to the Boleyn Ground with something to prove and he was never going to do that as a number two to Bonds. He was not a convert like Bonds and would have been more in tune with 'selling the game' than might be the case for the managerial aristocracy that had preceded him at Upton Park. In short, Redknapp was a cultural match with the forces of commercialisation that imposed themselves on football in the 1990s, even though he looked like 'one of the family'.

CHAPTER 4
BOND BOMBSHELL

*The 'what should be' never did exist, but people keep trying to
live up to it. There is no 'what should be', there is only what is.*
LENNY BRUCE

The great battle of Brown's time as a board member, before
his elevation to chairman of West Ham United Football Club,
was the bond scheme. This encounter, which resulted in what
looked like a face-off between those who owned the club and
its supporters, left an indelible mark on fan consciousness that
persisted throughout Brown's involvement in the running of
West Ham.

Following the Hillsborough disaster of 15 April 1989, in
which 96 Liverpool supporters were crushed to death in the
Leppings Lane cages, football found itself obliged to respond.
The majority of grounds were dilapidated and in more than a
few cases unsafe, although the straightforward removal of fences
around the country following the tragedy in Sheffield probably
meant that the kind of carnage that took place that fateful spring
day would not reoccur. The Prime Minister, Margaret Thatcher,
launched an inquiry into the future of the sport, to be chaired
by a High Court judge who (somewhat predictably) had never
attended a football match in his life.

BROWN OUT

The football virgin, Lord Justice Taylor, was tasked with creating a blueprint for the game. Although now, in a TV-drenched environment, English football is marketed on a worldwide scale and the Premiership is flooded with vast amounts of money, at the end of the 1980s football was, in fact, in the throes of a disastrous decline. Attendances had never been lower, supporters were perceived as worthy of little more than minimal consideration and the product itself was practically bereft in terms of entertainment value. The notion of 'attractive football' was considered either a contradiction in terms or an effete South American aberration. You played football to win! Graham 'Kick It!' Taylor's Watford were runners-up in the First Division in 1983! He was the man who told his England team to get the ball into touch as often as possible because every time the opposition take a throw they only have 10 men on the pitch!

The newly appointed Lord Justice of Football saw that the fans had tolerated or simply accepted poor services from the clubs for as long as anyone could remember. Conditions were almost barbaric at times. When I stood on the West Ham North Bank on Monday, 24 August 1964, I was part of what was to be the biggest crowd of the season at Upton Park; they crammed in an 'official' 37,070 but the actual number might have been over 40,000. During such a match, from the centre of the North Bank, it took about a quarter of an hour to get to the disgusting toilet blocks below the stand. The 'call of nature' usually came at some point before or after half-time, given the tradition of the pre-match bevy and/or the half-time bevy and the primeval state of the pies and hotdogs slopped out in and around Upton Park on match days. Of course, it took about the same time to return from the stinking urinals and filthy pans to where you started out on your expedition. With the time it took to 'take a leak' (for which you sometimes had to line up), it was possible that the most modest of pees would take somewhere between half and three-quarters of an hour to deal with. Those who reminisce about the 'days of the terraces' nearly always forget this intriguing facet of being crushed on the steps of the decaying football grounds pre-Taylor.

Consequently, it was not unusual, although not altogether common, for spectators to urinate where and when they could, sometimes where they stood, causing sparkling streams to trickle down the terraces for those below to ponder. These creeks could swell to small ponds at the foot of the stands which is where the youngest fans often stood.

Taylor favoured the practice of supporter representation and recommended that clubs should consult their fans as part of their decision-making processes. He told Thatcher that her compulsory football ID card scheme was unfeasible. The idea of ID cards was something that Thatcher had been very enthusiastic about, born out of the grubby aftermath of Heysel, another grim day for English football, the consequence of which was that clubs from the English League endured a five-year banishment from European competition.

Regrettably, the Taylor Report is remembered only for the resolve that terracing should be replaced by relatively expensive all-seater stadiums. Taylor naively thought that the abolition of standing and the provision of seating would result in a safer environment. Not really understanding the business that is football, he failed to realise that clubs would squeeze as many seats as possible into their grounds, putting income before legroom. Take a look around the next time you go to a game and ask yourself what your surroundings, littered with melting plastic seats, would be like in a panic. But the government and the football authorities supported the suggestion (which reflected UEFA recommendations) and stipulated that by August 1994 all major club grounds in the top two divisions should make the transition to all-seater facilities.

BROWN OUT

IRON BARS DO NOT A PRISON MAKE ...
BUT THEY DON'T HALF HELP

It is true that before the Hillsborough disaster West Ham were the only London club not to put their supporters in what were effectively cages on the terraces (Len Cearns had fought hard to keep Upton Park free of these inhumane pens) and many fans have expressed a kind of retrospective gratitude for this. The architecture of the Boleyn Ground, up to very recently, made pitchside fencing dangerous for the players; in the early 1990s the crowd at Upton Park were no more than a couple of feet from the pitch. As such, a fence in front of the stands would have presented players hurtling down on goal with the prospect that the slightest mistake or diversion by a defender would send them smashing into a wall of iron railings. Although I can think of a few players who would have just bounced off as long as their heads made first contact!

WEST HAM FIRST

West Ham declared that they were in the process of devising a scheme to redevelop Upton Park that would make the Hammers the first major club to come to terms with the funding of all-seat provision. The supporters, knowing football better than Taylor perhaps did, were understandably suspicious that the scheme would inevitably mean that they would have to dig deeper into their pockets to watch football (they weren't wrong, were they!). But there was a measure of assurance given when, contrary to some reports, it was claimed that the scheme would not mean moving to another ground. The notion of West Ham becoming a public limited company was also rumoured. Some were attracted to this idea and the possibility they would be able to purchase shares in their football club.

Nothing was heard of the plans for Upton Park that the West Ham board had spoken of until November 1991 at which point the club's fans were preoccupied with their side's poor showing back on the Division One stage. As winter approached, the board disclosed (firstly via newspaper reports) that they were considering a debenture scheme. Not too many of the club's fans were anything but apprehensive about the possibilities.

It was when expectations were raised and the Irons' fortunes took an upturn with the defeats of Arsenal and Tottenham in the space of one week that the board took advantage of this brief window of hope to launch their scheme in the pages of the *Evening Standard*. The club's new ringmaster, Peter Storrie, who had recently become managing director of the club with a 1 per cent stake, despite being a board member for less than two years, took responsibility for the day-to-day running of the club, and so it fell to him to explain the scheme.

At first, the details of how the scheme would work were unclear but most supporters wanted to believe that, when the plan was officially unveiled, there would be significant benefits in return for 'investing' in a bond. The full picture was revealed in the Upton Park Sunday match-day programme a few days later (v Liverpool, 17 November 1991). It read like a hybrid of *Catch-22*, *Alice in Wonderland* and *The Hobbit*.

The board argued that the bond was the best option to raise the necessary funding for the required development involving the demolition of the North and South Bank terraces and the building of replacement cantilever stands. They had seen that a straightforward share offer was unlikely to be underwritten, and a successful flotation could only be guaranteed if it was effectively underwritten (Newcastle United had recently paid a high price when this had not been the case). A traditional bank loan was considered too expensive. The club could perhaps have borrowed the money, but the interest on the £15.5m in the economic climate that prevailed in the early 1990s would have cost West Ham in the region of £2m per year. Given all this, chairman Martin Cearns went a step further than his board and insisted that the Hammers bond was not just the best but the *only* feasible way of raising the necessary cash.

Significantly, the small print of the bond prospectus detailed that there was an underwriting agreement dated 27 November 1991 between West Ham United plc and the Bank of Scotland whereby the bank agreed, in certain circumstances, to underwrite up to a maximum of £11,634,000 of the £15,112,175 issue in return for a maximum fee of £211,510 plus VAT.

The board told the fans, 'We need to get the builders in. We've got no choice – not if we're going to stay at Upton Park. And we want to do that. But to make sure as many fans as practicable can see us play and to provide our supporters with superior facilities, we need to raise around £15.5m. And to make this happen we need the continued support of Hammers fans. If we club together, we can build a better Upton Park.'

It must be remembered that big moves like Arsenal's' shift to the Emirates had not yet happened and club relocations were not the accepted norm they are today. Charlton, for instance, had been deeply affected by their move away from the Valley in 1985 and were glad to put an end to their time as a roving club in 1992. The idea that West Ham might move from Upton Park, although it was a possible means to fulfil the club's potential financially, sickened the majority of fans, even more when the prospect of ground-sharing was mooted. Several top clubs, like Arsenal, Spurs and Chelsea, have in the past been linked with ground-sharing. However, during the majority of his time as chairman of West Ham, Brown saw this as an unlikely option for the Hammers. Especially after many of the improvements to the ground had been made, he thought Upton Park would serve the club for the foreseeable future. But, with the new ownership of 2006 and the coming of the Olympics, together with other clubs breaking the ground, for example, Sunderland and Arsenal (the financial advantage the Gunners gleaned was made eye-bogglingly obvious in 2007), that had to change.

There was a precedent for the kind of play the board were putting forward. Glasgow Rangers had raised £7m with a similar funding plan (Celtic were talking about a £50m-plus project) and Arsenal had introduced a £16.5m bond scheme to bankroll the building of their new North Stand at Highbury. However, unlike the West Ham plan, the Gunners' scheme wasn't compulsory and, although it would hit fans' pockets equally hard, the Arsenal board had committed £8m to the scheme. The West Ham board were contributing nothing. In fact, in straightforward terms, the somnolent, patient Irons supporters were impudently being asked to finance the redevelopment of an equally weary Upton Park and increase its net asset value to the benefit of the shareholders and, ultimately, the board. Having funded the building work, those supporters would then merely have the right to purchase a ticket to the directors' brand-new multi-million-pound stadium. This was something worse than paying twice for the same thing.

No lesser organ than the City Desk of the *Daily Telegraph* observed, 'Unfortunately, while Arsenal's bond might be a good investment for its fans, West Ham's looks like a straight cry for help. Arsenal "bonded" a quarter of its seats but West Ham is "bonding" three-quarters of its stadium and once three-quarters of the seats are "special" there are not many left to be ordinary. If West Ham needs to maximise revenue, the seat discount to bondholders is almost worthless. As an investment these bonds are hopeless.'

Ownership of a bond would give the bondholder the 'right' (priority) to purchase a match-day (including away matches) or season ticket for a designated seat for 50 years. Their seat would have a plaque with their name on it and they would get a certificate and be able to have a photograph taken with a player or the manager. Bondholders would also have the opportunity to buy bond merchandise and the possibility of becoming mini-property speculators in their own right by selling the bonds in the future 'when' they increased in value.

The whole idea of the 'Hammers Bond' (as it was initially christened) was premised on some massively uncertain principles. First, the club would stay at Upton Park for the foreseeable future (half a century at least) and that attendance would remain at a maximum level – this was another way of saying that the club would remain in the top flight of English football. Football would also need to maintain the level of popularity it would have in the mid-1990s. Any diversion from this multi-dimensional path would have meant the bonds would have lost some, most or all of their supposed value.

Two great fan heroes, Trevor Brooking and manager Billy Bonds, were recruited to promote the board's plans. *Hammer* (West Ham's match-day programme) was stuffed with images of them smiling like the stars of a toothpaste advert, looming above a model of the projected new stadium. The 'editorial team' filled the programme with the virtues of the bond scheme, telling readers of the exciting world that becoming a bond owner would open up to them.

Following a photo-shoot with Bonds and having inspected a prototype of the new-look Upton Park, Trevor Brooking commented, 'I'm very optimistic that this will work.'

But then he had expressed something of the same attitude with regard to the 1982 World Cup.

Billy Bonds said, 'Upton Park is a special place for supporters and players so I'm delighted that we're staying … I'm always looking for more new players and obviously the more money that can be made available in the future the better it will be for me, the team and our fans.'

By 1994, West Ham intended to construct a state-of-the-art,

25,500-seat stadium at the cost of £15.1m, a staggering sum at the time. The work would start with what is now the Bobby Moore Stand, using the money that would come from selling the bonds. To cover the entire sum needed, including allowing for ongoing costs, the club wanted to raise £19m through the sale of bonds to supporters. A total of 19,301 bonds were offered in three price bands related to the quality of seating; there were to be 2,182 £500 bonds, 11,866 at £750 and 5,253 going for £975 (at least five times the price of a season ticket at the time). The ambition was that the funds raised would allow the board to finance the redevelopment without paying a penny itself, thus improving the infrastructure of the club (creating a more marketable/profitable product) without the inconvenience of venture investment; a capitalist's dream and what might be thought of as constituting 'perfect exploitation':

- the customer pays for the improvement in the product (that belongs to the board/shareholders);
- the improved product is then sold to the customer (by the board);
- the customer pays more for the improved product than they did for the original product; and
- the customer pays for what they have already paid for but at a continuing cost (they pay season on season).

Ever the cheeky chappy, Peter Storrie confirmed this analysis: 'We felt the debenture route offered everything we are looking for in our fundraising. We raise the money, we do not take on huge debt, the club remains under internal control, and monies for the team are not affected.'

For many, this appeared to take the Hammers supporters as 'Mugs Inc'. Irons fans were at that point disillusioned by the club's form. Watching the team struggle and, with only Mike Small, Kenny Brown and Mitchell Thomas to show for the previous campaign's promotion and FA Cup run that had taken them to the semi-final, they had long been demanding an answer to the question: 'Where's the money gone?' However, the board did reveal financial figures that showed a net deficit of over £2m. Operating costs had increased by far more than income from ticket sales.

For a brief interlude, the club worked under the strap-line 'We shall not be moved', which appeared in the match-day programme. Looking like something lifted straight out of the pages of Orwell's *Nineteen Eighty-Four*, the Big Brother rhetoric played on the possibility of West Ham needing to move away from Upton Park:

> The club had the choice of moving to another ground or redeveloping Upton Park.
>
> So we recently asked you, the fans, what we should do.
>
> The answer was overwhelmingly clear: Upton Park is our home – we must stay here. So let's state here and now – West Ham United is staying at the Boleyn Ground.
>
> To ensure we can accommodate as many fans as practicable and give our supporters much better facilities, we need to raise around £15.5m.
>
> And to make this happen we need the continued support of Hammers fans.
>
> You can give us this support by buying a Hammers Bond.
>
> It'll guarantee you the right to buy a season ticket for your own seat in the new improved Upton Park.
>
> I/we club together, we shall not be moved.

This appeal called on another cherished myth that (particularly before the coming of the bond scheme) West Ham were a 'family club'. Personally, I have never understood what this meant. Ron Greenwood is often quoted as saying that West Ham were 'a little bit different from everybody else'. For sure, even after generations of underinvestment, the Hammers maintained a huge fan base, despite humiliating defeats under Greenwood's command by the likes of Swindon and Hereford United. The West Ham board clearly had a culture that seemed to be premised on a lack of ambition, which probably went back to the club's first relegation in 1932 and right up to the Redknapp years, when Harry saw success for West Ham being a top-half finish, or even the meagre avoidance of relegation. This said, there was never any real effort to be rid of the lacklustre regime led by 'Mr Len'.

The emphasis of the above statement arose from the results of a poll of 2,000 fans. According to Martin Cearns, at that point the chairman of the board (having recently taken over that post from his father Len), West Ham's 'Looking Forward' survey had shown that 94 per cent of those questioned wanted the club to stay at Upton Park. This was hardly a surprise as most fans of top clubs at that time would have had similar sentiments. For example, Celtic issued questionnaires to supporters and received similar results. 'Looking Forward' also found that 85 per cent of those surveyed wanted to be involved in some way in the redevelopment of the ground and 70 per cent indicated that they would be interested in buying a bond. But, of course, these statistics would never be translated into actual bond sales.

However, the survey didn't ask any questions about the idea that without a bond fans would be obliged to take their chance of getting hold of one of the 6,199 tickets available to members and visiting fans.

In reality, the very notion that the supporters would pay up to almost a grand just for the guaranteed 'right' to buy a ticket for the next half-century at additional cost − a season ticket that would give them the 'right' to sit on the seat they had occupied for so many years – was simply unbelievable; and that realisation gave a cogent meaning to the bond affair.

The aim was that all the club's season-ticket holders would become bondholders; and, even though the take-up of the scheme was well below target, it was adequate for the club to secure the underwriting of the scheme.

However, the fans understood that the scheme was trying to sell them something that was already theirs (the 'right' to buy a seat) and this was pushing their devotion to the club beyond reasonable limits; in fact, many saw it as taking advantage of their loyalty and turning it into a commodity. As we read the details before the game with Liverpool, the group I was with began to laugh out loud. Was Storrie one of the Pythons and this another version of trying to pass off a dead parrot as 'only sleeping'?

> Fan: 'Ello, I wish to register a complaint about this bond what I purchased.
> Pete: Oh yes, the, uh, the Hammers bond … What's, uh … What's wrong with it?
> Fan: I'll tell you what's wrong with it, my lad. It's just a ticket, that's what's wrong with it!
> Pete: No, no, it's, uh … a debenture.
> Fan: Look, matey, I know a ticket when I see one, and I'm looking at one right now.
> Pete: No, no, it's, it's a right! Remarkable bond, the Hammers bond, isn't it, eh? Beautiful printing!
> Fan: The printing don't enter into it. It's a ticket.
> Pete: No, no, no, no, no, no! It's an investment!

But generally the mirth soon transformed into resentment.

The three 'benefits' that came with the bond didn't seem to get anybody excited. No one seemed to be gagging to get their hands on 'bond merchandise' or care very much about having their photo taken with Bill (if you were desperate for this, it was available by hanging around Chadwell Heath after training). And why, if we were daft enough to buy one, would we sell our bond? That would mean we would not be able to go to matches which would have been the reason for buying a bond in the first place!

CHAPTER 5
HIGH FIDELITY

We are the facilitators of our own creative evolution.
BILL HICKS

The Taylor Report was published in August 1989 so, up to the board's announcement of the bond scheme, it took over two years for West Ham to react; but this was a swifter response than any other club managed. Ironically, it was in the season before the bond, as the board were hatching their plans for the scheme, that the Hammers fans demonstrated their deep feelings of fidelity to the great East London phenomenon that is West Ham United. An amazing show of allegiance during the Hammers FA Cup semi-final defeat at Villa Park in April 1991 exposed the soul of the Irons that transformed a time and a situation that would have been accepted as hopeless by many into a beautiful and glorious celebration of the progeny of the Blitz that evoked an ancestral spirit wrought in the fire of Nazi bombs and the unremitting, unforgiving shipyard furnaces that roared day and night on the banks of the Victorian Thames.

West Ham were thrashed 4–0 by Nottingham Forest in a match that was over as a contest in the opening minutes after referee Keith Hackett sent off Tony Gale, a pivotal player in the

Irons' defence. What seemed a harsh decision in effect put the encounter beyond the reach of the East London side from the Second Division. Forest were then in the top flight of the English game, under the leadership of Brian Clough and League Cup Winners of 1990. But the West Ham supporters who had made the trip to the Midlands (I was one of their number) not only took it all in their stride; they actually made a carnival out of the disaster with an unparalleled expression of loyalty rarely seen even in the most passionately supported of games.

Throughout the half-time break and the whole of the second half, 20,000 claret-and-blue-clad Cockneys chanted 'Billy Bonds's claret and blue army' with a stirring intensity and volume, many doing a sort of rain dance to the rhythm as the hapless Irons were being overrun and battered; we never wavered, the chant didn't falter or alter as Forest's fourth went in. It made no difference at all, we just went on and on: 'Billy Bonds's claret and blue army'.

As the intonation of the chant seeped into the entire atmosphere of the stadium, the Hammers players began to take long gazes into the heart of the crowd, incredulous at the will and the endurance of the hymn. As the word 'army' ended, it was shadowed by a repeat of the word coming out of the ether until there seemed to be no separation between the phrases: 'Billy Bonds's claret and blue army, army. Billy Bonds's claret and blue army, army ...'

It was a mantra of inner power, the external was irrelevant. 'We-ness' prevailed; that which was 'us' overcame the rest of reality. The game itself had transformed into something symbolic; a means to show Cockney defiance and our total self-sufficiency as a community. 'Billy Bonds's claret and blue army, army.'

It reminded me of a story I once read about a Confederate military band that were surrounded by a crack Union regiment in the American Civil War. The Union commander sent a messenger offering to take the surrender of the band; the answer was a passionate rendition of 'The Yellow Rose of Texas'. 'Billy Bonds's claret and blue army, army.'

After the game, hundreds of fans took to the pitch to make merry. Most were West Ham supporters. Ian Bishop, the Irons captain that day, looked bewildered as the travelling Hammers carried him shoulder high off the field in front of the massed ranks of Billy Bonds's still chanting claret and blue army. 'Billy Bonds's claret and blue army, army, army, army!'

There are more than a few Hammers fans who were around at the time that the West Ham bond scheme was initiated who saw that bright Birmingham afternoon when Villa Park became the site of the commodious, sacred Cockney ritual of joyous insubordination, the 'knees-up', as the moment when the board became conscious of how much they might take advantage of the club's loyal support; seeing the fan base as vulnerable to maximum exploitation, seemingly ready to put up with anything. If this was the case, they mistook defiance for compliance and solidarity for stupidity.

We didn't *celebrate* defeat that day; we were demonstrating that we *could not* be defeated. No one has ever really beaten West Ham; not *the* West Ham; those who *are* the club and the area. These people were not beaten by the starvation brought by Victorian capitalism and being whipped into the docks as industrial slaves; they were not defeated by the Kaiser and the hell of the Western Front (the nickname given by the Germans to the British soldier had that telling Cockney ring: Tommy Atkins was the warrior the enemy revered and respected). They were not destroyed by the poverty of the Depression but stood firmly, disallowing Mosley's brown-shirted fascists to walk through 'our manor', with another repeated chorus: 'They shall not pass!' Hitler, Goering and the Luftwaffe were met with a similar force of attitude. Despite the murder of tens of thousands of East Enders, the destruction by fire of homes and workplaces, the evil of fascism was resisted on the streets. Thatcher's destruction of the union protection that had long been looked to by those who have inhabited the Docklands as their one defence against the past did not overcome us. So, the idea that the board were going to be an exception to this particular tradition was and is ridiculous – the real tragedy might be that the board could fail to recognise this. But I don't believe they did. History suggests that they understood and relied on these qualities of endurance to take the club through a very sticky patch, although the men in the boardroom would have to take some abuse in the process and, as it turned out, long after.

ADDING INSULT TO INJURY

It was to the likes of those who sang and danced at Villa Park that the West Ham board seemed to want to flog bonds, which were essentially pieces of paper. Concretely, what the board were seemingly trying to 'retail' to fans was a minimal guarantee for the purchase of future season tickets in return for a non-returnable 'loan' of up to £975 (equivalent to about £3,000 at the time of writing). This is exactly the same thing as you coming round to my house to buy my old car and me telling you that I want £500 for it, but in order to pay me the £500 you need to loan me £975 that I won't be giving you back! In plain old-fashioned East End parlance, that is a blatant attempt on my part to 'half-inch' your 'dosh'.

As such, the board's offer to supporters was insult enough, one would have thought, but, even more than this, they were in effect apparently looking to take what the fans saw as their birthright and market it. It seemed the ambition was to carve off a piece of the supporters' own soul and sell it back to them. Many understandably found it hard to see the advantage of such a transaction. And, as such, the bond scheme exemplified the adage that you 'can't fool all of the people all of the time'. However, it is very unlikely that any member of the West Ham board, seasoned businessmen, with a wealth of experience of the behaviour of West Ham supporters, would think they might.

THE WEST HAM WAY/THE FAMILY CLUB

Just four weeks after the FA Cup semi-final, in the spring of 1991, the Hammers timidly yielded the Division Two Championship to Oldham Athletic, after a 2–1 Upton Park defeat by Notts County (who would gain promotion via the play-offs). But the post-match celebration was nearly as enthusiastic as that which had so recently taken place in Birmingham. The Boleyn Ground's announcer wrongly broadcast that West Ham had won the League, prompting around 10,000 supporters to invade the playing area and indulge in 10 minutes of uncontained jubilation. But, even when the man with the mike announced that Oldham had, in fact, scored a last-minute winner to snatch the trophy, the festivity, peculiarly, continued unabated. The fans chose to focus on their team's impending promotion to the highest rank of English football and not another uninspiring disintegration and the loss of glory involved in being merely runners-up.

However, as the 'Hammers-bond saga' continued, the Cearns clan became increasingly unpopular. When the board made the decision to launch the bond scheme, the fable of the 'family club' was finally exposed as a charade. Of course, there had been indications that this was the case in the past; the shock sale of prolific goalscorer and local boy Syd Puddefoot to Falkirk in 1921 caused uproar among the West Ham fans. In 1963, the removal of Phil Woosnam to Aston Villa was seen as yet another example of duplicity. However, transfers had always been passed off as 'harsh necessity' and consistently linked with building works. You always know when a big name is about to leave Upton Park; there are protracted denials that one player is leaving, then another one goes. With Puddefoot it was Ruffell; with Rio Ferdinand it was Trevor Sinclair.

The bond scheme for many Hammers supporters felt like the first assault directly on the literal place of the fans; it was felt that the very seats they occupied were being held to ransom by a group who had historically portrayed themselves as trustees rather than the owners they were. The club was only a 'family' in the sense that it had consistently applied the 'domestic model' of management, which was all about paternalism, platitudes, patronisation and the direct administrative progeny of the age of colonialism (in which most of the board had been born and raised) when those in the empire were often thought of and referred to as 'family' or 'children'.

However, the board seemed to have badly misjudged the mood and attitude of the club's supporters, which demonstrated to many that, far from being a family, the figures that inhabited the boardroom at Upton Park were totally unfamiliar with the West Ham fan base. Perhaps one of the painful, yet healthy side-effects of the whole bond-scheme affair was that it ended the lie of the supposed 'kith and kin' ethos that was traditionally claimed to pervade Upton Park. It appeared to be markedly closer to the relationship between the British Raj and those they colonised.

This is not to say that there had never been efforts on the part of players and others to reach out to the community that surrounds the Boleyn Ground. John Lyall visited my home as a boy when I wrote him a letter and, later in life, after he retired from football, I was a guest at his farm. Ron Greenwood had a policy of sending out his first-team players to coach in local schools, and I will never forget Clyde Best teaching me and my mates over at Southern Road Playing Field, just a five-minute walk from the 'Home of the Hammers'. When I ran a youth club in Bethnal Green, both Pat Holland and John Lyall came to present the kids with prizes and stayed all evening to sign autographs, etc. A few years ago, I was giving a series of free lectures about the history of West Ham at Bethnal Green Library. After the final one, I was approached by a woman and her daughter who had attended every session. They told me they were lifelong fans of the Hammers but, as they were a single-parent family and the girl needed specialist medical treatment, they could not afford the price of a ticket to Upton Park. The next day I wrote to Terry Brown, telling him of this family's plight. A few weeks later, the woman wrote to me and told me that she had received tickets for a top match along with a compliments slip signed by Brown. But West Ham United never were, and never will be, mainly in business as a sort of community-service provider (although West Ham in the Community and the West Ham Learning Zone have made huge contributions to East London); it is, and always has been, a business. In itself, this is not a problem; the real problem is that it's not the way the board has portrayed itself throughout the history of the club. As such, when the stark capitalist nature of the organisation that is West Ham United was revealed by way of the bond scheme, many fans, who for generations had been brought up with tosh like the 'West Ham way' and 'the family club', felt betrayed.

It is often the case with working-class institutions that those who breathe life into them, the mass of those who use the institution, tend to give the credit for what they have created to small and detached elites. In the Church, this is the clergy; in industry, it is shareholders and directors; in politics, it is MPs and party workers. This trait has been damaging in the past to working-class-based movements. Unions have been made impotent by the removal of their leaders; the black community in the USA had its voice effectively taken away by the slaying of their figureheads (Martin Luther King, Malcolm X). But, like West Ham, all of these entities would not have any existence whatsoever without the 'rank and file', 'the grass roots', 'the people' (hence the Black Panthers' motto 'All Power to the People'). West Ham, the community of football which has its centre at Upton Park, has been created by generations of supporters; its existence has very little to do with those who sit on the board, although they are needed in terms of the physical development of the ground and the team, etc. Every one of them is expendable. They can be replaced individually or a whole new structure of management can be put in place. This is not the case in terms of the fans. They are irreplaceable. You can't ship in 40,000 people to pay exorbitant amounts of money to *support* something unless they feel in some way that what they are 'supporting' belongs to them. Hence, what makes what we recognise as West Ham – the feeling, the fraternity, the soul and spirit of this phenomenon – is the fans. They are its congregation, its workforce, its foot soldiers, its crew, the membership, the life's blood, 'the people'. It is among and between each of 'us' that West Ham exists. Understand that and, historically, apart from all other considerations, the Hammers board have been part of that, you begin to have a real grasp of the nature of what might be called the culture of West Ham United. However, the contemporary rise of the insistence on success and football clubs showing a profit consistent with alternative investments means that more than ever it is those of us who give our support to our team who will foster that heritage. The situation of the modern game has made boards more or less irrelevant in the task of 'keeping the faith'. We, the fans, are now the sole definers of difference and identity that our clubs embody.

CHAPTER 6
BROWN MEANT BUSINESS

Did you ever hear of a kid playing accountant?
JACKIE MASON

I think there was more to the bond scheme than the usual straightforward analysis of the events that has surrounded this particular 'innovation' suggests because I believe that at least some members of the West Ham board had much more business acumen than they have been given credit for. So much in the world of boundless commerce (here I'm not referring to the ethics of small business or organisational management) is premised on 'craft' and guile. As in war, you don't let your enemy (competitor) know what you are doing; in fact, you get them to believe you are doing one thing and then you do another. A day at the office may entail setting up ruses, laying false trails and setting diversionary tactics in place. If you inhabit this world, this becomes a way of life more than a job; it takes you over as it becomes your way of 'being'. It may be true that some of the West Ham directors believed that the bond scheme in its public incarnation was the answer to West Ham's financial needs, but, given Terry Brown's background, it seems highly doubtful that he was ever convinced that such a crude mechanism could of itself be adequate. However, it might well have been a tool that provided a means to an end.

Brown was and is more than a businessman. He has an exceptional devotion to West Ham that it would be hard for many fans to better. While a board member, and more so as a chairman, on the worst days of East London winters, he was consistently to be seen watching West Ham teams at any and every level, from kids to stars. At the same time, he is also a proud man with regard to his own business record. These two facets of his make-up would prove to be great assets to West Ham United.

At Southwold Primary School in Hackney, Terry passed the 11 plus, and so was taking his first step up the post-war educational ladder. However, his marks were good enough for him to be offered a scholarship at a public school. His mother turned down the opportunity, but the young Brown attended Parmiters Foundation Grammar School, a former public school that had been established in Bethnal Green in 1681 (in 1977, it relocated to Hertfordshire). It is one of the highest-performing schools in the country and was and is highly selective.

While he was at Parmiters, Brown also studied classical music at the London College of Music, a leading independent music conservatoire founded in 1887, in Great Marlborough Street in central London.

The Brown family owned a caravan in St Osyths, a seaside resort about five miles west of Clacton, Essex, and this allowed Terry and his brother Ken to experience a different environment. But the Browns needed to let the caravan for holiday rents to meet the costs of keeping it as a family holiday resource. It was quite a trek from East London to Northeast Essex in those days, but, during the football season on 'changeover days' (when one family of holidaymakers would leave and another arrive), Terry and his dad would drive to the site to clean and tidy the caravan, and on the way home stop off to watch Colchester United, Clacton Town or, occasionally, Ipswich Town. Terry had seen Mike Grice play for Colchester United several times and was pleased when he joined West Ham in 1955 to be part of the 1958 Second Division promotion-winning side that included such Hammers legends as Ken Brown, Noel Cantwell and John Bond.

Whenever possible, Terry's dad recruited him as a 'van boy' and, having grafted on the great square Dennis lorry, emblazoned with 'Sylko Crepe Paper Mills Ltd., Lea Bridge Road, Leyton E.10. Ley 1015/6', Terry grew up with an understanding of hard work and with plenty of incentive to 'better' himself, as he would have witnessed the toll taxing, laborious toil took on people who earned their living by muscle and sweat.

There was a dramatic change in Terry's family life when, as he hit his teenage years, his mother began to suffer from nervous exhaustion (what today might be recognised as a nervous breakdown) as a result of working as a machinist, doing piecework during the day, then cleaning in the evenings. By this time, she also had to maintain the caravan at St Osyths and travelled there every weekend to make it ready for the new occupants. In the end, everything caught up with her and she became seriously ill. This meant Terry had to leave school at the age of 15.

Given his academic gifts, Terry could have seen this as a bitter loss, but from a relatively early age he had the ambition to make the move into business. However, he was obliged to start his working life sweeping up in a factory in Dalston. The industrious Brown lad progressed to magnetising magnets and soon identified a business opportunity. Terry had earned his pocket money at school by selling football programmes, so it was natural for him to continue to pursue his business instincts in the world of work. The factory had a workforce of 660, and Terry was able to make use of his father's lorry and buy goods that could be sold to those workers in the tradition of the post–War East End 'informal trading' culture. My own father started up in business in much the same way and, like Brown's dad, hired himself and his lorry out to local businesses, although the chocolate teddy bears portrayed on the side of his first vehicle probably attracted a different type of business.

After a while, Brown managed to establish a very useful trading company and eventually ended up with over 30 'agents' not only selling in the factory but also in other factories and offices throughout East London. This is how Brown developed the simple ethic that guided the rest of his life: he found the harder he worked, the more successful he became. He recognised that luck always plays a part in any success, but, of course, luck comes more readily to those who look for it.

Slowly, Terry built up quite a useful cash fund, which he later invested in tenanted properties. His ability to understand the law of supply and demand enabled him to see that land was only going to get more expensive over time as God wasn't making any more of it. Every time he accrued £600 of profit, Brown used it to buy a house and that was the basis of the business he subsequently developed. He then progressed on two fronts.

Terry left the factory to join the Royal Exchange (opposite the Bank of England) where he would have fitted in quite well given that his education would have done much to expunge any obvious traits of his East End roots. In this fulcrum of British capitalism, Brown was able to teach himself how to invest large sums of money in major publicly quoted companies.

After leaving the Royal Exchange to become assistant company secretary at Ridgeways, the tea and coffee merchants, Brown then moved into the property industry, where he was assistant to the chairman of what was then one of Britain's largest property companies. Terry later became involved in acquiring companies for Bovis, an organisation whose foundations were 10 years older than West Ham's, having been established in 1885. In 1972, Bovis Homes were the second largest house builder in the UK and two years later became part of the P&O Group, a major international logistics and transport company.

While moving up the business ladder, Terry and his brother spent seven years studying. The first two years were taken up in obtaining the National Certificate in Business Studies at the East London College of Commerce in Whitechapel. They qualified as company secretaries with both the Chartered Institute of Secretaries and the Corporation of Secretaries. They then qualified with the Institute of Taxation and, finally, with the Association of Certified Accountants.

For Brown, his experience as a teenager trying to build a small enterprise helped him understand how business worked. Alongside his brother, he continued building up his private property company, acquiring houses and building lock-up garages.

By their mid-twenties, the Brown boys had found a financial backer in the improbable shape of the Duke of St Albans and were able to purchase a packing-case-manufacturing business in Sheffield and a large timber merchants trading throughout Surrey and South London, and developed a housing arm, renovating and building over 500 houses a year, while also setting up various other businesses.

While involved with West Ham, Brown continued to retain other business directorships and shareholdings. When West Ham's controlling shareholders asked him to become the paid executive chairman of the club in 1996 – arguing that they had deep concerns for the future of the club unless Brown was prepared to commit himself to it full-time – together with Paul Aldridge (who took on a full-time role at Upton Park at the same time as Terry), Terry's wife Jean took over the management of the Sussex

Beach Holiday Village and it became an American-style vacation park with 300 bungalows let on 21-year leases. Brown also managed a large office complex on the Isle of Wight. Terry's brother took over the management of other businesses: a large industrial estate in Kingston, Surrey; 200 retirement homes in Lincolnshire; a caravan park in Skegness and a residential portfolio, which included large blocks of rented luxury apartments in Kensington and Knightsbridge as well as various other luxury flats and houses in and around Hyde Park, Chelsea, Sloane Square and Westminster. There was also the residue of the houses purchased for £600 each in the 1960s. The Brown property empire housed an impressive list of well-known tenants. But, for Terry, his most significant tenants continued to be those who had originally called on his services four decades ago.

This background certainly does not suggest 'dodgy stall-holder'. Brown is a classy businessman and a slick entrepreneur. Not only does he have a head for trading and the market on a grand scale, but he also has the knowledge that comes with qualification and experience. To understand him as a common, unsophisticated shyster (as some detractors have implied) is a mistake that could only be made by those who are either ignorant of his personal history or totally naive about the way modern business and financial management proceeds.

There are a number of things that a successful businessperson must know in order to take best advantage of investments over the long term. Four of the most important of these things are:

1. Know and, over the long term, satisfy customers and employees
2. Understand and keep on good terms with product suppliers
3. Be aware of the market and what competitors are doing
4a. At any one time promote at least two ideas that might be the same idea

4b. Plan 'B' is often Plan 'A' – maintaining control, keep everything flexible

4c. Plan 'A' is often part of Plan 'B' – maintaining control, keep everything flexible

I don't think that Terry Brown ever thought for one minute that West Ham fans, in their tens of thousands, were going to buy the deal that the Hammers bond scheme offered. But, whether they did or not, I believe he understood that he would get what he set out to achieve in terms of redeveloping the stadium. Most successful businesspeople in their maturity do not want to simply make money; they want to create successful businesses. People who are just money oriented are usually not very creative, and therefore cannot create successful businesses. A successful business will of course make money, but that becomes a feature of the businessperson's enterprise rather than its purpose. West Ham United is a successful business in that it has more or less maintained its position as one of the top-20 organisations of its type in the most lucrative football market in the world over decades. It could, of course, be more successful and, if a business does not look to develop (change), it will, like all organic entities, enter a state of entropy and eventually die.

CHAPTER 7
BATTLE OF THE BOND

Don't follow any advice, no matter how good, until you feel as deeply in your spirit as you think in your mind that the counsel is wise.

Forty for you, sixty for me. And equal partners we will be.

Never floss with a stranger.
JOAN RIVERS

Terry Brown was eventually to say that the way the notion and aim of the bond scheme was mediated to the fans constituted a public-relations disaster. But in truth there was no 'good' way to put the plan over. Hardly any of the club's supporters saw it as much more than a scam. Most long-term fans were offended by the implication that they were required to purchase a bond or lose the right to renew their season ticket.

It soon became clear when only 300 bonds had been sold that the scheme was going to be drastically undersubscribed, but crucially the initial sales had somehow been enough to secure the underwriting of the finance needed to redevelop the stadium. However, the feelings of hurt and anxiety engendered by the bond, together with the poor results attained by the team, sparked a wave of unrest among the most loyal of fans. On-pitch protests and demonstrations ensued as supporters expressed their frustration and sense of betrayal in what became West Ham's winter of discontent. A direct, immediate and damaging consequence was that attendance figures plummeted (as low as 11,000).

The original aim that all season-ticket holders would become bondholders was always overambitious to say the least, given the cost of the bond and underlying messages it communicated. Following the scheme's poor reception, talks were held with representatives of the bondholders, resulting in the board relaxing the very limited conditions of the scheme. They offered more in the way of benefits, including a decade-long discount on season-ticket prices for bondholders (to conclude after the 2001/02 season).

Brown fully supported the bond scheme and, throughout his tenure at Upton Park, he continued to insist that the scheme provided the necessary resources to build the stadium that West Ham fans know today. As such, for Brown, the bond was critical for the regeneration of the club. Although the anger of the fans gave Terry his first personal taste of mass fan unrest, he was aware that the club had been through periods in the past when the board and the fans failed to see eye to eye.

However, Brown believed the supporters never totally understood or, in some cases, were completely unaware of the importance of the underwriting agreement West Ham had with the banks; for a fee of £145,375 the club was able to underwrite the cost of building the Bobby Moore and Centenary Stands. In retrospect, Brown is probably correct that most supporters did not appreciate this, although it is difficult to see how they could have fully grasped this point, which was hardly advertised in lights. This said, it is likely that, in order to secure the underwriting, it was not possible to widely publicise the strategy Brown might have been deploying. As such, the supporters may at no time have been in a position to be fully conscious of what was going on. They, for the most part, took the information that was given to them by the board and reacted to that. But even the obviously failing bond achieved the basic aim of the scheme; development costs were underwritten.

BATTLE OF THE BOND

According to Brown, he knew of no other way to finance the development of both stands and, even with the benefit of hindsight, he could not see any other alternative given the work that needed doing. The cost of land alone was £1.6m and Castle Street (at the rear of the Bobby Moore Stand) also had to be acquired and closed. At that time, Britain was in the middle of a severe economic recession; interest rates were touching 18 per cent, and, as such, Brown believed the money could not have been raised in any other way.

Billy Bonds believed that the bond scheme had a detrimental impact on West Ham's on-field performance. After four games, the Hammers were in 10th place, two points behind Coventry City in third spot, equal on points with Leeds United and Liverpool. Following a difficult phase, West Ham staged something of a recovery in the autumn with consecutive victories against London rivals at Highbury and Spurs at the Boleyn Ground. At the start of November, after four straight wins, West Ham looked pretty secure in 14th position. Pre-season recruits Mitchell Thomas and Mike Small seemed to be finding their shooting boots, Small hitting the net 10 times in 15 starts. The next game saw the Irons hold Liverpool to a draw; that was the day the scheme was announced. By the New Year, the Hammers hung one place and one point off the bottom of the League and a defeat at White Hart Lane on 1 April left the East Londoners stranded under the weight of 21 other clubs at the foot of the table. West Ham's demise correlated almost precisely with the coming of the bond scheme.

It is not altogether clear how the bond could have affected on-field results. However, it does seem as though the bond wove a destructive spell over Upton Park. There was a string of protests that did impact on the players. Perhaps the bad feeling between the board and the crowd was enough in itself to divert the players from what they were doing.

However, the way some of the club employees went about things certainly had the potential to leave a bad taste in anyone's mouth. At the height of the fan unrest that followed the coming of the bond, a goalmouth sit-in took place on 14 March 1992 at the Boleyn Ground match against Arsenal. This motivated Storrie to invite some of the 'revolting fans' into the boardroom to discuss their grievances. But such was Storrie's devotion to the promotion of the scheme that the seeming peace talks were no more than an attempt to transform shows of discontent into an opportunity to reiterate the benefits and necessity of the bond scheme. As with everything else connected to the bond, it failed in the making.

Hammers captain Julian Dicks, together with Billy Bonds, declined a request by the board to openly support the bond scheme. Bonds was to declare that he would never have placed himself in opposition to the board or the fans on the bond scheme. He was ready to accept that it was what the club wanted, knowing that he had a responsibility to the board, but he also understood that he had an obligation to the fans. As such, Bill felt he could never give unqualified support to the bond scheme. He did take part in a photo-shoot with some bondholders, but stated this was not giving his agreement to the way the club was intending to treat its supporters. For Bonds, it was 'diabolical'. To add to the strife, Bill was suffering emotional turmoil as the season progressed, with both his father and father-in-law passing away during the course of the campaign.

More than anything else, the bond scheme had provoked antagonism among the fans towards the club, but at the same time a wave of alarm went through the body of West Ham's support. People felt almost blackmailed by the possibility that, without a bond, no supporter would be able to purchase a seat, and many fans would have rather paid the monetary price than take on the personal cost of losing a part of what they perceived as their identity. This particular fire was stoked by the prospectus that was sent out to season-ticket holders, which carried the threat that 'missing out' entailed, and some fans dug deep in their wallets to allay their anxieties.

Prior to the launch of the bond scheme, there was no organised body of West Ham fans apart from the official supporters' club. That organisation was well known for its canine-like devotion to the Upton Park administration and, as such, it began to look like many would wander blindly into taking part in the scheme. But, even if no more than a large minority of the supporters became bondholders, it was feared that non-bondholders would become a sort of second-class citizen in the Upton Park empire.

From the very first whispers about the bond scheme, the three West Ham fanzines of the time had set themselves against it, and *Over Land and Sea* (*OLAS*), *Fortunes Always Hiding* and *On The Terraces* (*OTT*) founded the Hammers Independent Supporters' Association (HISA) and provided spokespeople from HISA with publicity and support.

Prior to the club's official announcement of the scheme, the three fanzine editors, Gary Firmager of *OLAS*, Steve Rapport of *Fortunes* and Marc Williams of *OTT*, were asked to attend a meeting with club secretary Tom Finn and Peter Storrie to give their views about the bond scheme. Dutifully, they voiced their doubts but also came up with an alternative set of ideas, involving a mixture of a private limited-share issue, a more modest debenture scheme and longer-term season tickets. Storrie and Finn told the editors that they valued their views and that the meeting was 'the beginning of a new and historic phase in club/supporter relationships'.

Another meeting was scheduled and HISA agreed not to carry out its first 'Red Card' protest that had been planned for the Liverpool match that was broadcast live on ITV on 17

November 1991. After HISA's members saw that details of the scheme had been published in *Hammer*, they felt the meeting had been a bit of a diversionary tactic, designed to deflect their attention and stop the scheme from being attacked in front of a massive live-television audience.

The response was to open the membership of the HISA committee to supporters. Anyone seeking a role was asked to put their names forward for election at a public meeting at the Boleyn pub, the famed hostelry a minute's walk from the main gates of Upton Park on the corner of Green Street and the Barking Road. In the fanzines, as part of a recruitment advert, HISA announced their intention to oppose the bond scheme and requested a £5 donation from readers to fund operations. In their initial full-page message, HISA declared, 'In short [it's] a club happy to call its fans the best in the land, but continually refuses to treat us as such. We want all West Ham supporters to join HISA so that we can have one united voice and ultimately have a bigger say in what happens at the club, both on and off the field.'

Leaflets handed out to supporters outside Upton Park that detailed HISA's aim to resist the board provided the fans with the opportunity to consider what was being put to them and probably prevented sizeable numbers of supporters from panic-buying bonds.

It was uncertain how many people attended HISA's inaugural public meeting, but it was a crowded Boleyn that saw fans make their dissatisfaction and anger clear by way of money and pledging their allegiance to withstanding the bond scheme. HISA, encouraged by the response, began to organise the first of a succession of protests, the aim of which was to undermine the bond scheme.

The Boleyn meeting was more about letting people know HISA's agenda than framing policy or tactics, as the founding members had put a strategy together prior to that first gathering, starting with the aim of getting the maximum number of supporters to sign up to the cause and offering them a determined leadership to push what was a single-issue manifesto.

Although drumming up a surprisingly beefy membership, HISA was not a democratic organisation, as, from the start, it was thought that voting on issues would mean delayed action and perhaps compromise the strength of protest. An elite group, the committee made all the tactical decisions and passed instructions to probably, at the height of HISA's action, about 150 activists 'on the streets' who acted as distributors of literature and agitators on the terraces and around the ground. This allowed HISA to keep its intentions secret, and so foil any possible attempts the club might make to insert moles in the structure, although quite why the board would want a mole or what they would do with one is unclear. In any case, it was not hard to find out the information about HISA action.

The initial HISA protest involved the distribution of A4-sized red cards carrying the slogan 'Resign' among the fans prior to matches at Upton Park with instructions to hold them aloft at half-time. On the other side of the card, HISA detailed their concise policy, describing the bond as 'attempted blackmail'.

From the point of the bond's launch, over the next two months, the team did not win a game in the League and had dropped into the relegation places. Following a 3–0 Boxing Day defeat at Notts County, the visiting supporters staged a 20-minute sit-down, chanting, 'Sack the board.' By the time Champions-elect Leeds United left Upton Park with a 3–1 victory on New Year's Day, the Hammers found themselves second from bottom of the table. After failing to better non-league Farnborough Town at the Boleyn Ground in the third round of the FA Cup (4 January 1992), a mass of supporters took to the field of play, chanting the now familiar refrain 'Sack the board'. For Irons skipper Julian Dicks, the club seemed to be at an all-time low: 'The mood is bad and the morale is low, probably lower than at any time since I have been here.'

This demonstrates that the protests certainly had a negative effect on the players.

Long-time stalwart Steve Potts was to reflect, 'The supporters weren't happy and quite rightly so in my opinion.'

Several hundred fans refused to leave the stadium for some two hours before half-a-dozen supporters were invited to meet the board.

This type of event was to become a feature of games at Upton Park. A week later, West Ham were held to a tedious 1–1 draw by Wimbledon. As the final whistle blew, a fan dashed to the centre circle and just sat down in the mud, and this one bloke seemed to express the feelings of angry despair shared by many thousands of fans.

He was soon joined by a group who had vacated the east side of the ground (the Chicken Run) in such large numbers that stewards were unable to prevent their movement. This was followed by waves from both the North and South Banks (now the Centenary and Bobby Moore Stands). This advanced guard (close to 3,000) was supported by around 10,000 fans who stayed in their seats for over an hour after the match (principally those in the upper stands). All were chanting 'Cearns out' and singing to the melody of John Hughes's 'Cwm Rhondda':

We won't take,
We won't take,
We won't take this shit no more,
(This shit no mo-ore),
We won't take this shit no more.

I was among those who took to the pitch that day and, as in most protests, there was a sense of jubilation. An impromptu kick-around was instigated at one point, with a ball made out of crushed match-day programmes. I had managed to loop the 'ball' out to the right and the guy who picked up the subsequent cross killed it on his chest with a grace that would have done Budgie Byrne proud. He beat a steward who was looking to protect the goal and hit a shot high into the net. It was the best West Ham goal all season.

This went on for the better part of 90 minutes after the last kick of the game (the one with Wimbledon!) and even continued when the board gave instructions to switch off the floodlights (neglecting to first dim them and so risked damage to these expensive and delicate illuminations). The event was concluded with a huge – somewhat predictable but necessary – Hokey Cokey.

At another point, a group of supporters stormed the directors' lounge and 'Mr Len' then felt the rancour of the fans. Seeming not to have a clue about what was going on (the whole situation was entirely outside anything in Cearns's experience), Lenny made a few rather pathetic attempts to mollify the unhappy claret-and-blue faithful. Although he got absolutely nowhere, he persisted in trying to 'discuss matters' with the hurt Hammers fans long after the other directors had made their retreat to the interior of the stand and left him to his fate. The police requested that Bonds make an attempt to quell the situation, but the West Ham manager wasn't entirely convinced that the majority of those arguing with Cearns were, in fact, West Ham supporters. Looking up at the group from the North Bank, I was inclined to agree. Although it was impossible to be definite, I got the impression that the whole thing was staged. Bill was handed a microphone (which was predictably faulty and made him sound like Norman Collier) and sent out like the Fifth Cavalry to the directors' box with orders to pour oil on troubled waters. The reaction to Bonds gave the game away for me, as no long-term or committed West Ham supporters would have reacted to him in the way this group did. There was little difference between their response to the two-time FA Cup winner and their tirade at Cearns.

While Bill indulged in a bit of semaphore pleading for calm, the pitch was lit up with little bonfires.

The protest made the following day's newspapers. An image of the frustrated throng on the field, one of whom carried a placard that proclaimed 'Lying Thieving Cheats', was lodged between the headlines of many of the Sunday papers.

The club claimed that seats had been broken and stewards injured, and as such a huge police presence was organised to prevent any such action during the FA Cup replay with Farnborough.

The pitch invasion had not been part of HISA's plans, although, as it probably had more impact than anything else, they did take advantage of it. However, Len's last stand had looked aggressive and seemed to have the potential to turn violent. HISA wanted to avoid any such association with naked and forthright hostility that might have aligned them with simple hooligans in the eyes of the media, and, of course, there was always the danger of criminal charges being brought. This attitude was something of a problem for HISA. They wanted to harness the raw anger of the fans and championed the cause in emotive language, portraying themselves, albeit suggestively rather than overtly, as the defenders of the 'working-class' supporter. But, at the same time, HISA adopted bourgeois values, set by their organisational structure, which blended elements of oligarchic and autocratic control with a reluctance to show genuine anger, instead looking to channel it into what their elite leadership deemed 'peaceful protest'. At the same time, the HISA committee fostered media contacts, informing them of the stunts they had instructed their followers to initiate.

These included the 'Stand Up, Sit Down' protest during the FA Cup tie against Wrexham (4 February 1992). As the match started, most of the supporters on the terraces sat down for around six minutes. At the same time, many hundreds in the stands took to their feet. On the plus side, it drew some attention, although not everyone understood what it was about and it also looked very silly. It felt like a middle-class stunt that in a way diminished the protestors; they had literally become the HISA committee's puppets.

Peter Cullen and the HISA committee were quick to distance themselves from West Ham's tragic season on the pitch. Cullen told the press before the Wrexham game that the protest was not intended to be an attack on the team, but a protest against the board. However, not all of those standing up and sitting down made this distinction. Many of those I spoke to during and after the game didn't see much of a division between the team and the board, and saw themselves as protesting against the club's overall failure to meet expectations. A few were openly aiming their anger at the players and/or the manager, while others thought it was 'just a larf'.

On 10 February, around 200 people attended HISA's second public meeting at the Denmark Arms, East Ham (there was something unintentionally sardonic about this choice of venue, a place where Hammers players of the 1950s used to get a 'free lunch'). The club had declared that the plans for the bond scheme would not be changed and claimed that the number of bondholders had reached the four-figure mark while 10,000 enquiries from supporters interested in purchasing a debenture had been made.

However, although Peter Storrie denied this, the newspapers were telling how, in order to raise funds, the whole of the West Ham side had been put in the shop window, which didn't really correspond with the boasts the club were making about the popularity of the bond scheme. It all looked a big mess from whatever angle one cared to look at things. However, one of the great ruses of battle is to confuse the enemy on the field. This gives the advantage to the generals who initiate the chaos.

Storrie took up an invitation to attend the meeting at the Denmark Arms along with John Ball, the stadium manager at Upton Park. On arrival, Storrie was offered a worryingly shaky chair to address the fans who had turned up. Plaistow Pete (Storrie had been born within a short walk of Upton Park) was certainly seen as an object of disdain among a certain strata of Hammers fans as exemplified by a popular ditty at the Boleyn Ground at the time; to the tune of 'Knees Up, Mother Brown', it went,

Who's up Cearnsy's arse?
Who's up Cearnsy's arse?
Peter, Peter Storrie is!
Peter, Peter Storrie is!

Although understandable, it was unfortunate that the little bloke was more or less pilloried by a torrent of accusations. Pete was eventually allowed to speak and, to his credit, he talked to his unsympathetic audience unprompted by a script, acting out his concern. But he didn't convince me. He hung around for around 40 minutes, including a question and answer session. Storrie didn't really compromise anything the club had done so far, but for some inexplicable reason he was given generous and seemingly grateful applause when he dismounted his unstable podium.

When Storrie left, the HISA committee announced it had plans for mass protests during the next two games at Upton Park but declined to provide any details about what shape these would take. The meeting, rather strangely, concluded with a rendition of 'I'm Forever Blowing Bubbles'.

This secrecy was indicative of the way HISA operated. Captain Manwaring like, reasoning that there could be 'fifth columnists' among those gathered at the Denmark, knowledge about intended action was kept within a very restricted circle. I had seen this kind of secrecy before during the miners' strike of the 1980s and always got the impression then that it was more about the organisers keeping power and influence to themselves than anything else. If the club did know about any protest, there was very little anyone could have done about it. How do you stop people holding up red cards for instance?

While not telling its own members of its plans, HISA did inform the *Daily Mirror*, at that point the self-appointed representative of the football proletariat, with enough information to fuel a two-page editorial on the morning of the West Ham v Everton match (29 February), telling supporters to 'Stand up and be counted'. Those attending Old Trafford, Maine Road and Highfield Road brandished red cards. At Anfield, the Scousers collectively declared, 'We all hate seats' and 'You'll never seat the Kop'. It looked like the bond issue had got a bit lost in a protest about seating.

HISA committee members such as Peter Cullen and Shane Barber had turned up on BBC and ITV regional news programmes and Sky TV. A 6ft 'HISA chicken' made her appearance on ITV's *London Tonight*. 'Chicken Ron', as 'it' called itself, may have caused many viewers to have a chuckle, but, when I saw this figure on my television screen, I just squirmed. The thought came to me: 'Is this necessary?' Chicken Ron made light of the issue and made anyone associated with his cause look like to fools.

Before the Upton Park game with Everton, HISA, as part of what had become a national protest against all-seat stadiums, stationed people at every turnstile handing out over 10,000 red balloons and organised the waving of red cards at half-time. This association, with what was in effect an 'anti-Taylor' sentiment, did little for HISA's cause as the push against the bond got hijacked by the debate outside of the East End. This said, many of those involved 'on the ground' with the resistance to the bond seemed to convince themselves that it was their issue specifically that was being supported by 'the family of football'. I found this a macabre sort of wish-fulfilment, to say the least. It has been argued that the two issues were related and that, from the start, HISA had been against both the bond and seating. But it was the principle of the bond that had provoked anger and fear among West Ham supporters and was the major motivating factor for any bedrock of support HISA might have boasted.

Looking from a wider perspective, it seemed that what was going on at Upton Park among the fans was much more a part of a national disenchantment with the rulers of the club game than a mere 'local issue'. But at the same time I heard HISA activists talking about how 'anti-bond movements' were 'sprouting all over the country'. Working in the Midlands and the North, I was congratulated as a West Ham fan for 'fighting for the terraces'.

The balloons were released by the crowd just before the start of the match with Everton. It gave the next day's newspapers lines like 'THE BALLOON GOES UP', and photographers, given the tip-off by HISA, were able to capture some predictable pictures. A Sky TV camera also found its way into the West Stand.

During the game, the great Welsh international goalkeeper Neville Southall spent a good deal of the opening minutes of the match bursting the balloons that threatened to impede his performance. But Everton were 2–0 in front when a West Ham supporter plucked a corner flag and made a dash for the centre circle, 'replanted' it and then sat down, with his arms folded. The Hammers skipper, Julian Dicks, put an arm around him, and uprooted the flag for its return to its original plot. Martin 'Mad

Dog' Allen began negotiating with the pitch invader. But it was too late. Dozens of supporters were now on the pitch, mainly congregating under the directors' box, demanding, 'Sack the board.' The police finally turned up, but there was now such a crowd on the field that referee Arthur Smith was obliged to call both sides off the pitch. It was almost 10 minutes before the game could be resumed.

Of course, the Sunday newspapers lapped it up. Peter Cullen, speaking for HISA – once more distancing himself and HISA from the action of the fans, not seeing the incursion on to the field of play as a 'proper protest' – expressed his fear that the pitch invasion would have negative repercussions for the anti-bond campaign. In the *People*, he argued, reminiscent of the whining quality of a school monitor, 'We organised the balloons as a proper protest. Invasions [during the game] destroy everything we're doing.'

It appeared that the supporters weren't keen to be controlled by HISA after all and that it wasn't providing much in the way of 'leadership', and it seemed to at least some fans that HISA didn't like the fans doing anything that they didn't want them to do. There had been an on-field fracas between Birmingham and Stoke that day, and, although the St Andrew's encounter had nothing to do with the general protests against seating, a few newspapers conflated it with what happened at Upton Park. But, overall, the storming of the Boleyn Ground pitch did not meet with total condemnation by the media. More than a few sports journalists were Hammers fans and were unhappy with the way the board were managing the club. The likes of Jack Steggles, an esteemed correspondent, in an open letter to the board in the following Monday's *Daily Star* wrote, 'Dear Sirs, I have a simple question to ask you, the people running – or should I say ruining – West Ham: What the hell are you doing to the club I love?'

Tony Cottee, the former West Ham and England star, who had been in the Everton team on 29 February, gave his support to the Hammers fans, telling reporters, 'What has happened to all the money they had from transfers, like the £2m they got from me? Of course I feel sympathy for the fans. If you've got a family of four, how the hell are they meant to pay out for those bonds? What this club needs is for the directors to dip their hands in their pockets.'

Julian Dicks also backed West Ham supporters when he declared, 'I agree with what they [the fans] are doing, even if I don't agree with the way they are doing it. Their actions could cost us points but it's their way of showing the club they are unhappy. I think they are totally justified in doing that. They pay our wages and pay to keep this club alive. The bond scheme is wrong; you can't ask an ordinary bloke to fork out up to £975 just to watch his favourite football team. Something has to be done, and quickly.'

This amounted to a shocking public censure for the board. The Terminator went on to make it clear that, if he weren't an employee of the club, he might have joined the protest: 'The unrest has been there for a long time. I'd like to help, but there's nothing I can do.'

During the week following the Everton game, it was reported that Peter Storrie got himself to the West Ham training ground in Chadwell Heath to reprimand the club captain. Oh to have seen that particular encounter: Bud Abbot's Lou Costello v *Die Hard*'s John McClane. Poor old Dicksy; it must have been like being mauled by Paddington Bear. Demonstrating the effectiveness of Storrie's tongue lashing on the Hammers skipper, a few short weeks later, Jules reiterated his point of view in a fanzine interview and told how other players were in agreement with his position saying he 'wouldn't buy one [a bond] because they are a lot of money and are morally wrong.

BATTLE OF THE BOND

There is a lot said by quite a few of the lads, but they won't say anything in public. I was the only one that spoke up, so it was obvious that I was the only one that would get spoken to.'

The protest of 29 February is seen by some as the incident that put an end to the bond scheme. But it was an open secret that only around 500 bonds had been sold at that point. However, the board still didn't admit defeat but rather opted to relaunch the bond with a few inconsequential adjustments. One incredible alteration was that potential 'investors' could get 'preferential loans' to pay for bonds. Originally, it had been deemed that prospective bond buyers could purchase bonds over a five-year period. Now the club was prepared to provide loans to pay for the bonds (loans for a loan!) that needed to be paid back over two years. So the wonderful new option was you either used your own money over five years or you borrowed money from the club that needed to be repaid in two years. There was also the offer of up to £100 discount per season to bondholders who purchased a season ticket for the next decade (but there was no guarantee that the price of the season ticket wouldn't go up by £100 at any point or over a number of years). Of course, that made all the difference!

At the same time, the club informed fans of a huge increase in season-ticket prices for the coming season. Supporters were told that this was going to happen even if the club were relegated. The board announced that bondholders would be able to purchase season tickets for the following season at that season's prices while the rest of the club's supporters would have to pay the increased prices. This seemed like business madness as the club appeared destined for Second Division football, and, as such, even without any hike in prices, season tickets were going to be hard enough to sell.

During the Upton Park meeting with Arsenal (14 March), close to 25,000 balloons were handed out by HISA and the

Independent Arsenal Supporters' Association (IASA). IASA, led by Gooners Tony Willis and Dyll Davies, were demonstrating against the Highbury bond scheme. West Ham fans were given red balloons while Gooners got claret ones. Even if, unlike me, you were not colour blind, it was hard to tell the difference, but it was a nice touch that attempted to move beyond the simple partisan influences of competition and create a feeling of solidarity between football supporters. The Arsenal fans also had a banner demanding 'Ban the West Ham Bond' which was hoisted in the away end. However, a little while ago, I was told by a Gooner that I had *his* lot to thank for saving us from the bond ... and he was serious.

West Ham were beaten 2–0 while two goal-line sit-ins and another corner-flag protest went on. A big placard displayed in the stands referring to the board proclaimed 'Wanted for the murder of West Ham'.

The demonstration at the Arsenal game received much press coverage, while a fall in attendance and match-day programme sales that HISA claimed was a consequence of their boycott (nothing to do with the crap football, of course) began to hit the club finances. This was accompanied by a drop in takings on West Ham merchandise (and, with relegation threatening, one could hardly expect a boost in retail profits!).

At the same time, fanzine sales were benefiting from their increased profile and HISA had developed their own coach service transporting fans to away games which undercut the official club fares by almost a quarter. In retaliation, bailiffs were set loose on HISA's merchandise stall and HISA's use of two crossed hammers in the design of some T-shirts was challenged. Other unlicensed stalls that surrounded the Boleyn Ground on match days did not receive the same treatment.

On 23 March, a 2–2 Boleyn Ground draw against Queens Park Rangers left the bottom-placed Hammers eight points adrift of safety with 10 games left to play.

HISA arranged a number of 'unofficial' meetings with Storrie, who had been given the job of placating the fans while continuing to stick to the club's line. The then managing director was seen by the HISA high command to be genuine, but having little real power, although the majority of supporters saw him as a prime mover in most of the club's affairs.

By now, even the HISA elite understood that red cards and balloons had their limits as effective weapons against the board and, seemingly having run out of ideas, decided to moderate their rule-from-the-centre inclinations and ballot members at what was to be the third and last public meeting, which was convened at the Broadway Theatre, Barking, at the end of March.

At that meeting, in a search for some inspiration, a microphone was passed around the theatre. But anarchy reigned as irritation grew, and the gathering all but collapsed. HISA did manage to propose that fans should stand outside Upton Park for the whole of the match against Norwich City on Saturday, 11 April, but the idea was dismissed. However, after some frustration, there was a tacit agreement to implement a walkout at half-time during the following Tuesday's match against Southampton at the Boleyn Ground. Unsurprisingly, this made the concept of a total flop feel like the height of ambition. It was clear that HISA were impotent and that their notion of peaceful protest was coming to the same end as most demonstrations of that species. In fact, HISA's plan for the Norwich game was so peaceful it died.

The relative success of football protest has always been linked to what is happening on the pitch, which overrides all else in most cases. The failure at the Norwich match was probably quite correctly attributed to the West Ham team putting in one of their best performances of the season, thumping Norwich 4–0 and sparking some hope of a revival in the process. The first half against Southampton went pretty well for the Hammers and, with no score at half-time, few fans took the opportunity to protest at that game either. Inevitably, Southampton got the game's only goal in the final minute of play.

HISA's swan song that season followed the Irons' final home game. Nottingham Forest were the visitors when supporters were instructed to rip up their season tickets on the pitch, which was not exactly in the 'we shall overcome' league. It had been a week since West Ham's relegation had been finalised and many fans were concerned that the Hammers might have to wait many years to get a taste of Premiership football. The number of unsold season tickets was rumoured to be in the several thousands, and they would not be sold before the start of the following campaign. Large numbers of supporters chose to make the game against Forest the last match they would see at Upton Park.

Fearing that the match would end in violence, an *OLAS* editorial appealed to fans, 'I've heard a lot of talk about violent action at the last match – violence towards members of the West Ham board, stewards and the Old Bill. I have also heard reports that the ground is going to be smashed up. Come on, gang, do us a favour. What the hell do you think that will achieve? I'll tell you. Nothing. All that will achieve is more than likely the end of West Ham United.'

Noble sentiments indeed that were hard to argue with, but the fact is that anyone who had it in their mind to cause any trouble during that game would not have been deflected by the warnings of a fanzine, and everyone knew that. The *OLAS* statement was an understandable pre-emptive public disassociation with anything that might have been construed as 'unreasonable'. But, in the end, no one wanted to be associated with anything too 'bad'. Nothing happened except that Frank McAvennie ended his time at West Ham with a second–half hat-trick and West Ham finished the season rock-bottom in 22nd place with 38 points from 42 games. Some people got on the pitch and tore up their season tickets as HISA had ordered. Wanting to see what happened, I took to the field of play and have to say I didn't see many renewal vouchers being thrown to the winds.

West Ham were relegated in 1992 for the second time in three years. The Hammers had finished at the foot of the First Division for the first time since 1932, but they at least avoided equalling a club record number of League defeats set in that relegation season 60 years earlier. Peter Storrie told how the club was at 'an all-time low' but saw indeterminate 'long-term planning' as the way forward rather than any undefined 'quick-fix' measures — essentially meaningless platitudes.

Not long after the season ended, the club sent a letter to a few season-ticket holders to let them know they had given their seats away. The letter from the ticket office read, 'We regret to inform you that a bondholder has requested and been allocated your seat. Therefore it will not be available to you for renewal in the future.'

As the number of bondholders would reach little more than 800, it is pretty certain there weren't too many of these letters.

By the end of May, Martin Cearns, the fourth generation of the Cearns family to be a West Ham director, had resigned as chairman, but made himself vice-chairman. Commercial manager Brian Blower lost his job, the biggest casualty in the club's huge cost-cutting exercise implemented by Storrie.

The new number one was the holiday-camp tycoon Terence Brown, who no one knew very much about except that he had bought around 30 per cent of the club's shares for £2m to become the largest shareholder. So ended the dynastic rule of Upton Park. In 2006, Brown wrote (in the club programme), 'When I got the job … it was the proudest day of my life.'

Brown had been on the board at the time the bond scheme was announced, but had more or less avoided any flak, with the Cearns family having been almost entirely the focus of fan hatred. It was said that Cearns had been motivated to stand down by a group of angry fans who had surrounded his car in the club car park following a game. It seems they had rocked it violently and had at one point been looking to overturn it.

Brown's appointment appeared to be a face-saving means for the board to make a retreat. However, it was probably more about financial timing, making future decisions look detached from previous policy. It seemed as if the club was under new leadership, but, in fact, the Cearns family continued to exert a great deal of influence on the board and this would not change for some time.

Two months into the 1992/93 season, seemingly under Brown's 'new broom', the board backed away from the bond scheme, and the directors were left to mull over how they would ensure that the Boleyn Ground would be fully seated by August 1994. The financial state of the club was looking grim. Its sponsorship by BAG Windows had ended, and it was little more than a week before the new season began that a replacement was found (Dagenham Motors – the arrangement with the Ford dealership was believed to be worth just £100,000 a year, a relative pittance in relation to former deals, but that was mostly the cost of being out of the top flight).

West Ham had spent £1.3m on advertising the failed bond scheme, money that many thought would have been better used to buy players in an attempt to avoid relegation. However, this is a complete misunderstanding of how commercial advertising budgets are structured, expressed and met and of how financial audits work.

FOOTBALL ECONOMICS

Most of us are limited in our financial knowledge to the domestic situation wherein money is quite a 'liquid' (if never abundant) resource. It is wonderful to look at company costs like £1.3m and imagine that they are like petty cash that can just be lifted from one spending stream and plopped in another. The reality is quite different. Without going into a thesis on corporate accountancy, it is worth pointing out that organisational costs can be made up of a number of factors, only one of which is cash. Non-cash factors (and cash for that matter) cannot, unproblematically, simply be transferred from one element of a company's expenditure and realised in another at a moment's notice.

The idea that West Ham or any other football club have ever spent less than they should or could have on players really needs some thought. Why would a group of shareholders contrive to not spend, say, £2m to stay in a market where they can be guaranteed an annual income of, say, £20m? Put another way, why would people with long-standing investments in a company purposely allow that company to enter a market that will negatively affect profits and so their return on their investment? Why would they damage their own income in that way?

The reality of the situation is that football clubs in the modern era hardly ever spend too little on players. It is much more often the case that they spend too much. Leeds United are a recent case in point. They actually spent more on players (in transfer fees and wages) than they had the capacity to earn. If more clubs had looked to match their spending, more clubs of the Peacocks' standing would have fallen with them. This is why Chelsea should be given an Asbo. The West London side have created a highly volatile market that pushes clubs who want to compete with them to the very edge of financial reason. At some point, it will all go bang because all markets rise and fall; the bigger the rise, the sharper the potential fall. But survival in this market during its meteoric climb has demanded that football clubs produce financial ingenuity of the highest order. Apart from all other considerations, West Ham, with Terry Brown first in the background and then at the helm, have achieved this.

There were some suggestions that more attractive options to the bond were possible, a returnable, interest-free loan to the club for example. It was mooted that this might have taken the shape of a £1,000 bond, guaranteeing a priority choice of a seat. Part of the cost of the bond, it was argued, could have been reimbursed over a number of seasons by way of a discount on season tickets. It is probably true that this idea would have been marginally more attractive to fans than the Hammers bond, but did 30,000 supporters have £1,000 to loan to West Ham free of charge in 1992? A £50,000 house in London at that time would be worth nearly £192,000 in 2007; that's a rise of 284 per cent. The price of football has gone up faster than the cost of housing, but even a conservative estimate suggests that a grand in 1992 would be roughly equivalent to £3,000 today. Apart from this, all the club had to do was to up the price of season tickets to effectively turn the loan into the original bond. The supporter would have been trapped because the only way they could even hope to get their money back would be to keep on buying season tickets.

This said, the club weren't looking for an interest-free loan; it was looking to be *given* money. So, the 'returnable loan' was never a starter and, from the point of view of anyone who knows anything about corporate finance, it felt like yet more financial naivety.

PREMIUM BOND

The board never quite conceded that the idea of the bond had failed but the brutal rise of season-ticket prices for non-bondholders was taken as a significant message. At the same time, the board were looking to at least raise finance to redevelop the

South Bank and Chicken Run with the minimum effect on profits. But the economics of the First Division quickly kicked in with relatively few supporters being ready to pay more to watch what were in effect second-class teams. (Would you pay Gordon Ramsay prices for George's pie and mash?) Season-ticket sales fell by 50 per cent and, even without any HISA suggested boycotts, attendances at Upton Park plummeted to an historic low. Gates of 11,921 against Watford, 11,493 for the game with Derby County and 10,326 to see Sunderland must have provoked high anxiety in the boardroom. In only six months, attendances at the Boleyn Ground had halved and there seemed no reason to expect a recovery.

The club that had threatened its most loyal fans with effective banishment could do nothing but watch as support drained away. In October 1992, Terry Brown wrote personally to former season-ticket holders who had withdrawn their patronage and apologised, albeit guardedly, but not for the bond scheme. However, he admitted that the rise in the cost of season tickets had been a mistake. Prices were slashed for anyone who decided to return to the fold. For the fans who had renewed their season tickets, there was a £50 refund and admission fees were lowered for the Upton Park meeting with Swindon Town on 24 October 1992. HISA, along with the fanzines and the local newspapers, asked fans to come back to the Boleyn Ground, and the following week the Hammers had their highest gate of the season. However, it seems obvious that this was due to the lowering of prices rather than the result of appeals to the fans. Close to 18,000 were at the Swindon game, but it was West Ham's involvement in the fight for promotion that really brought crowds to regularly better 15,000, a figure still well down on the previous season.

Eventually, Peter Storrie announced that fans would not need to buy a bond to purchase or renew season tickets. The few supporters who had become bondholders would receive all the promised 'benefits'.

As the East Londoners began their fight to get out of the Barclays League Division One, the Irons' former manager John Lyall was leading Ipswich Town in the newly formed Premiership. John felt no urge to revel in his former club's misfortune, but sent his sympathy to Billy Bonds. Lyall had brought his Second Division Champions to the Boleyn Ground before the start of the new season for Ray Stewart's testimonial match. In the ranks of the Tractor Boys were former Hammers Mick McGiven (then a coach at Ipswich), Paul Goddard and Steve Whitton (part of Lyall's title-winning squad).

Unlike the hapless Irons, Ipswich would milk the lucrative riches of the Premiership that was close to signing a £304m contract with BSkyB. That would have gone a very long way to solving West Ham's problems.

Although Peter Storrie came out of the post-bond-scheme period as the 'littlest devil' in the pack, the bond is remembered as probably his greatest mistake at West Ham. Over the following years, it was not unusual at Upton Park for the mere mention of his name to give rise to laughter or sneers.

The scheme has come to be accepted as an error of judgement on the part of the board that seemed to show that they were hopelessly out of touch with the nature, sentiment and interests of the club's fans. West Ham, the 'family club' that had sacked one of their most successful and popular managers, a devoted servant of the club, just three years earlier, were seen to have attempted to do to their fans something very similar to what they had done to John Lyall.

But, for the 808 supporters who took up the club's bond offer, the investment was rewarded with the discount and priority for the purchase of away-match tickets. In addition, the executive committee of the Hammers Bond Company regularly meets the board of directors to talk about issues that interest or concern bondholders and many other lifelong West Ham supporters who do not have such representation.

HISA claimed the victory as theirs and also took credit for 'calling off the dogs', seeing themselves as playing a major part in persuading the fans to return to Upton Park. But this is not living in the real world. West Ham fans, en masse, do not do anything that does not suit them; hence the dismal failure of HISA's final efforts to demonstrate against the bond. In truth, the major reason the bond scheme failed was that, first, the supporters saw right through it and, second, the team were not attractive enough for the fans to make the sacrifice. The HISA elite had little in common with the average supporter and its active membership wasn't that much more impressive than the number that purchased bonds. The fanzines had played the most powerful part their potential allowed, being the conduit of information to the fans. These tough little journals probably came out of the whole affair as the most noble of the combatants and certainly with an enhanced reputation for integrity that awards them a deserved place in the strong tradition of the 'people's press'.

In the long run, the club did raise enough money to redevelop the stadium and, at the time of writing, a season ticket at the Boleyn Ground (if you can get one) will set you back £745. It costs close to £100 for my family to attend a match at Upton Park if we can buy legitimate tickets, which is practically impossible unless the Hammers are playing Dagenham and Redbridge in one of the early rounds of the League Cup. If that's winning, what's losing?

When the bond eventually died, West Ham were not able to publicly announce its passing as the banks that had underwritten the scheme could have withdrawn their investment. It was the underwriting of the bond scheme which allowed West Ham to redevelop Upton Park the following season. Peter Storrie confessed this in an interview in November 1992 in *On The Terraces*: 'Clearly if we could put the clock back, we wouldn't have done the bond scheme. However, some pluses have come out of it, notably the underwriting. That is a very important aspect of the bond.'

This leads one to wonder if indeed all or some of the Hammers board had ever really expected to sell the bond scheme to supporters. In fact, what actually needed to happen for it to 'work' was to convince the banks that West Ham believed that they could sell bonds to supporters.

As angry as the club's supporters might have been, Brown thought that the underwriters would have been more annoyed about the way things went with the bond. One leading banker subsequently told him that every time he saw the bronze hammers in his office, which the club had presented to him on the completion of the development of Upton Park, he felt like hitting himself over the head with them for making such a bad mistake. Considering the whole affair in retrospect, you can see why.

The fact is that the bank's underwriting secured Upton Park as West Ham's home for at least a decade and now as prime building land it has provided a financial basis for a new super-stadium close to West Ham Underground Station (very close to the site of the Thames Ironworks Memorial Ground, the first home of West Ham United). The underwriting deal that the board quite amazingly managed to convince the banks to be part of was exclusively for the redevelopment of the Boleyn Ground. For years local newspapers had reported that the club was thinking about moving to Stratford (about two miles from Upton Park, close to where the Olympic Stadium will be built and the proposed site of the new Hammers stadium). But, if the club had moved in 1992, the banks could have demanded the return of their £15m, probably with interest.

Put simply, the underwriting scheme provided West Ham with the financial means to transform Upton Park into an all-seater stadium at relatively little expense. The crucial element was to convince the banks that the board were going to make the bond work (even if some or all of them secretly believed this would not happen). In the last analysis, this is what happened. And that has to be seen as good business for West Ham, however it came about.

This scenario has been more or less confirmed by Brown, who has said he felt it was regrettable that such a financially advantageous arrangement, from the club's point of view, has been so misunderstood by the Hammers supporters. According to Brown, the banks controlled the marketing and obviously didn't want to sustain a loss from the underwriting agreement, and therefore decided to create an advertising campaign that put pressure on people to take up the bonds. Terry has argued that the only way West Ham could have changed the marketing would have been for the club to forgo all or part of the underwriting. But, whoever called the shots in the marketing, it would have had to be done aggressively to convince the banks that West Ham meant business with the bond. It might be a hard pill to swallow for all those who have made Brown and the board hate figures over the years on the basis of the bond, but it may be the case that West Ham as an institution have at least something to thank Brown and his 1992 colleagues on the board for.

The final move, to bring in Brown as chairman, was the coup de grâce. Any blame the banks or the fans might harbour could be channelled at the old regime, although it may be that the chairmanship was passed to Brown, at least in part, in recognition of his role in 'pulling the Irons out of the fire'. Storrie came out with his job intact, and he and Brown were able to portray themselves as the 'new face' of Upton Park who restored justice and sanity. This of course couldn't last, but it did allow fans who had vowed never to return to the Boleyn Ground while the Cearns family were in charge to come back to Upton Park feeling at least partially vindicated. It would have also encouraged many disillusioned supporters to see what was probably a genuinely new start and give the club a second chance.

HISA finally disappeared but it is still viewed as having been instrumental in defeating the big boys of the board and their evil bond. *OLAS* are now the only non-virtual fanzine of any size, but with its online sisters they have become the mature and trusted lines of communication for supporters; this has done more in terms of giving the fans a voice than a sectional pressure group like HISA ever had the potential to do. At the same time, the democratic and slightly anarchic nature of these combined mouthpieces is part and parcel of their being, and as such they retain an inner integrity not always accessible to organisations premised on a ruling committee that many football supporters equate with the officialdom that dominates most of us in our everyday lives.

Perhaps the most lasting legacy of the bond scheme was the realisation that a meaningful relationship between the West Ham board and the main body of the club's supporters cannot exist. The fans, although still drawing on the power of identity that is implicit in supporting West Ham, are now largely aware that, first and foremost, the board perceives them as consumers of a product. That I believe to be a good thing. We all know where we stand. The board are permanently regarded in the same way as any shop or service provider and that is healthy; *caveat emptor* – buyer beware. As fans, we have consumer power and we can choose not to attend matches because they are on the television anyway, and even big games can be taken in down the pub. We can withdraw our labour. The likes of *OLAS* and the web-based fan sites make our feelings known and this is, for better or worse, 'real' power and, in the best Lutheran traditions, it is set in the individual. Our collective power is something else: 'Billy Bonds's claret and blue army'.

CONSEQUENCES

Although the club was promoted at the end of the 1992/93 season to make its debut in the Premier League, the start of a decade in the Premiership, it took most of that time for the Hammers to recover from the emotional, spiritual, social and psychological rift that the bond scheme precipitated. Harry Redknapp, who returned to Upton Park in the aftermath of the 'bond affair', several years later recalled how the experience of the bond-scheme season had left the players' confidence in tatters; poor old H had to contend with that too. Without this added pressure, perhaps he would have made us Champions!

Before the evening game between the Hammers and Manchester City in November 1993, the crowd at Upton Park were asked to observe a minute of silence for the passing of Will Cearns, who had died a few days before. The bond scheme was something of the past, with West Ham sitting halfway up the Premiership table. Before the practice of gaudy applause for the dead took over from the traditional dramatic and respectable silences that were given in memory of football's fallen, when quietness was asked for, you could always hear a pin drop at Upton Park. But not on this occasion; a loud chant of 'Cearns out' echoed around the ground, obliging the referee to blow his whistle before the minute was up for the start of the match.

Looking back, that seems very harsh; Will Cearns had always sought to be gentlemanly in his dealings and was not by any stretch of the imagination a bad man but I believe it was a symbolic end to the times when fans believed that they and the club's owners and directors were 'all in it together'. Supporters are now all shareholders in the game. We may not all pull in cash benefits, but, unless we get what we want, we have the option to withdraw our 'investment' (of time, payment, sentiment, etc.); behold the so-called 'Cockney Reds' and Chelsea supporters who live in Exeter. At least, we can now deal with the situation in a realistic way.

I know this is not the case for every fan; those like myself feel no alternative other than an affinity to West Ham and I would not change my allegiance even if the team fell to Ryman League status (and there are no guarantees that won't happen one day). For supporters like me, it is the Hammers or nothing, 'West Ham till I die'. But that again is down to us. It is what we take from the game.

As it was, West Ham became a sort of test case for other clubs throughout the country and there can be little doubt that, whatever angst the Hammers went through, in the long run, football did benefit. But the bond scheme might be most accurately understood as a symbol of self-destruction. Its coming and going was a civil war at Upton Park. But, from the vantage point of 15 years later, I wonder if it was really all about the bond. The debenture was indeed a useful focus for bitterness and resentment, and it did unmask the nature of the football business for many West Ham fans. The meaning of that time (or, indeed, any time) is perhaps best judged by its outcomes. It was when the last vestiges of the notion of 'the family club' and the 'West Ham way' were swept away. It was the start of the end of the 'Academy of Football' epithet that was to be replaced by the label of a 'selling club'. After all the shouting and recriminations, the stadium that emerged – with its pretend turrets and its cold Meccano stands, where we sit relatively quietly compared to the days before the bond – was probably built on a ruse that replaced the illusions of the past. We are left with stark reality and, as usual, it is up to us, the fans, to make that into something more, by way of our passion and will to make something in which it is worth celebrating our collective identity. This will not be what it was in the past; it might not be as good, but it can be even better. That, I really believe, is down to us.

CHAPTER 8
AMAZING DISGRACE

They always lost but he didn't blame me because, to a
gambler, a bad tip is better than no tip at all.
PHIL SILVERS

Terry Brown's early football experiences are steeped in the core values of the game and he has known of the disappointment that football can generate. He was 10 years old when he was rocked by England's first home defeat by a foreign team; the 6–3 win that the Hungarians took away from a depressed Wembley dealt England's sporting morale a painful blow. Brown found he shared the trauma with everyone at his school (where, in play, he had often imagined himself leading out the England team) and the rest of the nation. Many years later, Brown was in a position to tell three of those winning 'Mighty Magyars', Gyula Grosics, Nándor Hideguti and the 'Galloping Major' Ferenc Puskas, about his feelings after that historic match when a team made up of Hungarian MPs played their British counterparts at Upton Park. Terry was surprised that the legendary trio had very little idea of the effect their victory had on England's football fans of the time.

Like many young men of his generation, Brown kept a few scrapbooks focusing on his passion for football. His were themed on West Ham's progress (and otherwise) during the 1950s and early 1960s, but this wasn't a committed interest. However, in those days Terry and his peers were fervent programme collectors and he built an impressive collection of these match-day journals as well as a remarkable anthology of the *Charles Buchan's Football Monthly*, another enthusiasm of many a young football fan at the time. Although collecting autographs of favourite players was popular when Brown was a boy, this wasn't part of his youthful experience. They didn't give the insight that *CBFM* and the Hammers programme offered. It seems football had something to tell Terry. I do understand this, as my attraction to the sport is much the same. Saying 'football is a metaphor for life' is not only a cliché, it is also one of those phrases that do not really mean very much. What human activity isn't a metaphor for life? Activity is what life is. But the game can be read and studied; it reflects and is part of society; providing its tests and questions, it can enlighten the watcher with its many lessons and ethical paradoxes.

As such, Terry's basic education in football was influenced by respect rather than the kind of cult following that arose in the 1960s that made idols of players. The game's influences on the young Brown were about the rewards of discipline and an appreciation of individual skill set within a tactical framework. There was something quite sophisticated and civilised about the football in the 1950s that was founded on an ethical and moral structure wherein players were admired more for their sportsmanship and/or gentlemanliness than their ability to feign injury or succeed in delivering sly digs at opponents. The men in football had integrity and, although it was a far more physical game, it was played in a spirit of individual adult responsibility rather than as it is today, when players often seem incapable of self-control, having to be watched from all angles as they deceive and grumble like small spoiled children.

AMAZING DISGRACE

In the spring of 2006, I was at a function in central London organised by a company fronted by a popular former England international striker. It was attended by many top footballers along with the inevitable hangers-on. People had paid about £30 for their tickets, but the queue outside was hundreds of yards long. Young women with WAG ambitions were trying to enter through fire doors and toilet windows all around the building, but were mostly foiled by the security staff.

There was a group of dinner-suited men inspecting the queue and every now and then they would select individual young women from the line-up and direct them into the several large ground-floor and basement rooms used for the event, each with their own bar and sound system. If you were male or failed to pass the beauty inspection, you weren't getting in and many people who were standing outside when I went in were still there when I came out.

Inside, a players' lounge had been arranged, a sort of inner sanctum at the heart of this extremely crowded hive. I couldn't tell if this was a formal or informal arrangement, but some of the same troops who were selecting the girls outside were also patrolling inside. They judged what they thought to be the best of the best girls and guided them to the players' lounge.

I witnessed widespread drug-taking – no shock for any experienced clubber, but not something one would expect to be a tolerable diversion at an event attended by top English professional footballers (I saw no foreign players).

I am told to be 'reasonable'; why should I expect young, rich men to behave any differently to this? 'Kids have a right to let their hair down.' Fine, but let's not pretend that these people are honed and fit athletes capable of competing against other young men who put excessive social activities on hold, knowing that they have only a few years to capitalise on the best of what they have, and make a concerted effort to live up to the expectations of the people who pay to appreciate them. Let's not call them 'artists' and 'geniuses' but regard them as ordinary and unexceptional lads. Then we have a case for not paying £50-plus for a seat to subsidise young men and women degrading themselves and watch a half-hearted tedious 90-minute display. And let's acknowledge that we rely on Emile Heskey and Michael Owen, with a combined age of nearly 60, to lead England's football assault force for the next decade, men who can outrun and physically dominate strikers 10 years their junior because they have dedicated themselves to fitness.

Football players in the mid-20th century were associated with a certain type of chivalry that demanded a particular blend of manliness, honesty and respect. Managers, who demanded deference, were, above all, seen to direct rather than restrain their players and few coached, although the better ones did (for example, Alec Stock, Walter Winterbottom and Arthur Rowe) and were known as intelligent and informed strategists.

This being the case, at times it must have been difficult for Brown to preside over some of the fumbling managerial errors and chaotic player personalities exhibited at West Ham during his watch as chairman. I have detailed just five instances of this kind of turmoil that give a taster of the culture of carelessness, indiscipline and foolish deception that occurred over a nine-year period at Upton Park. Any Hammers fan could add to this account (there are many others detailed in this book) with their own favourite list of gaffes, mistakes, sham excuses, bogus reasoning and infantile unruliness, but the following suggest a certain line of ineptitude that smacks more of a lack of management than anything else.

Ain't that a Kick in the Head?

Early in October 1998, the Professional Footballers' Association demanded that West Ham make public John Hartson's punishment for kicking Eyal Berkovic in the head at the

Hammers' Chadwell Heath training ground. This had happened the day before the Irons were due to play Southampton in a Premiership fixture on 27 September. The incident had been captured by a television crew and Berkovic, known as the 'The Magician' in his native land, was clearly wronged by the great lumbering mass of Welsh flesh that was Hartson at this point. A week before his attack on Berkovic, Hartson had been convicted in Swansea for kicking flower baskets around a shopping centre.

When news of the Chadwell Heath incident first surfaced, Harry Redknapp denied anything serious had occurred. When challenged by the evidence, he responded by saying, 'It was nothing.' After the gravity of Hartson's actions became undeniable, Redknapp confessed that what the Welshman had done was 'totally out of order, absolutely terrible'.

H's unwilling confession resulted in calls for Hartson to be sacked. But Redders argued that he wasn't going to simply dismiss a multi-million-pound player.

Peter Storrie, at the time the chief executive at Upton Park, told of his determination to address the situation and that internal disciplinary action would be taken after Berkovic returned from international duty. But the FA requested a copy of a videotape that has since become famous through television and internet exposure, which showed Hartson, having ploughed into Berkovic, sending the player crashing to the ground, seemingly mistaking the midfielder's head for the ball, landing a 'slap-kick' just under his team-mate's chin as the Israeli crawled around in the Essex mud.

However, Redknapp was putting forward his plans for peace, saying that he would be looking to 'get the two players together and get it all sorted out … once and for all'.

H also told how, after the incident, Berkovic had asked him not to fine Hartson, but later Berkovic claimed that he was 'very upset with the West Ham board. They tried to cover up what happened.'

Early in October, Peter Storrie claimed that, in conversation with Berkovic, the Israeli had explained, 'He could not believe how it had been blown out of proportion and I think he was a bit shocked and embarrassed about it all.'

Storrie told how he would arrange further talks with both Hartson and Berkovic before deciding if any action would be taken and asked the Football Association to stay out of the matter and allow West Ham to manage things their own way. He argued, 'This is surely an internal matter for West Ham to deal with and I am sure the FA will trust us to do the right thing ... They know I have not been in the game for just five minutes and they should know I am capable of dealing with it in the appropriate way.

'I shall be contacting the FA to let them know very clearly my feelings on this issue. If they start looking at videos from training-ground incidents, then it will lead to cameras being banned by every club in the country.'

Redknapp backed up his chief executive: 'If the FA think there is not some kind of fight or incident on a training ground somewhere in the country every week, then they must be dreaming. I don't condone what Hartson did and I am not saying that kind of incident happens every week at a training ground. But somewhere around the country, there will be a fight, or punches will be thrown because players are competitive and these things happen.'

Hartson's agent, Jonathan Barnett, went to the newspapers with the offer of an exclusive interview with his client for a reputed £20,000 which would have more than covered any fines Hartson had to pay.

Here it is ... Merry Christmas

Shortly before Christmas 1998, two West Ham players appeared in court charged in connection with an alleged incident at the club's Christmas party.

AMAZING DISGRACE

Defender Neil Ruddock and midfielder Trevor Sinclair appeared at Havering Magistrates Court in Romford, a town whose cultural demographic bridges West Essex and East London, along with a third man, youth worker Richard Nelson (who did not train with the YMCA ... I've checked that).

The appearance was related to an alleged attack on a Mini car and its 19-year-old driver, beauty therapist Belinda Knowles, who claimed she was ambushed by 20 partygoers and that two men ripped bits off her car in South Street, Romford, in the early hours of Sunday, 20 December 1998.

Ms Knowles and her female passenger were waiting at traffic lights when she alleged three pedestrians blocked her path. She told police that one man rolled across the roof of the Mini and damaged her windscreen wiper, radio aerial and wing mirror. Another man was said to have climbed on her bonnet, but she drove off when he jumped off. She said, 'I ended up crying because I was so upset by what happened.'

Former England international Ruddock was charged under the Public Order Act with affray, having allegedly thrown a glass bottle at a Mini. Sinclair was charged with criminal damage to the car while Nelson was charged with using threatening, abusive or insulting words and behaviour.

Earlier that night the Hammers players had held their Christmas party (called by one journo at the time 'a boozy 70s fancy-dress bash') at the nearby Secrets nightclub.

Harry Redknapp commented, 'They have let themselves down. They were out on their Christmas party ... I just told them to enjoy themselves and to make sure they behave. It appears a couple of them have got themselves into a bit of trouble by getting arrested ... If it is right that they have misbehaved, then you can be sure we will read them the riot act.'

All three men were remanded on unconditional bail to appear again at the court on 12 January 1999.

Ruddock was eventually acquitted by Havering Magistrates due to conflicting evidence, while Sinclair was fined £250 and ordered to pay £225 compensation.

Drink-related incidents were nothing new at West Ham, but one would have hoped that, towards the end of the 20th century, the impact of the modern game might have drawn a line under the Hammers' propensity to mix striving for athletic success with excessive boozing. However, the man who took West Ham into the new millennium was a product of his era.

In 1999, Harry Redknapp said of a report that West Ham players were drinking until 4 a.m. before a match on the same day, 'I tell you it is absolute rubbish. That sort of thing does not happen.' He claimed that, on match days, he didn't allow alcohol on the coach or in the players' bar.

However, not long before this declaration, Harry was reported to have complained that foreign players refusing to drink had a detrimental effect on team spirit. He confirmed the well-known adage that West Ham was home to a 'drink culture' from the mid-1960s by telling how his playing days were dominated by drink and gambling. He echoed what self-confessed alcoholic and Hammers defender from the 1960s John Charles had told me, 'You could say our motto was "Win or lose, always on the booze".'

H's approval of drinking frustrated Ragnvald Soma, who was with the Hammers for a short spell between 2000 and 2001. The Norwegian international protested about players turning up for training reeking of booze. Redknapp's answer was: 'They don't drink at West Ham. The players' bar is completely alcohol-free and has been since I've been here. I stopped that years ago.'

Manny, a Tear has to Fall

Just before Christmas 1999, Harry Redknapp was, in his own words 'too upset to talk' after finding out that Aston Villa were demanding reinstatement into the Worthington Cup as the Irons had used an ineligible player, Manny Omoyinmi, during the quarter-final tie between the two clubs at Upton Park. But Graham Mackrell, the Hammers club secretary, stated that the club had believed Omoyinmi had been eligible for the game. He told the media, 'West Ham United now acknowledge this was not the case but wish to emphasise that the club acted in good faith … Manny appeared for only six minutes against Aston Villa and had no influence on the result of the tie. West Ham United firmly believe that the tie was won fairly, that the result should stand.'

On Wednesday, 15 December, Harry had sent Emmanuel Omoyinmi on as a substitute with eight minutes of extra-time left to play in the match that his team were to win 5–4 in a penalty shoot-out following a 2–2 draw. After Shaka Hislop saved Gareth Southgate's spot kick, it seemed that West Ham had made it to a Cup semi-final for the first time since 1991. West Ham were scheduled to meet Fulham or Leicester in the last four.

However, only hours passed before Villa lodged an appeal against the result. Manny had turned out for Gillingham in both legs of the Kent club's second-round tie with Bolton and as such was officially cup-tied.

Villa demanded at least a replay with West Ham. Villa club secretary Steve Stride commented, 'We've lodged a complaint with the Football League. We're treating this as a serious breach of regulations. We trust the outcome will reflect the seriousness of the matter.'

Manny had been brought on to replace Paulo Wanchope in an effort to change the pattern of the game and perhaps take up a few precious seconds. H would later say that the decision to use Omoyinmi would 'haunt' him 'forever'. Many Hammers fans who lived through that season will share his experience. The substitute had little, if any, impact on the match.

Although West Ham insisted that fielding Manny had been a

'genuine administration error', they were obliged to replay the tie. At full-time on Tuesday, 11 January, the score stood at 1–1, but the Birmingham club returned to the Midlands with a 3–1 victory. The defeat meant that the Hammers missed out on the opportunity of millions of pounds in revenue that could have been generated by winning at Wembley and taking a place in Europe.

Eventually, Mackrell took the blame for the error and resigned along with the club's football secretary, Alison O'Dowd. Coming from Sheffield Wednesday, Mackrell had also worked for Luton and Bournemouth. He had arrived at the Boleyn Ground only the previous summer to replace Peter Storrie.

Mackrell said his decision had been 'sad but somewhat inevitable' and that he felt 'in the light of the circumstances regarding the decision to make the club replay that I am the person who is ultimately responsible for administration and it was the honourable thing for me to offer my resignation to the board. I'm conscious of the supporters' disappointment at the game having to be replayed and, in the light of that, I felt that something along these lines was appropriate.

'Eventually you have to take some responsibility in life for the actions that go on and the people that work for you.

'Obviously we would not have played the player unless we'd thought he was eligible to play. It has transpired that information was wrong and we are now paying a heavy price for that. It was a little error but unfortunately it has had large consequences for the club.'

Mackrell continued to insist that West Ham, on the conclusion of Omoyinmi's loan to Gillingham, were led to understand by the club that the striker had not been cup-tied. But officials at the Second Division side had not agreed with this version of events.

When asked if Omoyinmi should take part of the blame, Mackrell told West Ham's ClubCall, 'You would have to ask him that. At the end of the day, he's paid to play football and that's all water under the bridge now.'

Terry Brown kept his comments short and diplomatic: 'We feel Graham has made an honourable decision but it seems a high price to pay for what was a small and genuine administration error.'

(In August 2006, Mackrell got the job of chief operating officer at QPR. In November of that year, he was sacked following a row over compensation for former assistant boss and ex-Hammer Tim Breacker.)

Supporters from both clubs who still had their ticket stubs from the first game were able to obtain free tickets for the replay. Others had to pay the full admission price, although profits from the game were donated to charity.

Manny was born in Lagos, Nigeria (28 December 1977), and, when he was eight, his parents moved to Custom House, part of the West Ham heartlands. As such, he was a local boy and he became an English schools international. He appeared a dozen times and scored twice for West Ham.

A product of the Hammers Youth Academy, and one of the young Irons that claimed the South East Counties League Championship at the end of the 1995/96 season, Manny was also in the side that contested the two-leg FA Youth Cup Final that term alongside Frank Lampard and Rio Ferdinand.

The 5ft 6in, 10st 11lb Omoyinmi made his Premiership debut in the March 1997 encounter with Leeds United. During May 1998, after coming on for Samassi Abou, he scored two marvellous point-saving goals in the 3–3 draw at Selhurst Park against already relegated Crystal Palace.

But first-team football was not a regular expectation for the diminutive wing-back (who preferred an all-out attacking flanker role) and his career began to look like a patchwork of loan deals. In September 1996, Manny played seven League games for Bournemouth; during February 1998, he made four appearances for Dundee United. Between March and April 1999, he scored one goal in four outings for Orient and, in November 1999, he netted against Oldham on his debut for Gillingham. He also scored the winning goal for the Gills that stunned the Oxford United defence. But Omoyinmi's most remembered appearance was to be at Upton Park on 15 December 1999.

Harry had avoided any blame, telling how Omoyinmi hadn't mentioned that he had played for Gillingham to anyone at West Ham. But this was not to be the end of the matter.

Hate mail and threats began to be directed at Manny. He was shunned and ridiculed in an unprecedented way that left the club with no recourse other than to effectively exile the player via loans. He had half-a-dozen games with Scunthorpe United (he scored a goal while at Glanford Park) and made six appearances for Barnet on loan. In July 2000, Manny went to Oxford United as a free transfer, forever to be regarded as a pariah at Upton Park.

But Omoyinmi could not regain anything like the form he was capable of and was not able to command a regular place in the Us side; he scored nine times in 77 run-outs. His first season for Oxford could have been better; he scored just three goals in 24 appearances, although two of them came in one virtuoso performance during a 4–3 victory over Rotherham, who went on to win promotion.

However, Manny and his team-mates in the 2000/01 season sank to the foot of the Second Division. With 97 professional games behind him and 15 goals to his credit, in the 2003/04 term he was loaned to non-league Margate and then Gravesend and Northfleet, where he was given a contract starting on 25 May 2004. He played for Ebbsfleet that same year. But, by August 2005, Manny was with Canvey Island playing in the Conference and was with Lewes in December of the same year.

A tricky, seemingly tireless player with skill and pace, since leaving the Boleyn Ground, he had given some wonderful, inventive displays. But Manny was prone to injury and protracted loss of form at times. How much that fateful substitution took from his future will never be known, but it surely did him no good at all.

Doesn't it Get Right up your Nose?

On Wednesday, 19 July 2006, it was announced that West Ham winger Shaun Newton had been banned for seven months by the Football Association after testing positive for cocaine.

The 30-year-old had provided a positive test on 23 April, following the Hammers' 1–0 FA Cup semi-final victory over Middlesbrough. He had come on for Matthew Etherington in the 89th minute. This being the case, it was perhaps thanks to slow administrative procedures on the part of the FA that West Ham were not disqualified from the competition or at least forced to replay that game. The ban started on 20 May, when the former Charlton and Wolves man was suspended by West Ham.

The ban applied to matches but Newton was allowed to take part in training and other football-related activities. The FA further declared that Newton would be 'target tested' throughout the period of his suspension. He did not travel with the rest of the Hammers team when they left for a pre-season tour of Sweden, and he was relatively lucky as three months of his ban took place in the close season.

West Ham stuck by the 30-year-old, who admitted he had let down his family, friends, supporters and himself and was 'truly sorry'. Manager Alan Pardew declared that the club would not turn its back on Newton, but he would still face additional disciplinary action from the club.

Pardew said, 'I have seen at first hand the emotional and personal hell that Shaun Newton has been through in recent weeks, and our priority must be to help him – not abandon him. I hope his experience serves as a lesson to any sports person … I would like to express my disappointment and sadness at the situation … West Ham United has always had a reputation as a family club and our belief here is that, when a member of your family is in trouble, you look after them.'

However, he went on to say that the situation had put a stain on his team and that he and the club's sports scientist, Niall Clark, felt 'very let down' as they had 'always taken such care and concern with the health, condition and well-being of our players'. He continued, 'It infuriates me to hear of drug use in any sport – there is absolutely no place for it. It is a belief I have always held, so for it to occur at West Ham United is something that hurts and saddens me … we are also acutely aware of our responsibilities as a club, and he will face internal disciplinary action when all of the information surrounding his situation is clarified.'

A father of three young children, Newton claimed his drug taking had been an 'isolated incident' but that he felt he had to face up to his responsibilities. He said, 'I in no way condone the taking of drugs and hope that my experience will act as a deterrent to others.'

Had Newton been a participant in almost any other major sport, he would have faced a two-year ban for a first-time offence that might have been reduced to 12 months if mitigating circumstances were identified. But the FA applied their own rules which require a minimum six-month ban for a player found to be using cocaine.

Newton's case was the most high-profile football-related episode of cocaine taking since 2004 when Chelsea dealt with Romanian Adrian Mutu. The striker was sacked following his admission of failing a test for cocaine and was fined £20,000 and banned for seven months by the FA.

AMAZING DISGRACE

Racist Hammers

In the spring of 2007, the *Sunday Mirror* claimed that two West Ham players were caught up in a 'race hate hell'. It was reported that Nigel Reo-Coker and Shaun Newton had to take flight after being targeted by 'racists' in the Upton Park crowd. The report stated that a group of 30 turned on the pair during the home game against Spurs on Sunday, 4 March. Reo-Coker and Newton, who were watching the game from the stands, were said to have been racially abused, physically threatened and as such obliged to leave their seats. It was the second time that season that Reo-Coker had allegedly experienced racist abuse. It had been claimed that he had been the recipient of hate mail a few months previously, although the offending letters were seen only by the player and his agent.

After the Tottenham game, a number of exhaustive searches of the hundreds of comments included on the various West Ham internet forums failed to identify a single report from anyone witnessing the alleged racism directed at the Hammers club captain. This was odd, given that Nigel would have been sitting in a prominent position and a relatively large number of people were said to have been involved.

Neither of Reo-Coker's reported accusations regarding racism at West Ham resulted in the bringing of any charges and, as such, all West Ham supporters stand accused, but without recourse to any defence, as sectional racism indicts the whole when it goes unchallenged by that whole. It seems that no one in the almost 35,000 crowd did a thing to confront or report the alleged racist abuse. This includes the police and West Ham security that had the full range of modern surveillance equipment to call on.

Reo-Coker had been disenchanted at West Ham for most of the season. It was rumoured that, after finding out that Arsenal had come in for him after the Cup Final, he was annoyed that

Alan Pardew had not informed him of the Gunners' interest, and he had put in a transfer request before the start of the 2007/08 season. For many fans, it appeared Nigel more or less went on a go-slow from the start of West Ham's second campaign after promotion back to the Premiership, seemingly in a sulk about his situation. While I was writing *Black Hammers*, Nigel told me, 'I personally haven't come across any racism in the game.' It is sad that this experience changed so suddenly.

Early in July 2007, West Ham United sold Reo-Coker for £8.5m to Aston Villa. The England Under-21 captain was seen by sizeable sections of the media to have been one of a number of Hammers players responsible for the team's poor performance on the pitch after a fall-out between him and the club. However, when he got to Villa Park, Nigel made it understood that he felt he had been hung out to dry by West Ham. As such, he was thrilled to sign a four-year deal with Villa, happy to get away from the misery he experienced at Upton Park and elated to be working under Martin O'Neill.

I wish Nigel all the best but not a few Hammers fans have seen his accusations about racism as a sorrowful and shameful end to his time at West Ham, where he had experienced a great deal of positive support and had achieved much with the Hammers including supplanting Bobby Moore as West Ham's youngest ever captain.

MEN BEHAVING BADLY

The above catalogue of immature behaviour, risible 'man-management' and poor decision-making is difficult to find replicated at any other top football club in Britain or Europe over a similar time. Placed within the period from the sacking of John Lyall up to the final days of the Brown administration, these events are part of the East London farce that continued for

Left: John Lyall – arguably West Ham's greatest manager – held the position for 15 years until he was sacked in 1989.

Above: Billy Bonds – The Hammers legend's reign as manager ended in August 1994.

Left: Harry Redknapp, dispensed with at the end of 2000/01 season.

Above: Anguish on Green Street.

Left: West Ham fans' 1996 response to the news of Michael Tabor's (racehorse owner and former bookmaker, and friend of Harry Redknapp) £8 million offer to take over the club.

Right: Hammers fans invade the pitch to vent their anger at the board.

Above: The Egg has landed – Eggert Magnússon gives it the thumbs-up.

Right: Kia Joorabchian, the businessman linked to a takeover bid who was also behind the controversial transfer of Tevez and Mascherano.

Above: Tevez can't believe he's sitting on the bench at Upton Park. Mascherano can and leaves for Liverpool and the Champions League.

Below: On his mobile is Richard Scudamore, the Premier League executive chief who came under fire for his handling of the Tevezgate affair.

almost two decades. From May 1992, when Brown became chairman of the club and Harry Redknapp took over as manager, Upton Park became an almost manic exhibition of chav crudity, lack of sophistication and panic-induced deception. Through it all, the likes of Harry Redknapp and Alan Pardew ducked responsibility, managing to unload culpability on to club officials, fans or players.

How on earth did Pardew not know his players well enough to see the signs of drug abuse? Of course, this malaise is everywhere, but I have known many individuals from the world of football imbibe drifts of snow, including ex-players that one would have thought immune from such indulgences. I have not seen them day in and day out for years as their manager, but I could still see the signs of use. Once you know the signs, you can tell sooner rather than later on regular contact.

Why might Pardew apparently feel that he should not inform a player of another club's interest in him? All that betrays is a lack of self-esteem and an inability to deal with a player leaving, and thus it is all but saying that the player is bigger than the club.

Why did Redknapp get off scot-free with his appalling decision to even include Manny Omoyinmi in his Worthington Cup quarter-final squad? Was it not part of his job as the *manager* of the club to *manage* and to know whether the player was cup-tied? Was he not interested in what Omoyinmi was doing while he was away on loan? This oversight, which I have heard called a 'straightforward and crass piece of stupidity', potentially cost the club astronomical amounts of income, but Harry was not fined or even publicly reprimanded.

And Harry's initial response to practically deny and then try to downplay John Hartson's vicious attack on a team-mate in a training-ground situation that was ultimately his responsibility while Sky TV cameras were rolling almost beggars belief.

It is too easy to pick out the fact that Terry Brown was the one constant throughout this procession of incompetence, seeming apathy and apparent neglect of professional duties. In my view, what happened after the Worthington Cup quarter-final of 1999 is telling. Brown was focused on what his job required. He had to get the club and his staff through what was a calamity and, putting all recriminations and blame aside, he did get on with this. There is an adage I have used when teaching 'people management' at MA level: 'There are no vacuums in management. You are either managed or you will be managed. If you do not manage yourself, you might find one day that you will be managed right out of the window.'

Brown refused to be managed by the situation; Redknapp succumbed to being managed by it. Many close observers of the Hammers might have believed that was not the first or last time this happened at Upton Park during Brown's tour of duty.

CHAPTER 9
OUR 'ARRY

Ability is of little account without opportunity ...
I think knowing what you cannot do is more important than
knowing what you can do. In fact, that's good taste.
LUCILLE BALL

In the spring of 2001, Terry Brown, along with the long-suffering West Ham fans, watched as the Irons struggled once more to secure their place in the Premiership, scrambling around in the bottom third of the table following the bitter disappointment of the Upton Park defeat in the FA Cup quarter-final at the hands of Spurs, having defeated Manchester United in the previous round. In truth, everyone had seen enough good players making their exit, the millions made in their departure squandered and heard the cries of 'bare bones' too often.

But Harry Redknapp, with just one game of the 2000/01 season to play, arrived at his meeting with Brown on 9 May in the chairman's office at Upton Park in a surprisingly cheery frame of mind, having worked out the details of a new four-year contract with his chairman. It was worth £10m; his annual salary of £1m would increase by £600,000, as well as a range of other benefits that had been tacked on. H was looking forward to signing on the dotted line that morning, although his side had

127

suffered a series of poor results. He explained the situation from his point of view by saying, 'You haven't got the players and can't afford to buy them.'

West Ham had been badly affected by the loss of Rio Ferdinand not long after John Hartson joined Wimbledon for £7m. That transfer had been followed by half-a-dozen losses. But, according to Harry, he had been buoyed up by Brown telling him, 'Harry, I want you for ten years, not four.'

H had delayed signing the contract for four months, feeling that, as he had two years left on his existing paperwork, he had no need to rush into anything.

According to Redknapp, the conversation with Brown went something like this:

Brown: I'm not happy with you, Harry. I'm going to call it a day.
Harry: OK, if that's the way you feel. But I've got two years left on my contract. You'd better make sure that you sort me out.

Brown was willing to pay Harry for what remained of his contract and, as H tells it, within five minutes he was gone with a good reference from the West Ham chairman, which Rupert Lowe called 'fantastic' just before H left Portsmouth to join Southampton (before leaving Southampton to rejoin Portsmouth). Despite the allegedly gleaming testimonial, Harry was to claim that Brown had told him that he was unhappy about the language Redknapp had used in an interview with a fanzine. Apparently, the problem hinged on Brown's views about the amount of money H had spent on players. Harry had responded by suggesting that the trained, well-qualified and vastly experienced accountant and successful businessman couldn't 'fucking add up'.

In fact, in his time as manager, Harry had spent almost £58m on a staggering 67 players. Rumours circulated alleging that some of even the most expensive of these players had been bought on the strength of video evidence or single-match judgements. He recouped just over £67m, selling 68 players; that seemingly made him £9m to the good. But £24m came by way of the sale of Marc-Vivien Foe and Rio Ferdinand in the final season of Redknapp's reign at Upton Park. Another £7m had come from the sale of John Hartson. Ferdinand, of course, just a couple of years after departing the Boleyn Ground, went to Old Trafford for over £31m. Had his months in a Leeds shirt really increased his value by 60 per cent? The painful and seemingly endless list of flops and 'old pals' has also to be considered: Marco Boogers, Scott Mean, Neil Ruddock, Scott Minto, Gary Charles, Leon Britton, Ragnvald Soma and Rigobert Song just for a taster. Along the way, the Hammers had lost or given away assets like Matt Holland, Tony Cottee (an England international striker that apparently could not be used at Upton Park after his peak years), Marc Rieper and of course Ferdinand. Over 130 players passed through Harry's office during his reign. But, perhaps worst of all, Harry had negotiated player salaries of astronomical proportions, many by way of short-term, short-sighted and wasteful loan deals with players like Dieter Eckstein, Chris Whyte, Mohammed Berthe and Hannu Tihinen – mostly anonymous, all ignominious. The 'Harry years' had been the most profligate in the entire history of West Ham United, during which time the Hammers averaged around 11th place in the Premiership (even finishing as low as 15th) and their best performances in domestic cup competitions had got them only a couple of quarter-final places. Under Redknapp, West Ham never managed to score more goals than they conceded over a season.

While always insisting that football was in essence a sport that was English in character, Harry's record in the market, looking back from August 1996, showed that he had bought 11 foreign players for £4m. West Ham, having the biggest cohort of overseas players in the UK, were being called 'Harry's Foreign Legion'.

Florin Raducioiu was one of Redknapp's most noteworthy blunders. The Romanian came from Espanyol in 1996 for £2.4m. According to H, he had 'followed his career for years before I signed him, so I know what he can do'.

Agent Dennis Roach was a mover and shaker in the signing. Not long after landing on Planet Harry, Raducioiu was spotted rehearsing his body swerve round Harvey Nichols when he should have been on his way to Stockport with the rest of the West Ham team. Redknapp said of the man whom he had 'followed for years', 'His displays were worth about two bob.'

Following half-a-dozen appearances, Raducioiu was flogged back to Espanyol at a £900,000 loss, reputedly earning Roach £300,000 commission on the deal.

Marco Boogers was another (as Harry put it) 'disappointing' buy and, after Ilie Dumitrescu was salvaged from White Hart Lane, H complained, 'I have to buy at the cheap end of the market … I was buying second-hand players with no MOTs.'

By the time Redknapp had been in charge for two years, West Ham's record had deteriorated. Choruses of 'What a load of rubbish' and 'Redknapp out' regularly rang around the Boleyn Ground, while Brown and the directors were threatened on the streets, causing the chairman and his wife to run to Upton Park Underground Station to escape attack.

Trying to mollify the club's supporters and fight off the peril of relegation, Brown made finance available for new players, although a dozen of the 19 faces in the official team photograph of the previous season were no longer at the club. Gary Charles came from Benfica for £1.2m in 1999, and the defender played only four games.

Redknapp's relationships with a select band of agents, such as the likes of Dennis Roach and Willie McKay (who H called his 'representative in France'), continued to be a disturbing feature of his management profile, and he seemed happy for them to use the Chadwell Heath training ground as a sort of office, reportedly gossiping to players about wages at other clubs and transfers. It was also reported that McKay was Redknapp's host at a selection of expensive London restaurants, in one instance celebrating Marc-Vivien Foe's transfer. When asked about his dealings with these individuals, H said, 'I don't know how an agent can be dishonest.'

Redknapp allegedly responded to the FA bringing a case against Roach for taking money from both sides in a transfer by claiming, 'It's not a big deal if an agent earns from both sides. If you want a player, it doesn't matter what happens to the money. All that matters is I think the deal is good value for the money.'

Perhaps H just didn't make good deals then?

With the benefit of hindsight, Brown has suggested that he would have avoided the huge financial commitments he oversaw in the transfer market and the liability of the long-term contracts negotiated between Redknapp, players and agents. Brown admitted that Harry's time at the club suggested that just spending in the transfer market did not guarantee success on the field. This was diametrically opposed to Harry's own philosophy of management, 'If you've got the dough, you've got more of a chance to be the "best" manager.'

This said, Brown has acknowledged Harry's contribution to West Ham, saying that he provided some seasons of excitement and that, at his best, he was able to wheel and deal with anyone in football. But, annoyed by H's lack of discipline, demands for money and the rumours about his dealing with agents, Brown told his fellow directors that Redknapp was 'not a proper coach'.

BROWN OUT

It is perhaps an indication of how much Redknapp's assistant compensated for Harry's deficits that Brown has made a point of giving credit to Frank Lampard Sr. Terry believes that Frank has not received the recognition he deserves for his contribution during Harry's time as manager. Brown believes Lampard is an authentic 'West Ham man' who brought Frank Jr to Upton Park and was responsible for bringing Rio in for training when Ferdinand was a young player. Brown has never forgotten that Lampard worked without payment with the Academy before becoming Harry's right-hand man.

However, Harry also has to get credit for working his magic on many fans, making them feel grateful for top-half finishes or even for just staying in the Premiership. Helped by the media, a mood was fostered that portrayed West Ham as the inherent poor relations of football, which seemed to be more or less taken on by the club in the shape of a latent inferiority complex on and off the field of play. We were happy to scrape a draw at Highbury and thought ourselves favoured by God when we managed to defeat Manchester United anywhere. This was not quite but almost a defeatist attitude. Limited ambition alongside the perky pessimism of Redknapp made supporting West Ham a trial by misery at times. Invariably I would listen to half-time conversations that started with provisos that seemed to tie West Ham to their pedestrian fate: 'OK, we might never win the League, but …' or 'You've got to be realistic … West Ham are not Arsenal …' That is like saying 'Up the 'Ammers (but not too far up)'. Is it me or is it perverse that West Ham supporters are sneering at the Hammers' new owners talking about Champions League placings? Why can't we have ambitions or even hopes? Why can't we want to be or try to be the best?

Every time I make this point, I seem to be told to be 'realistic' but, if folk support football for 'realism', haven't they missed the point? As Sir Geoff Hurst once said, 'Football is a game of tomorrows'; it is about hope more than realism. Football is a kid kicking a ball round the street imagining they are in the World Cup Final; it is facing Real Madrid at the Bernabeu and *believing* you can win; it's going to Old Trafford without the thought that, 'if we're lucky, stop 'em playing, we'll come away with a point'.

The wasted money and the uninspiring platitudes that seemed to be rife during Redknapp's time as West Ham manager are nothing compared to the job he did on the general attitude of the club and the way everyone involved in it looked at a proud East End institution. It was as recently as 1965 that West Ham were regarded as *the* London club. Even in the 1970s we were still seen as 'up-and-coming' and 'fashionable'. John Lyall and Billy Bonds at least gave us the mindset that we could take on anyone (beating Arsenal at Wembley in 1980 proved that). West Ham punched above their weight and gave football lessons to the barbarians of the game. Harry made us humble and, in sport, that is often the path to mediocrity.

Redknapp, who once described himself as 'bullet-proof', after getting his marching orders from Brown, didn't say goodbye to his players and didn't enter into any verbal exchanges with his chairman. Later, Brown suggested that the board's unanimous decision to get rid of H had been due to the team's dismal 2000/01 campaign and the cash haemorrhage via the mad salary structure that extortionately rewarded average and journeymen players who never justified the money it took to get them to deign to come to Upton Park. But only Manchester United's Alex Ferguson had managed his Premiership club longer than the 54-year-old Redknapp, and it wasn't as if his spending was anything new or wasn't subject (in the last analysis) to the veto of the chairman.

Still, the next day's headlines told us that old 'mutual consent' story.

Harry's claim that some interviews with *OLAS* contributed

to his dismissal merely amused Brown, and he later told how Harry's interaction with *OLAS* was something he might have thought about doing himself if he were more prone to spin-doctoring. He declared that, overall, he and Redknapp – although very different characters – had a good working relationship, but the board had been concerned at the start of the 2000/01 campaign with Redknapp's negative attitude with regard to the coming season. But it was Harry's general dissatisfaction and the nasty arguments that arose as a consequence that really got Brown down. It seems Redknapp's moods would vacillate wildly from euphoria at the prospect of spending money to gloom when defeats were blamed on financial constraints. For Redknapp, Brown did not make enough money available for him to consistently field a decent team. And it appears Harry's love of the transfer market goes on unabated.

Brown was to say that the fact that West Ham had only just managed to keep their Premiership status by defeating Southampton 3–0 in the final Boleyn Ground match of the 2000/01 season had been another factor in the board's thinking about Redknapp. It seems it had slipped Terry's mind that the Hammers finished eight points clear of relegation, but the Hammers only achieved the same number of points during Harry's last season as were gained during the 2002/03 term, when the Irons were relegated from the Premier League.

Even Harry's most ardent admirers would stop short of calling him a strategic genius or a great coach. Harry's career has been premised on the notion that he has been a canny wheeler-dealer. But, as shown above, this is a bit of a myth, although Redknapp's propensity to generate a traffic in players has been astonishing wherever he has gone. His relationships with agents has made H's name synonymous with – for want of a better expression – the cutting edge of football's trade and transfer system. But, during Harry's time at West Ham, there wasn't any evidence of foul play in the market.

Peter Storrie (who would again team up with Redknapp at Portsmouth) once commented that Harry preferred to have a turnover in his playing staff as he liked to 'freshen up the dressing room'. Redknapp's fuel-injected activity had troubled Brown and he has been reported as asking Peter Storrie on a number of occasions, 'What is Harry up to?'

Storrie was said to have reassured his chairman that there was no evidence of any dishonesty by Redknapp. But, according to H, 'No one gives a monkey's about you once your career's over.' As such, Redknapp believes that, while doing 'your best', a manager should take advantage of their situation 'because it doesn't last for ever'.

Harry has said that, as West Ham were relegated and he had just won the Championship with Portsmouth, he thought to himself, 'What goes around comes around,' and that he wouldn't lose sleep over what West Ham fans thought of him. I guess he should be envied for that. Indeed, in 2006, even as the FA were in the process of conducting an inquiry into the extraordinary number of bets that surrounded his reappointment as Portsmouth manager in December 2005, Harry seemed untroubled. In August 2006, when Harry was in his second stint with Portsmouth, the FA questioned H and Milan Mandaric over an alleged £16.5m betting coup. Redknapp told the press that he and the Pompey chairman had been shown a list of names who had bet on the appointment of the Portsmouth coach after he left Southampton. The list was believed to include the name of at least one Barclays Premiership football club director.

Redknapp claimed that he had not bet on Betfair's 'next Portsmouth manager' market, in which £16.5m was traded. He commented, 'I didn't have a bet and that's the end of it. But unfortunately this just keeps dragging on and to be honest I could do without it.'

Mandaric denied that there had been a leak of insider information about the final decision to appoint, which was only taken 20 minutes prior to the move being announced. However, *Sports Betting Update* later revealed that at least a further £56,000 was traded in the 20 minutes before the suspension of the market. FA spokesman Andrin Cooper confirmed the investigation would be continuing.

In March 2007, the FA dropped charges against Redknapp. But the saga seems to be never-ending. Late in November 2007, Redknapp, Storrie and Mandaric were arrested in connection with alleged corruption in football, just as H was being mooted as the next manager of England. For sure, the nation will never find his like. As the Pompey fans quite rightly tell us of their erstwhile Cockney treasure within the confines of Fratton Park, 'There's only one Harry Redknapp.'

HARRY OVERVIEW

From the start of the 1994/95 season until 2001, Brown propped up Harry Redknapp as the Hammers ambled through a string of moderate campaigns in the Premier League. West Ham achieved three top-10 seasons between 1997 and 2000, which made things look better than they actually were. Redknapp signed overly expensive players and, at the same time, sold quality players like Rio Ferdinand and Frank Lampard Jr to rival clubs for what turned out to be a fraction of their subsequent value. The money from these sales was spent on a new stand for the stadium and on players who often looked unlikely to make the grade.

The club's wage bill soared at an alarming rate, while results on the field didn't improve. Harry made some disastrous buys throughout his time as manager of the club, entering into contracts that in retrospect look foolish. Yes, he also made some astute deals and was lucky in bringing the likes of Paolo Di Canio to Upton Park, a move that could have gone very wrong given the Italian's behavioural record both before and after his time at the Boleyn Ground (since leaving Upton Park, he has called himself a fascist, albeit a non-racist one).

There is no denying that Redknapp supervised a high-spending, low-achieving regime that drove West Ham almost to the point of bankruptcy, seeming to destroy much of the infrastructure and ethos of the club set in place by Ron Greenwood and built on by John Lyall. As Harry's Youth Cup-winning skipper from 1963, John Charles, who played alongside Redknapp and watched his career develop, said to me, 'What the fuck does Harry Redknapp know about football?'

CHAPTER 10
RIO 500 GRAND

I just don't want to die alone, that's all ...
It would be nice to have someone care about me, for who
I am, not about my wallet ... Everyone carries
around his own monsters.
RICHARD PRYOR

Although it was seen as controversial at the time, according to Terry Brown, it was correct to take what Leeds United bid for Rio Ferdinand in 2000, but it was rumoured that the board were of the opinion that the £18m income from the sale of the England defender had not been spent wisely. The fee was a record for a British defender, but those who helped the transfer go through provoked queries about the negotiations and there were more questions about how the fee was spent. There was no independent regulator at that time and, as such, the 'interesting' phalanx of 'accomplices' in the deal fell under the camouflage of confidentiality and vanished.

By 2000, Rio Ferdinand had assumed a place in the consciousness of the Hammers fans that made him a symbol of West Ham's future, but he was also a pictogram of the club's historical lineage. He had risen through the Academy under the tutelage of Tony Carr from his earliest years, and had been honed by the club's coaches to become a shining example of a proud Upton Park tradition. As a stylish defender, his path into the ranks of the best of the Hammers echoed the rise of Bobby Moore and this, added to the fact that he looked every inch a future captain of the side and maybe a skipper of England, caused Ferdinand to become a beacon of hope that shone over East London like a gleaming promise of tomorrow.

The tale of Ferdinand's departure from his footballing alma mater is a complex and murky one, and I'm grateful to Tom Bower's *Broken Dreams* in the following analysis that goes some way to exposing the grimy underbelly of the financial chicanery that is the football transfer market.

In 1999, Rio was four years into his seven-year contract with West Ham. An exceptional graduate of the Hammers youth system, his salary stood around £1.5m a year. Harry Redknapp had declared, 'The day I would want to leave West Ham is the day we start wanting to sell the Ferdinands.'

Brown was in full agreement with this stance, seeing Ferdinand as having a crucial part in what West Ham had achieved over the previous few years.

Pinhas 'Pini' Zahavi, Rio's Israeli agent, had told Brown about a £12m offer for the player from AC Milan early in 1999. Liverpool had put in a bid of £10m, while Real Madrid had also expressed interest, although Pini and Ferdinand had decided that, after his time at West Ham, Rio would play his football in England.

(Zahavi would go on to introduce Roman Abramovich to Chelsea and Alexander Gaydamak to Portsmouth.)

Terry asked Pini if he could stall any moves for Rio for a year and the Israeli agreed to play for time, but, just a few days on, Brown was told by Zahavi that Ferdinand wanted a transfer. This took the chairman by surprise as Rio had given every impression that he was going to stay at West Ham, a view also widely held in the media until the *Mirror* signalled that the England defender was on the cusp of moving to Leeds United. Newspapers pay impressive money for such 'leaks'.

For Brown, this apparent and sudden change of heart had the stamp of surreptitious work on it, but, as Terry understood that H would be against the transfer of Ferdinand, he was almost as concerned about dealing with his manager's reaction as he was about the consequences of Rio's impending move to a Premiership rival.

Rune Hauge – a Norwegian agent who had been disqualified by FIFA from operating as an agent in 1995 for providing a 'bungs' service to several British football executives – had been assured of a 5 per cent share of the transfer fee if he brought Ferdinand to Elland Road. Brown never spoke to Hauge. Leeds chairman Peter Ridsdale talked to his West Ham counterpart's answering machine. But Brown was in Kennington, at the Oval watching cricket, when H contacted him by telephone to tell his chairman that Leeds had made a £15m bid for Ferdinand. Brown was perplexed it was his manager rather than he who had received the bid. He asked what Harry thought about the offer. Redknapp replied by saying he understood that Brown could not turn down Leeds as it was the best thing for West Ham. Brown told Harry that he was surprised that, all of a sudden, he was prepared to part with a player that he had just recently seen as central to his plans. He told Redknapp, 'This doesn't sound like you to let Rio go.'

Harry, seemingly taking pains to consider his response, said that he thought it was in the club's interest to accept the offer as the transfer market was about to collapse.

However, Harry's account of the events leading up to Ferdinand's move from Upton Park does not concur with Brown's version. According to Redknapp, he was totally unaware that anything to do with Rio moving was going on and he didn't make the Oval telephone call. Harry claims that the first he heard of the bid was when Brown told him about it and that Zahavi had informed him that his centre-half was 'happy' at

Upton Park and didn't want to move. Redknapp also claimed that he was amazed that Hauge had any part in the situation.

At Elland Road, after the Irons' 1–0 defeat of Leeds on 18 November 2000, Ridsdale asked Brown what he wanted for Rio (who had performed brilliantly). The Hammers chairman told the Leeds man that £18m was needed to take Ferdinand away from Upton Park. Brown saw this evaluation as deliberately setting Ridsdale a high target. The Yorkshireman accepted and Brown instructed him to fax the offer to him on the Monday morning.

An initial payment of £12m would be followed by a final payment of £6m. But both Ridsdale and Pini must have known that the player was worth much more on resale. Pini earned around £1m, and Hauge's 5 per cent came to £900,000, not bad for a few minutes on the phone. However, you can't help asking why a canny Yorkshireman and a sharp Cockney needed an Israeli and a Norwegian involved in what they were doing. It seems hard to believe that Ridsdale was happy to pay the costs involved.

Ridsdale claimed he had no knowledge of Hauge's involvement until after he had made arrangements with Brown. But Brown asserted that the initial approach with regard to Ferdinand was made by Hauge, which he as good as ignored. According to Brown, his first conversation about Rio moving was with Zahavi. Terry had not responded to Ridsdale's calls and messages, and it was weeks before the West Ham chairman talked with Ridsdale about Ferdinand joining Leeds. This version of events was confirmed by the Israeli agent.

After Ferdinand's move was announced, Hauge told Ridsdale that the deal would fall apart unless Leeds paid an increased commission of 10 per cent (£1.75m). However, Leeds had no contractual obligations to Hauge; Ferdinand's transfer was agreed, but Ridsdale felt he had to pay up, although the Leeds board were reportedly not told about this payment.

Later, Ridsdale claimed that Zahavi had put pressure on him to pay the increased commission, threatening to scupper the transfer, although Zahavi has denied this. Ridsdale also told how the Norwegian needed the extra money to pay other unnamed people involved in making the transfer possible.

Further extraordinary payments were made. Ferdinand was given additional cash; he spoke of his lack of enthusiasm for joining Leeds, having only agreed to move after being persuaded by Zahavi. Brown agreed to compensate Rio to the tune of £500,000 in lieu of the remainder of his contract. West Ham also paid Harry £300,000 as an 'incentive' not to push for a dash to the market, demanding that the income from the sale of Ferdinand be spent on new players. Brown told H, 'Every business needs a bit of luck.'

Redknapp replied, 'Your luck was when I arrived.'

So everyone was lucky!? Why didn't *I* feel lucky at the time?

Unluckily, Ferdinand's departure resulted in a depression at West Ham and the side started to slip down the Premier League, and the £300,000 did not stop Redknapp spending. As the Hammers nose-dived down the League, he demanded that a defender be brought in to replace Ferdinand.

After £6m had been blown, H slapped down nearly £5m for Titi Camara and Rigobert Song. Brown thought Pape Diouf was the agent involved; he was associated with Willie McKay (who was also arrested at the same time as Redknapp in November 2007 in connection with similar issues). Liverpool's chief executive Rick Parry was quick off the mark to unload the French-speaking African and seemingly jumped at the offer that would rid Anfield of a player who had brought a deal of disruption to the club. His delight doubled when he found out that Rigobert Song could also be dumped on West Ham. McKay collected commission from Terry Brown for bringing this pair to Upton Park.

Harry was very pleased with the deal, but both players

somewhat predictably flopped badly. Camara cost £30,000 a week but this was a drop in the ocean within Upton Park's £23m salary maelstrom in 2000 (which rose to £30m in 2002).

Following a 3–2 Upton Park defeat by Spurs, H demanded another £12m. After Ferdinand's move, Harry had brought in 10 players at a cost of £10.3m. Half of them (£5.3m worth) had made 48 appearances between them. At almost half-a-million pounds per appearance, Camara's three-outing career summed up the situation, but this was just the tip of the iceberg. None of the new players even came close to impressing and there were 10 wage packets, all down to McKay, that needed filling.

With appreciable income from Ferdinand's transfer gone, Redknapp merely shrugged his shoulders and looked forward to the next round of spending. He seemed to have learned nothing, leaving the board with little option other than to instruct Brown to get him out straight away.

Redknapp's own story of his sacking differs greatly from at least one other version that told of him sobbing as Brown fired him. But no one argues that he walked away with £1.6m, which was paid over 20 months.

Not too long after Redknapp left Upton Park, he was leading Portsmouth at the top of the First Division while West Ham struggled in the Premier League, at least partly as a result of the damage he had done. The Pompey crowd celebrated their saviour's prowess, while his failure, squandering and doubtful behaviour seemed to be either forgotten or ignored, as was the double betraying move to and from Portsmouth's greatest rivals Southampton. But perhaps that story isn't over yet. Truth is a slow-moving storm.

But I for one am glad that the East London days of Harry Redknapp are over. When he got the bullet, I could only be thankful to Saint Jude, football's informal patron (in general he covers lost causes/cases despaired of), that we had finally seen the

back of him. It seemed I had suffered him for too many years —
most of my life in fact — from the days when he dashed down
the wing, crossing the ball either too high, too long, too short or
too low.

I recall seeing H score a rare goal. A low cross struck him on
the left cheek of his arse and went in. Tellingly, he was facing the
opposite direction from the centre that had come in from his
left, thus he hadn't even seen the ball coming his way. Harry
went nuts. The celebration went on for what seemed like hours.
That kind of sums him up for me. Whenever I saw his snowy
white, stickman frame gangle out on to the pitch, my heart sank
and I couldn't help but groan along with the rest of the blokes I
used to stand with on the North Bank, 'Oh gawd! It's Harry.'

CHAPTER 11
ROEDER, RELEGATION AND ROTHERHAM

I consider myself to be a pretty good judge of people …
that's why I don't like any of them.
ROSEANNE BARR

The sacking of Redknapp met with much criticism as it seemed that the club didn't have a ready-made replacement. Brown has said that Alan Curbishley and Steve McClaren were both considered for the post, but neither was in a position to take up the job. In June 2001, Brown made an 'in-house' appointment as coach Glenn Roeder became the club's manager, having been caretaker manager since May, following Harry Redknapp's sacking.

The move didn't go down well with the club's supporters, many of whom believed that an experienced manager was required, and that Roeder's appointment was a money-saving ploy more than anything else. It was also perceived that the board were taking the soft (cheaper) alternative in appointing Roeder, who said himself that he was as surprised as anyone to be offered the job after apparently being told originally not to even bother applying.

However, Brown claimed that Roeder was never a cheap option as he was paid a good salary. He also points out that the man from Woodford took the Irons to seventh place in the 2001/02 Premier League, his first season. Roeder had been given a new three-year contract in February 2002, and, for Brown, he was the appointment that the board had wanted, an experienced coach who could retain and develop young players. Roeder also brought the advantage of being able to continue his work with the England squad. Terry saw Glenn's first season as confirming his coaching skills, but later admitted that the board might have failed to foresee the reluctance of the West Ham fans to accept Roeder as manager. That disinclination was combined with a poor start to his initial campaign, which gave rise to a deep-rooted problem in terms of Roeder's image.

It was Harry Redknapp who brought Roeder to the club, having offered him a job following their meeting during a dinner in London. Harry didn't know Glenn well, but he said he felt sorry for him (as he was out of work) and invited him to Chadwell Heath. Roeder took the young Hammers to the Youth Cup Final, showing his talent as a coach and tactician.

REL-LEG-A-GAY-SHON TIME, C'MON

Roeder's second season as manager was a disaster. He seemed out of touch with his dressing room and unable to revive the Hammers as they slumped to defeat after defeat. Although there was general agreement that the team were too good to be relegated, following Christmas things looked bad with a long list of injuries, poor performances and debt of around £44m that put a stop on buying. Brown took much of the resulting recrimination from the press and the supporters, with the focus on his dismissal of Redknapp.

In April 2003, Roeder had to receive treatment for a brain tumour. It struck me that the life-threatening illness he suffered towards the end of the 2002/03 season could hardly have been helped by the pressure he was under. According to Brown, the board's decision to keep faith with Roeder was unanimous. He felt Leeds United and Sunderland had spent millions of pounds appointing and sacking managers but that was not seen by the board to be the solution to the Hammers' problems. Brown told how the board wanted to invest as much as possible in the side during the January transfer window and felt assured that this would work for Roeder, which, to a certain extent, it did. West Ham passed the 40-point mark that would usually mean safety, but the Irons were relegated with the highest number of points ever achieved by a team relegated from the Premier League.

Brown believed West Ham's destiny relied on the penultimate game against Birmingham City. The Irons required other struggling teams to produce five losses; instead, there were four wins and one draw. Bolton Wanderers came back from 2–0 down against Arsenal and were awarded a 94th-minute penalty against Spurs. Leeds United also somehow won at Highbury. Brown confessed that, on the last day of the 2002/03 campaign, he had been certain that Bolton would avoid defeat against Middlesbrough. The Wanderers were quickly 2–0 up against the north-easterners and, from that point on, Brown said he knew the battle to survive in the Premier League was over.

On the day West Ham were relegated, Brown recalled that Hammers fans reacted in an incredible manner, particularly as the Birmingham City fans were chanting, 'Going down'; the Irons supporters replied with the chant: 'So are we!'

Brown had a great deal of sympathy for the Hammers fans at the end of the match and, indeed, felt that the team had failed them. He arrived home late at night and sat in his garden and tried to come to terms with the reality of relegation. He then ran 20 miles on his running machine. Terry finds running relaxing; he ran the 2002 London Marathon and has competed in many half-marathons. He also plays the occasional game of squash, but he sees running as the key to keeping himself sane.

Brown recalled that Billy Bonds had once said to him that 'if only' was the longest phrase in football and, as his team looked back on an awful season, Brown felt the wisdom of that statement. But he thought that the best had to be made of what was clearly going to be a very difficult summer and season ahead.

Brown issued a 10-page question-and-answer summary about the club's position following the Hammers' demotion in 2003, and the press focused on a single loosely worded suggestion that it was West Ham's 'turn' to be relegated. He replied to supporters – in great detail in a four-page letter – only to find that the letter was passed on to the press who subsequently extracted one sentence or phrase, or even a word, in order to ridicule Brown and West Ham. He remarked at the time that he had been told by politicians to produce just a short phrase, and to keep promoting that phrase in the media; he didn't want to be seen as a sort of spin doctor, seeing it as impossible to sell a negative. He understood that the club's problem was that it had been relegated with what was seen to be a very good squad, and, for Terry, no amount of PR skill could alter that.

Although relegation was a blow, Brown, like any astute businessman, had plans in place for all scenarios and West Ham were preparing for the financial impact of relegation from December 2002. Visits were made to all the clubs that had been relegated during the previous few seasons to inform the board's plans on how to manage relegation. But Brown always held on to the possibility that the Hammers would keep their Premier League status right up until the last game of the season.

Reflecting on the consequences of relegation in 2003, Brown described how it cost 19 full-time and 11 part-time jobs. The club's retail outlets took the brunt of the job cuts; branches were closed and the match-day hospitality department was 'rationalised'.

Trevor Brooking, then a director of the club, had successfully taken the role of caretaker manager during Roeder's illness, and there was talk that relegation might have been avoided if Brooking had been brought in to work with Roeder in the weeks and months before he had been taken ill. Brown claimed that Trevor had worked closely with Roeder and, once the club had acquired new players, and Paolo Di Canio and Fredi Kanoute returned to the team, West Ham's record improved; it is true that the Hammers lost just one of their last 11 matches and were second only to Manchester United during that period.

Some fans held Brown personally responsible for the club's position and called for his resignation. He reacted by saying that 'there are no bad soldiers, only bad officers'. But he fully accepted that perception is all, and understood why the supporters held him to account for what had happened to the club, although he felt that, in such a complex industry and being involved in a large company like West Ham, no one person can totally determine the future of the organisation.

FIRE SALE?

After Glen Johnson, Trevor Sinclair, Fredi Kanoute and Joe Cole left the Boleyn Ground, Roeder was always fighting a losing battle. The club's supporters were annoyed and upset when young favourites like Johnson and Cole departed Upton Park. Brown admitted to sharing that sorrow, having watched the likes of Johnson and Cole progress through the Academy and into the first team, as he had all the club's young players. However, Terry was aware that the business of modern football dictates that players no longer remain with a club until the end of their careers. Some thought that West Ham needed to take Chelsea's money or go into administration, but Brown claimed that there never was any likelihood of the latter. For him, West Ham had to raise funds in the transfer market to restructure the club after relegation but, as is generally well known, a big offer for Jermain Defoe was rejected at a fairly early stage.

After his contract expired in June 2004, Joe Cole had made it clear that he had no intention of re-signing for West Ham. Although amazingly many fans felt West Ham should have kept Cole at the club and simply allowed his contract to run out, it is puzzling that he was not sold much earlier, especially given the collapse of the transfer market before the coming of Abramovich. It seemed that Cole was always an asset that West Ham needed to cash in on sooner rather than later. But Brown argued that, despite what fans might have thought, the board had no wish to sell the club's players. He has claimed they did their utmost to persuade Joe to sign a new contract and it is true that, from the player's earliest years, Brown had taken a major role in guiding his career.

But the loss of star players caused a deal of anger as supporters saw themselves as being duped into buying season tickets for 2003/04 before the full scale of the summer sales were known. Brown later said that he didn't think that fans were tricked into buying season tickets, pointing out that he did say at the Extraordinary General Meeting – held before the end of that season – that West Ham would sell two or three players; in fact, four were sold. Refunds were made to 72 season-ticket holders who asked for them, and Brown believed this demonstrated that the club were aware that there was no advantage in misleading season-ticket holders in order to enhance sales. He said that he didn't want disgruntled season-ticket holders because of the negative effect this could have on the match-day atmosphere and, ultimately, the performance of the team. Terry claimed that he would not want anyone buying a season ticket to be under any misapprehensions.

CONTRACTS

It has often been said that the protection of modern contracts prevents players from taking the full consequences of their club's failures and that they should be held to account for their under-performance in the same way as most employees in other spheres would. However, Brown has made the point that there needs to be an understanding that, when a club signs quality players, it is the market that dictates both their salary and contract terms. If this is ignored, no chairman or manager is going to be successful in signing the players they think are needed to help their team succeed. For Brown, West Ham always tried to sign and retain good players. He has made the point that, having made decisions about player contracts, the board cannot simply change its mind because of relegation, although he has explained that many clubs, including West Ham, now include relegation clauses within any new contracts.

ROEDER'S RETURN

Roeder made an almost miraculous return to work in July 2003, but, four matches into the new season, Brown sacked him. To many, it seemed inexplicable that the club continued with Roeder only to dismiss him so soon after the start of the new campaign. The idea that the manager had been kept on out of sympathy for his illness became to be taken as a truth, but Brown has said that after relegation it was the board's intention to stand by Roeder and give him the chance to lead West Ham back to the top flight. At the same time, he told how everyone was concerned about the manager's illness; however, Terry denied that this played a part in allowing Roeder to continue in post.

With a Division One record of two wins and a draw, the Hammers visited Rotherham, and Brown identified events there as the last straw for the club in terms of Roeder's continued leadership. The players failed to get changed in the tiny dressing rooms at Millmoor, and this attracted another wave of adverse publicity. West Ham were portrayed as a side lacking the fighting spirit that rose above petty considerations like the conditions of dressing rooms, but Brown asserted that this had nothing to do with the players refusing to use the Rotherham dressing room. It seems Glenn had told the board the week before the match that the team would be partly changed when the coach arrived at Rotherham and would then warm up and finally prepare for the match in the dressing room. The whole affair did seem quite bizarre. The thought of a professional football team getting changed on the coach didn't strike anyone as the best preparation for a match, and that proved to be the case when the Irons lost 1–0 to a side that would barely escape relegation.

A statement on the Hammers' official website was made: 'West Ham United wish to announce that Glenn Roeder's contract has been terminated with immediate effect and he has been relieved of his duties as team manager.

'The board would like to place on record their gratitude to Glenn for his hard work and commitment to the club since his permanent appointment in June 2001.

'This was demonstrated by his desire to return to active duty so quickly after his recent illness and I am sure all supporters recognise how dedicated he was to the club.

'The board, however, feel that, following relegation to the First Division, the club's best chance of returning to the Premiership at the first attempt would be enhanced by a change of manager.

'Trevor Brooking CBE will once again act as caretaker manager until such time as a permanent successor is appointed.

'Interviews will begin immediately and Glenn's successor will be appointed in due course.

'Until that time the board has complete confidence in Trevor's ability to manage the team starting at home on Tuesday night against Bradford City.'

Roeder also issued a statement on the Hammers' website: 'I found the decision of the board of West Ham United to terminate my contract after only four matches disappointing ... However, I would like to put on record my thanks to the players, staff and fans of West Ham United, a truly great club, and wish them every success for the future.'

No one could doubt Roeder's courage when he fought his way back from brain surgery to take charge of a club like West Ham that were struggling on so many levels. Brown refused to fire him, perhaps for many good reasons, but, if Roeder could have made things work, it would have saved on compensation money. However, that pay-out figure paled into insignificance after relegation and the prospect of a prolonged stay outside the Premiership.

Brown never gave up his view that Roeder had great qualities. He wished him well after he departed the club, but was subsequently to admit that, when Roeder had asked for more funds at the start of what was to be a relegation season, the board had made a mistake in not giving him more resources to strengthen the squad that had overachieved in finishing seventh in 2001/02. But Brown also pointed out the need to remember that the club committed £14m during the summer of 2002, paying the second half of the payments due in respect of the transfers made during Redknapp's tenure the previous summer, adding players to the squad – who subsequently turned out to be unsuitable for the Premier League – and in renegotiating the contracts of players who had been tempted by other clubs. As such, for Brown, it was simply not possible to find any more money, bearing in mind the huge commitment the board had made with the new Dr Martens Stand.

Brown argued that West Ham's fiscal predicament would have been improved if the club had not frozen ticket prices for the second year running and that was certainly the case, but, at the same time, there were other factors that had as much, if not more, impact; not least was the woeful state of the Hammers' merchandising, which, while not untypical in football, would have done well to follow the way baseball and grid-iron football clubs market themselves in the USA.

As Trevor Brooking once more stepped into the managerial breach, the club looked desperately for a replacement for Roeder. Although, for many, it was clear that the board hoped that Brooking might take on a permanent contract, according to Brown and Brooking himself, the former Hammers star had made it clear that he didn't want the job on a permanent basis.

Brown explained that it was difficult to identify a new manager before firing Roeder, but the Hammers did get Brooking to agree to act as caretaker manager prior to Roeder being dismissed. Brown made the point that the club had needed to be careful about illegal approaches, and that, when a manager leaves a club, almost immediately they are inundated with applicants for the vacant post, many of surprising quality.

Terry also said he had to bear in mind the accusation that Glenn did not have a great record prior to becoming West Ham manager, so the board carried out meticulous research, looking at managers with good records. Alan Pardew was second only to Sir Alex Ferguson in terms of winning ratio and had achieved much of his success with Reading, a club at the Hammers' current level. According to Brown, when the Hammers board were finally allowed to interview Pardew, they began to appreciate why he had been so successful and the former Crystal Palace and Charlton man took over in October 2003.

CHAPTER 12
WHISTLE

*When you're constantly looking for things from other
people, you're not looking within yourself ...*
SANDRA BERNHARD

Terry Brown has said that PR is not just about releasing player-related stories in the press. It has to be said that, in the last few years of his chairmanship, he sometimes appeared to get as much press interest as any of the club's playing staff.

After West Ham's relegation in 2003, angered as well as frustrated about the sale of the majority of the club's best players, a pressure group calling itself 'WHISTLE', made up of Hammers' shareholders, season-ticket holders and bondholders, were critical of Brown and pressed for his removal via a boardroom coup.

WHISTLE outlined their main objectives for West Ham, a club they saw as having 'considerable potential':

Aim to be 'the best of the rest': while accepting that West Ham do not currently have the ability to take on the giants of the English game such as Arsenal and Manchester United, WHISTLE maintain that West Ham have the capacity to be 'the best of the rest', while achieving a top-eight finish in the Premiership every season.

Return to regular European competition: WHISTLE believe that, with the right management, the club has the capacity to enter European competitions on average at least once every five years – and reach a major domestic final also on average every five years. *Retain younger players*: the group strive to ensure that the young talent nurtured by West Ham would seek to remain at the club rather than leave at the first opportunity as is the case currently, by giving them a reason to stay.

The group planned to replace the West Ham board of directors, who they held as culpable for West Ham's dire financial situation. Money would be made available to the manager in order to strengthen the squad for a return to the Premiership. Thereafter, more funds would be issued to boost the playing side.

WHISTLE also revealed that a 'management turnaround team' was ready to replace the board. The group produced an eight-page document which was distributed to shareholders, detailing the group's plans for West Ham that started with a call for the removal of the current board members Terry Brown, Paul Aldridge and Nick Igoe.

The report proposed three options for change:

a. Appointment of a non-executive chairperson to structure and oversee West Ham plc
WHISTLE call for a CEO with a proven track record to replace Terry Brown as Chairman of West Ham United. The successful candidate would also be joined by 'one or more' non-executive directors with 'a deep knowledge of the game' (Trevor Brooking was cited).

b. A one-for-one public rights/share issue
WHISTLE are calling for the implementation of a new share issue scheme in order to raise much needed funds

for the club. The scheme would see 20 million shares issued at £1 each, in much the same way as the recent schemes announced by Norwich City and Ipswich Town.

c. The introduction of new private investors/owners
WHISTLE would seek a group of private investors to join the club as majority shareholders (a prerequisite being that their interests lie in the long-term success of the club, not personal profits). This group would be responsible for selecting the non-executive directors as mentioned above in section b.

WHISTLE concluded by stating:

It is the intention of this paper that one or more of the options be pursued and adopted to ensure that West Ham United plc is placed in the hands of professional and respected owners and management teams who conduct themselves along structured and accountable lines.

By implementing the proposals we believe that the club will have started the process of directing this potentially great club back towards the destiny it merits. We are aiming high because the club's devoted and special fans deserve to see their faith rewarded. Let us set the standard that others will be measured by.

West Ham's patient and loyal supporters have waited long enough – it is time to act.

Mike Hanna, who claimed to speak on behalf of a group of five shareholders in West Ham United plc who collectively held a total of 1,203 ordinary shares in the company (0.006 per cent of the issued share capital), announced that WHISTLE would table their resolutions at the company's AGM on 8 December 2003, proposing the removal of the three executive directors of the company – Brown, Aldridge and Igoe.

A long email was sent to all shareholders outlining WHISTLE's case, and it looked convincing:

> We are a group of businessmen and professionals who are West Ham supporters and fellow shareholders and are writing to ask for your support at the company's forthcoming Annual General Meeting ('AGM') as we feel that the current board of directors of the company have now proven they are unable to move this club forward.
>
> Although the exact date of the AGM remains to be announced formally by the company, as we have yet to receive the company's accounts for the year ended 31st May 2003, we understand that it will take place at 11am on Monday 8th December 2003 at Upton Park.
>
> The attached financial summaries show the position as at 31st May 2002, but not necessarily appreciated by the company's shareholders let alone its directors, who undersell the implications of the actual size of the debts and liabilities that are constraining (if not overstretching or even endangering) the company.
>
> We will update the information once we have received the 2003 accounts of the company and its peer group, which in our opinion will only confirm that the financial position of the company has worsened against its peers. If you are interested in receiving a copy, please let us know by writing to the above address or emailing us at tellmemore@whistle.lt
>
> Furthermore, as you are aware the football club have been relegated from the Premiership. However, the 2003 accounts that we are about to receive do NOT reflect in any manner the financial effect of relegation with the

concomitant reduction in income from Sky TV, sponsorship, et al.

Much has been made in the popular and financial press in recent days concerning the financial performance of Leeds United PLC and Tottenham Hotspur PLC, both of which clubs remain in the Premiership as well as Sunderland PLC who were likewise relegated with West Ham United.

In all cases, as well as there being changes in the football management, there have also been changes in the board of directors who ultimately have responsibility, irrespective of the performance on the football field, for the company's financial health.

In the case of West Ham United PLC there appears to be no such changes proposed, despite the company's financial position, being, in relative terms, considerably worse than the aforementioned.

The recent alteration to the Articles of Association of the club at the Extraordinary General Meeting, 'EGM' (the removal of the rule that borrowings were limited to a maximum of three times net operating assets), was a foretaste of the ultimate effect of the failed financial strategy that had been followed by the present board.

Some would argue that the current board refuse to acknowledge the true depth of the company's current financial position and perhaps even to mislead us. For instance, at the EGM the directors were allegedly unable to state whether the borrowing covenant had already been breached. This at the very minimum was a dereliction of their duties and quite possibly a breach of Section 221 of the Companies Act 1985, which requires the directors at all times to be able to produce accounts showing the financial position of the company.

One would have thought that the directors, having convened an EGM, would make this financial information readily available, but when asked the directors were allegedly unable to state whether the borrowing covenant had already been breached.

We are therefore tabling a motion calling for the removal of the executive directors, namely Mr Terence Brown, Mr Nicholas Igoe and Mr Paul Aldridge, and propose that the company instruct head hunters to identify and employ suitably qualified individuals who can be appointed to run a public company.

It is further proposed that Mr Trevor Brooking, in addition to being a non-executive director of the club, is also made, with his agreement, a non-executive director of the company and that the current non-executive director Mr Charles Warner be asked to stay for a period of 12 months to allow a new board to be appointed.

The cost of providing redundancy packages to the current executive board is nothing compared to the financial losses suffered by the company under their management, let alone the effect on the football club.

You may be interested to know that in the accounts for the year ended 31st May 2002 the chairman Mr Terence Brown wrote in his report that 'I do hope that, in due course, all our supporters will understand the need for "belt-tightening" which is taking place and realise that a priority for your board remains that of passing the club on to the next generation of stakeholders (supporters, staff and shareholders) in the best possible shape. What we cannot do is to gamble with 107 years of hard-earned history in the vain hope of achieving some unprecedented success on the pitch.'

The chairman's report was approved on 11th

November 2002, yet allegedly at a board meeting of the company held on 4th December 2002 it was recorded that the company's chairman Mr Terence Brown had been awarded a pay rise in his basic salary, excluding pension and benefits to £492,000 per annum effective from 1st June 2002. The other executive directors likewise received pay rises effective from 1st June 2002. This minute did not make any mention of the 'paycut' subsequently announced at the EGM and which Mr Brown refers to in the latest missive alleging that the 'paycut' had been agreed in December 2002.

You may also be interested to know that, if the club are successful in being promoted in the 2003/04 season, then the 'paycut' will be reversed and the directors will receive in full the amount that they are allegedly not currently receiving since 1st June 2003.

It is in this context that the enclosed motion has been drafted and we strongly urge you to support the motion by signing the enclosed Notice of Motion and returning to the club no later than 5pm on 17th November 2003 with a copy to ourselves.

We would stress that, in light of our understanding of the current shareholdings of the directors of the company and club and their related/associated business and personal interests, there is absolutely no chance of success of the motion being passed unless the club's directors Mr Martin Cearns and Mr Charles Warner and/or their interests/associates and family members vote in favour of the resolution.

However, it is important that the directors are aware that we, the shareholders, are not satisfied in the way the company is being run. We strongly urge you to support the Motion by signing and returning the enclosed Notice of Motion to the company no later than 15th November 2003 and make every effort to attend the AGM to make your feelings known.

Brown offered WHISTLE an Extraordinary General Meeting. His official statement read:

> However the Companies Act 1985 stipulates that requisitions for members' resolutions must be deposited with the company no later than 6 weeks before the AGM. Mr Hanna appears to have misinterpreted the Act as the requisitions have not been deposited with the company within the correct time limit, and for this reason the resolutions proposed by Mr Hanna cannot be included within the business to be dealt with at the AGM.
>
> However, the company is prepared to facilitate a procedure whereby the resolutions can be voted on even though there is no obligation under company law for it to do so. The company has made an offer to Mr Hanna that it is prepared to convene an Extraordinary General Meeting to put the resolutions to shareholders.
>
> The company has made this offer in the interests of maintaining an open dialogue with all shareholders and because it does not wish to be seen to defeat Mr Hanna's proposals merely because of his failure to comply with the provisions of the Companies Act. The board will however vigorously defend its management record at any EGM so convened and is confident of winning the support of the vast majority of its shareholders.
>
> A further announcement will be made regarding the EGM once Mr Hanna has accepted the company's offer.

WHISTLE refused the option of the EGM, but failed to win the necessary support from the club's major shareholders at the AGM; the existing directors retained the support of the influential Warner and Cearns families. Managing director Paul Aldridge and Charles Warner polled over 98 per cent each of the total number of shares in the votes, as expected.

But a show of hands prompted by one shareholder demonstrated that the majority of shareholders present, the numbers of whom were swollen by those who had taken advantage of the 'single-share' scheme, felt it was time for Brown and his colleagues to step down.

Brown took on a barrage of criticism from angry shareholders. Although obviously shaken by the response, he vowed to continue as chairman, telling those shareholders present, 'I will not force myself on this club – but will not walk out and let the club down.'

Later, Brown told how he wasn't surprised that WHISTLE had turned down the idea of an EGM. He said that he wasn't sure the WHISTLE group understood that, at the AGM, even if the votes controlled by members of the board had been ignored, the remaining shareholders would give massive support to the current board, demonstrating faith in their policies. Brown was happy that all resolutions had been passed by a huge majority of shareholders at the AGM.

However, WHISTLE didn't accept defeat and turned to the club's creditors. They sought the backing of the club's biggest lenders on the grounds that West Ham's debts following relegation from the Premiership still ran into several tens of millions despite the sale of most of the club's top players. At the same time, WHISTLE argued that about £20m had been promised to them by potential but unidentified City investors who were keen to put resources into the club by way of a share issue if major lenders (the largest of which was Barclays Bank) could oblige Brown to resign.

According to Hanna, WHISTLE were 'not proposing a takeover. We want a share issue that doubles the shares available in the company ... Certain people have undertaken to buy certain amounts of those shares, and their money would be used to appease the debt ... If the financial institutions come on board, you've got pressure. If the City loses confidence in a business, it has to change.'

But West Ham's managing director Paul Aldridge dismissed claims of a deteriorating relationship with Barclays and accused WHISTLE of jeopardising the club's promotion bid.

He said in a statement, 'The club's year-end accounts will show a substantial reduction in debt.

'We have had an excellent relationship with Barclays for over a hundred years and that relationship is stronger and better than ever.

'I'm afraid this is clearly just another alarmist story trying to destabilise the club at this very important stage of the season.'

WHISTLE published a dossier in April 2004 raising concerns about a possible increase in the club's debts, despite player sales of £27m. In the process, it accused the West Ham board of financial ineptitude. The dossier, which was sent to Brown, also contained 180 questions about the club's finances.

Mike Hanna was quoted as commenting, 'Despite selling all the crown jewels, which you can't sell again, Brown has failed to address the debt situation. We're now a Nationwide First Division club and we are not generating the revenue to handle our current financial position. The banks are begging for a credible alternative. They are waiting for an approach which will handle the debt. We have people associated with ourselves who are influential within the City and would offer the financial institutions an alternative.'

WHISTLE's dossier was also sent to the Football Association, Football League and the Department of Trade and Industry in the hope of an investigation into the club's finances, and was designed to cause maximum embarrassment to the West Ham board. Hanna said, 'If we don't get answers, what on earth does it do to the reputation of the business?'

The club were upset that a number of WHISTLE's questions implied misconduct on the part of West Ham by raising issues about preferential corporate hospitality and links with freemasonry. Brown was said to be furious about the allegations. After attacking the timing of the dossier – with the Hammers being on the threshold of the play-offs (Alan Pardew's side had to avoid losing by four goals at Wigan on the coming Sunday to guarantee a top-six finish) – Brown, the club and their bankers Barclays refuted claims of an increase in the club's £44m debt despite the sale of players. He also confirmed that there would be legal recourse against WHISTLE's members over 'untrue allegations'.

Brown said at the time, 'We do not have a financial crisis at West Ham and have not had one at any time since our relegation. It is unacceptable that, at such a crucial time in our season, someone should seek to undermine all the hard work of Alan, the players and our staff by issuing information that contains so many lies simply to mislead and demoralise our fans who have given West Ham such fantastic support throughout the season. We will be taking legal action against Mr Hanna and other members of the WHISTLE group to protect the club from these scurrilous allegations. May I urge every single fan to ignore this nonsense and back our boys.'

WHISTLE's claims about West Ham's financial position were emphatically denied by the club, whose lawyers said, 'In fact, the debt burden will have significantly decreased from last year.'

Hanna responded immediately. At the end of April 2004, he sent a letter to Alan Pardew detailing the reasoning behind the campaign to get rid of Brown and certain key directors and replace them with a new management team and told the West Ham manager, 'We are absolutely not trying to destabilise you or your team. If the club win promotion, you will need significant funds to buy new players. We fear those funds will not be forthcoming under the current management.'

The group also claimed that West Ham's board had resisted approaches from 'serious parties' for a much-needed cash injection. Again the board refuted this allegation, with the club's legal advisers, City law firm Herbert Smith, saying, 'There have been no serious offers of fresh investment.'

WHISTLE further alleged that West Ham's precarious financial position would force more player sales during the summer, even if they were promoted to the Premiership. Once more, the club's lawyers denied WHISTLE's claim saying, 'Such an allegation is defamatory and highly damaging.'

WHISTLE were understood to be determined to continue with their efforts to overthrow Brown, seize control of the club and appoint a new management structure regardless of the legal action.

On 6 May, West Ham threatened to sue WHISTLE members for aggravated damages if they continued to make 'untrue and defamatory' allegations about the club. Brown instructed Herbert Smith to begin a libel action against the 1,000-strong group.

In a strongly worded letter, West Ham's solicitors wrote, 'We demand that you immediately desist from making any further untrue and defamatory remarks regarding our client. If you fail to provide an undertaking confirming that you will do so, any further such statements will be used to support a claim for aggravated damages in the proceedings our client is going to initiate against you.'

During 2004, two WHISTLE members submitted public apologies. West Ham's official website announced during the 2003/04 season that a settlement with the group had been achieved.

Later, Brown said that he saw WHISTLE as having the right

to take any steps they wanted and that he thought the group meant well. He described how they had put questions to him at the AGM in a well-mannered and reasonable way. However, he believed that the group had scant financial backing and little experience in business. Brown pointed out that the resolutions proposed at the AGM early in 2004 were passed by average majorities of 99 per cent and argued that, for him, this demonstrated the situation. However, he said, while he had no wish to be impolite or show any lack of respect, he felt that, if a wealthy businessperson ever looked to purchase the club, they were most unlikely to approach the club through individuals like those involved with WHISTLE.

Some West Ham fans had complained that Brown had misled them by initially declaring that player sales were not necessary and then, after finding out the amount of money spent on season tickets, oversaw a multi-million-pound clear-out of players that resulted in the disappearance of 21 of the first-team squad.

However, Brown maintained that proclaiming that the club had massive financial problems would have encouraged other clubs to make ridiculous offers for players, which West Ham would have been obliged to accept. Terry managed to keep the supporters sweet with this argument, although the club failed to gain promotion in 2005.

WHISTLE really never stood a chance of winning over the West Ham shareholders. The manner of the shares distribution meant they would need to convince the Warner and Cearns tribes to turn against Brown, and realistically that was never going to happen. It seems unbelievable that they thought it might. It seems that forcing a vote at the AGM in December 2003 was a means of drawing attention to the situation, and, by undermining confidence in the administration of the club, they hoped to open the way for a coup by way of the creditors, or merely to embarrass Brown out of his seat of power. However, this again seems to demonstrate WHISTLE's woeful and unacceptable level of naivety.

In the end, Brown's battle with WHISTLE illustrated his strong position at the top of the Upton Park hierarchy, and resulted in a powerful vote of confidence in his chairmanship.

The WHISTLE debacle seems mystifying to any close observer of West Ham United. WHISTLE'S membership, having publicly expressed its contriteness, retreated into anonymity, while Terry Brown looked invulnerable, stronger than ever.

CHAPTER 13
PARDEW – THE CLINT EASTWOOD OF SE7

If you want a guarantee, buy a toaster.
CLINT EASTWOOD

Bringing Alan Pardew to Upton Park after the vital summer months – in which he might have had the chance to put over to the players how he wanted them to play and to prepare the team for life in the lower league – seemed at first to be a handicap. Brown argued that Pardew's earlier arrival might have made little difference because the team was changing constantly as players were released and new ones signed. However, as the months floated by, it became increasingly clear that the West Ham team of the time took little notice of what their manager had to say.

AL, THE PLAYERS' PAL

At Upton Park, Pardew liked to foster an egalitarian, somewhat matey attitude and encourage banter between him and his playing staff. He cultivated an image of the thoughtful tough guy, but was at his happiest promoting *esprit de corps* in a huddle with his players. This might have been influenced by his career

173

path in football. He came into the full-time game following
several years combining a career in the non-league realm at
Dulwich Hamlet with a 40-hours-plus-a-week job as a glazier
(very appropriate given his future Selhurst Park connections).
Pards was also a cabbie in his spare time and did go South of the
River. He joined Yeovil Town, working under Ian McFarlane,
and in 1987 moved to Crystal Palace for a fee of £7,500. Alan
was in the side that Steve Coppell led to victory in the play-off
final, which sent the Eagles back into the English football elite
in 1989. The following year, Palace got to the FA Cup Final
where they were beaten by Manchester United.

From 1991 to 1995, Pards was managed by Alan Curbishley at
Charlton. A move to Barnet in 1995 opened him to the
influence of first Ray Clemence (1994–96) and then Terry
Bullivant, with whom he worked as player-coach. It wasn't an
altogether successful partnership as the Bees were relegated to
Division Three. Bullivant moved on to Reading and Pardew
returned to Dulwich Hamlet for a short stint as their centre-
half, but soon he was Berkshire bound to join Bullivant as his
assistant. After a run of poor results, Bullivant left the Royals,
and, not long after, Al started his career as a manager just off the
M4. Having coined the rather cheesy motto 'Tenacity, Spirit and
Flair', believing this could give his team a 'psychological edge',
he led his side to defeat in the Division Two play-off final in
2001. The following season, he took Reading into Division
One, but once more he lost in the play-offs.

At West Ham, Pardew struck me a bit like a teacher wanting
to be one of the pupils and that didn't promote respect in him
as a leader or manager, perhaps because, as he was no longer able
to play, he had become a manager but had never come to terms
with that role.

It has to be borne in mind that Pardew was nearly 27 when
he came into the upper echelons of the game. Unlike most

managers, he had not grown up in a football environment. As such, his attitude appeared to me to be fuelled by an effort to compensate for something. This showed itself in a variety of ways. For instance, when his own players had bust-ups among themselves, he passed this off as a positive thing, showing keen competition in his squad and the character of the players. Reading between the lines, this meant that he either didn't know how to respond to such situations or he felt incapable of exerting any authority. But, whatever the case, the result was that he did nothing.

Another example of this flaw in Pardew's managerial personality came after League One Chesterfield knocked the Hammers out of the League Cup in October 2006. It was rumoured that, after the game, Brown, angry with Pardew and the players, went into the dressing room and told the team they had played 'like a pub team' and that the £16,000 spent on an overnight stay before the game had been a waste of money.

As soon as this story made the headlines, Brown told the club website, 'I went down the tunnel to make sure that Alan was OK. Nothing negative or critical was said.'

Brown told how he placed a supportive arm around his manager and let him know that everything would be fine. He went on to say that it was disappointing that some media reports had suggested that there was animosity between him, Pardew and the players but that it would 'not distract us from working hard to turn round the team's current situation'.

Pardew confirmed his chairman's version of what had occurred, telling how Brown had said to him, 'Come on, we've been here before; we'll sort things out and turn it around.'

Even accounting for the press habit of cultivating the worst-case scenario, Brown had never been prone to dressing-room visits in the past, so the mere presence of the chairman after the match could be seen to demonstrate that he was losing faith in his manager. And, with little evidence that Pardew had the inclination or even the ability to berate his underachieving side, it would not seem unreasonable for Brown to take matters into his own hands. But the reality is Brown really isn't that sort of man and would not compromise his dignity in such a manner. He is a deliberate and practical man much more prone to action than rhetoric. While he is capable of calculated and uncompromising action (as any good businessman must be), he is not a person to let his temper rule his purpose.

Pardew seemed more concerned with having a cordial relationship with his adolescent rebels than trying to instil discipline. To fans like me who can recall or know about the Upton Park administration of Ted Fenton back in the 1950s, it felt as if history was repeating itself. Fenton was squarely placed in a back seat firstly by Malcolm Allison and then by Ken Brown, Noel Cantwell and John Bond. When the team won promotion in 1958, while Fenton got the media credit, everyone in football knew that the 'BBC' had been the brains behind the triumph. For Pardew, team matters appeared to be dominated by a core of influential players who it seemed he dared not cross for fear that they might withdraw their labour, which in the end a few seemed to do anyway. His reported avoidance of telling his skipper Reo-Coker about Arsenal's interest in him seemed to verify many of the feelings some of us had about Pardew's character, his fears and insecurities.

In the end, Al could only watch as the players appeared to either sulk or simply ignored him. His spat with Arsène Wenger on Bonfire Night 2006 demonstrated that Al, as a character, was either not ready for or unsuited to his role. Although the slapping match was lauded by a body of West Ham fans as 'Al' 'aving a go!', it was embarrassing for those of us who have known the club under dignified giants of the game such as John Lyall and Ron Greenwood. There was no harder player than

Lyall, but he would never have got himself into such a position in the technical area. Taking kindergarten swipes at each other, Wenger and Pardew just confirmed that they had simply lost control. I know Wenger and Pardew might be said to be equally to blame, but it had been Al's 'giving it large' antics that had sparked the barney. Pardew's ridiculous posturing stance was ill disciplined and irresponsible.

Over the last eight years I have taken groups of students on regular tours of Upton Park as guests of the Learning Zone or West Ham in the Community. Shortly after Pardew took over as manager, the home dressing room was festooned with plaques inscribed with sayings, mottos and statements apparently designed to concentrate the minds of and/or inspire his young players. As I watched students, who were about the same age as many of the Hammers team, I noted that no one ever read these worthy snippets of literature. I made the effort to look at one or two, but found them tediously repetitious and convoluted. Each time I looked at these hieroglyphics, it seemed to me Pardew seemed to understand little of the young men he worked with.

According to Brown, Trevor Brooking had been an enormous influence on the board's decision to appoint Pardew. Brooking had welcomed Pardew and had been glad to give up the responsibility of management, but I'm not sure what the former England international would have found to particularly endorse about the new manager. He certainly was not in the same class as the managers Brooking had worked with during his time as a player.

Pardew has been described as one of the new breed of bright, young English managers making an impact on the modern game. He put his faith in sports science and the use of the highly detailed statistical and graphical information facilitated by modern technology. He employed an ICT person at the Boleyn Ground, who at half-time would download data gathered from the first half to Al's laptop that he then could hook up to a plasma screen in the dressing room, allowing Pardew to evaluate his players' performances as they chatted among themselves.

Brown told how he was not surprised that Reading chairman John Madejski vigorously fought against Pardew's move to the Boleyn Ground, saying that West Ham would have done much the same if he had been the Hammers' manager. Pardew spent so much time with 'gardening leave' between finishing as manager at the Madejski Stadium and coming to Upton Park that he could have applied for a job at Kew, while the respective chairmen went into all the legal ramifications of the move with Madejski muttering curses about poaching.

Brown saw Pardew as a strong, charismatic manager who believed the club needed to build a winning culture right from the supporters through to the team, the board and the staff. He also claimed that his new manager was well organised, ambitious and a determined individual. While these statements may seem heartfelt, they seemed to mirror something of Pardew's approach while at Upton Park and are more reminiscent of management-speak soundbites: what actually is a 'winning culture' and how do you 'build' one? And does declaring this in fact achieve anything?

BROWN – A GIANT IN RELEGATION

For all this, Pardew had a difficult start and, while excuses were made about him needing time to get his views and policies across to the players, it wasn't always obvious that he knew how to communicate with the team. A feature of Pardew's time at Upton Park was how, with each game, the players seemed to be organising themselves more. From the lower rungs of the Dr Martens Stand, you could hear and watch Pardew shouting and gesticulating to his seemingly oblivious players who quite often did the exact opposite of what he was instructing. He'd fold his arms as the blush of embarrassment covered his countenance. As one player told me with a smile, 'He says go left, go right, he says go back, go forward …'

Brown admitted to wanting more wins and that the club, having had to reinvent itself for the Nationwide League, was proving to be more difficult than he had expected but he understood that working through three managers and many new players was not the ideal start to a season, and that, while the fans were understandably frustrated, he recognised the need for the club to shake off the stigma of relegation and rebuild. Again, good words.

However, at the time, Terry was quite forward in saying that he did not see it as his place to tell the supporters to show patience. He obviously knew that the reaction of the crowd was an ally in terms of pressurising for success. But Brown told how he was conscious of the need to produce the results at home that would encourage fans to give the team the backing it needed and for which West Ham supporters are famous. Once more, the message to the manager was clear.

Brown said he did not believe West Ham could have asked any more of the fans and the fact they filled the stadium for a match against Wigan Athletic told everything one might need to know about West Ham United and its supporters. It also said exactly what Terry thought of Wigan!

Not long into West Ham's initial campaign in the Nationwide League, while conceding the Hammers had to learn from their mistakes, Terry said he didn't want to dwell on the club's past mistakes. He described how he looked to the players who had experienced relegation, and to those who had joined the club having never played in front of 35,000 fans. He also placed his faith in players emerging from the Academy, predicting that some of these would one day be great players. In praise of West Ham's historical record, Brown pointed out that only five teams have spent more seasons among the cream of English football than West Ham since 1958.

While this kind of rhetoric was heartening, it also helped to deflect resentment from the recent past, which is an essential tool in the control (and management) of any mass of people to provide hope for what is to come from a focus on the present. It is harder to dwell on what has occurred if one is preoccupied with what is happening or going to happen. I hope that this book serves to do the opposite of this, by considering historic events in order to make some sense of them and thus inform about the likely shape of future events, helping to make them as close as possible to what we want.

Relegation allowed West Ham to reduce debts and restructure financially. For Brown, none of that could have been achieved overnight but he said that, through improved performances, he wanted to persuade the fans to be patient to help the club return to the Premier League in better financial shape to ensure profits and therefore shareholder satisfaction.

HAPPY DAYS

In 2003, looking back on the previous occasion the club was relegated, Brown recollected saying to Len Cearns that West Ham's best days could be over. Terry remembered Cearns had looked at him in amazement and said that, although West Ham United had had both good and bad days in their history, as a man of then nearly 80, he realised they were *all* good days.

One doesn't really need too much convincing of that in the case of Cearns; win, lose or draw, he was going to score. The loyalty of West Ham's supporters had guaranteed consistently good attendance figures throughout his days with the club. Investment in players had for the most part been unnecessary (relative to most top clubs) as the East London area was a veritable goldmine of young football talent and the stadium infrastructure had been maintained at minimal cost. Yes, all old Len's days had been the best but, as a supporter of nearly half a century, I can't say the same. In fact, the good days have been good only in comparison with an awful lot of really shitty days: soaked and frozen, let down and taken advantage of, while more or less being told that I should be grateful for the insults meted out 'for the good of the club', another often used yet ultimately meaningless phrase.

Like so many supporters, this has made me realistic about football management and the way West Ham is and has been run. I know there is no alternative, but at least we can stop kidding each other. I have always known, since I was a kid, that West Ham is about the fans and the place where we come from. Everything else is a necessary evil and I have accepted that. What is harder to deal with is the soft soap handed out in massive slops. It is not so much the fact that this is meant to fool me that I resent; it is knowing that managers, and sometimes players and board members, *think* it is fooling me that really offends me. To his credit, Terry Brown is not as likely to indulge in this sort of thing as much as some of his peers. But West Ham have had their share of people that have more than made up for that.

THINGS DO GO BETTER WITH COKE?

As a Nationwide League side, West Ham were touted as a prime candidate for automatic promotion but could do no better than fourth at the conclusion of the 2003/04 season. This disappointment was compounded by a 1–0 defeat by Crystal Palace in the play-off final. Unable to bounce back in the following term, now in the Coca-Cola Championship, the fans laid the blame for the club's failure principally at the door of Brown and his board.

BROWN OUT

The restriction of the transfer window was not applicable in the Football League in 2004 for domestic transfers so this meant that the board could provide as much financial assistance to Pardew as possible. But Brown was conscious that, if the club had failed to achieve promotion at the first attempt, they would need to scale down the then £17m player wage tab, as most clubs in that division had wage bills of around £3m per year.

In 2004, Brown said that he and his colleagues on the board still had the appetite and energy to continue in their roles and remained very optimistic about the club's future. He claimed that they would never walk out and leave the club's future to chance. He pointed out that the Warner family could trace their involvement with the Thames Ironworks back to 1856 and that the Cearns family had provided directors since the company's formation in 1900. For Terry, the main concern for West Ham United, the last major British football club to be controlled by their founding families, was the future wellbeing of the club and, while a takeover bid could, of course, be structured in so many different ways, as far as the board at that time were concerned, they remained focused on returning to the Premier League in good financial shape. He claimed it was that task which dominated the board's thinking and, to be fair, he and his board succeeded.

In 2005, West Ham once more made the play-off final, only just getting there with a sixth-place finish. But a 1–0 win over Preston North End in the final eased the criticism that had been aimed at both Brown and Pardew. The success meant that the minimum increase in revenue, relative to the amount it would have received in the Championship, was estimated to be in the region of £30m (£18m from TV rights for the 2005/06 season plus £6m for the subsequent two seasons should the club not remain in the Premier League). Brown announced that he did not want to repeat the mistakes made in the recent past and made £20m available for player purchases in May 2005. He was re-elected as chairman in October 2005, approved by a vote of 14,461,566 shares in favour and 371 against. In the summer of 2006, West Ham made it to the FA Cup Final and were unlucky to lose to Liverpool on penalties.

It seemed West Ham were 'over the hump' but, hey, if you thought that, you didn't know West Ham.

CHAPTER 14
BROWN OUT

I love football. Football is, is, she's a cruel mistress.
She's, she's more than a mistress. She's a wife, she's a mother, she's
a daughter, she's an errant child. She can make you laugh, she can make
you cry. She can bring tears to me eyes. She can bring blood to me
shoulders. She can bring the kettle to the boil. 'Cause football is
about nothing, unless it's about something and what it is about.
ALAN LATCHLEY – FOOTBALL MANAGER (PETER COOK)

When the Queen (always a Hammers fan) opened West Ham's new West Stand, there were hopes that the Irons were in for a right royal future. But in 2002 Brown, alongside the club's supporters, was obliged to suffer the abysmal first half of the 2002/03 season, and the Hammers were rooted to the bottom of the Premiership at Christmas. The board didn't seem to recognise the danger of relegation unless drastic changes were made; no other club had been bottom at Christmas and avoided relegation from the Premiership. Around this time, the banners and the angry chants from the fans left no doubt as to who West Ham supporters held responsible for their club's plight. 'Brown out!' was the battle cry reverberating around the Boleyn Ground as the Irons supporters vented their frustration.

However, Terry claimed that the board were concentrating on raising as much money as possible in order to sign players during the January transfer window and were confident that, if the club could get hold of the right players, the magic 40 points could be attained.

BROWN OUT

A constant rant against Brown and his board was that they did not release funds for new players. This, together with his apparent indecisiveness and a lack of foresight in sacking and appointing managers, made him a scapegoat for a huge body of fans. His promises that after relegation there would be no 'fire sale' of players appeared to have been proved false, as the club's most talented and valuable players had been shipped out to pay off debts or because they just would not consider playing outside the Premiership.

With Terry accused of overseeing the decline of West Ham from an average yet self-reliant Premiership outfit to a struggling Championship club, the 'Brown out' campaign was the coming together of part of the Hammers crowd that resented not being where they thought they should be. But Brown refused to relinquish his status until he received an offer from someone who he believed could take the club forward.

The protests began with a few dozen people chanting 'Brown out!' in the Boleyn Ground car park after a pre-season game. But a modicum of organisation preceded the Upton Park Carling Cup game against Rushden and Diamonds on 13 August 2003, where some nostalgic 'activists' tried to resuscitate the halcyon days of HISA by seeking to boycott the evening game in protest against the board and, in particular, Brown.

Protests were planned prior to, during and after the match, wherein it was thought fans would express their anger at the demise of their team. Central to the proposed complaints was the sale of four players, principally the club captain Joe Cole, who had signed for Chelsea in a £6.6m deal the previous week.

Protest organisers urged fans not to enter the ground but to stand outside the Upton Park main entrance throughout the match. A press release issued the previous week by the organisers stated, 'We are urging all fans to attend at the ground but to remain outside and voice their disgust for the duration of the game at the way our club has been totally destroyed under the financial guidance of Terence Brown – a chairman that, despite pleading poverty when it comes to investing in players, has always found enough money to pay himself up until this year one of the highest chairman's salaries in British football.'

As if in preparation for what was to come, an email, allegedly from the chairman, was circulated in which a case was set out in Brown's defence, claiming that the club had no other option but to sell the likes of Cole and Johnson in the summer.

It was estimated that several thousand supporters would join the protests, which had been widely advertised in the local and national press. West Ham were thought to have sold less than 10,000 tickets for the game; as it was, nearly 14,000 attended the match, which would prove to be the lowest gate of the season. But that is traditional in the Hammers' first involvement in the League Cup of any season.

Further protests were planned to take place around the ground on the following Saturday, when West Ham hosted their opening Nationwide Division One League fixture against Sheffield United, before and after the game. Inside the stadium, a 'stand-in' (a refusal to leave seats after the final whistle) was planned.

Five years after the bond-scheme debacle, the chants of 'Sack the board!' and 'Brown out!' smacked of déjà vu. As Brown and Roeder set out the stall for a literal sell-out after relegation, things were probably worse than they had been in 1992. But during the 2003/04 season fan protest amounted to little more than regular chants of 'Brown out!' from the stands. However, the banners raised against Brown had a deeper significance and stayed in the collective memory of supporters probably because they represented something that was indicative of Terry Brown's time as the supreme power figure at Upton Park.

From the relatively subdued nature of the 'Brown out' campaign, some have argued that the Hammers fans no longer had the will to resist the board, that indifference had become the favoured response in the stands, and there is something to this. The seated, relatively quiet consumer of modern football is hardly the stuff of a revolutionary cadre. The cost of attending a match, together with a more 'family-oriented' environment, has produced a particular demographic of 'live' supporter; people who have the disposable income to spend at least a couple of hundred pounds a month watching football tend to be comparatively wealthy and 'choice-oriented' members of society, who can express their satisfaction by consuming products and their dissatisfaction by seeking alternatives. West Ham's 'football product' exists in a football market (which includes television and internet), which itself sits in a sports market, which in turn is part of a wider massive entertainment market. The competition is thus multilayered and historically extraordinarily competitive. For a growing number of supporters, there is no need to wave banners or stand outside the ground for a collective protest; they can, and do, just walk away.

On Wednesday, 19 September 2007, Stamford Bridge played host to the Norwegian side Rosenborg in the Champions League. There were close to 20,000 empty seats at what turned out to be the self-proclaimed Special One's last match in charge of the Blues before Avram Grant took over. In contrast, Arsenal's game against Sevilla in the same competition on the same evening in the same city was played in front of a packed Emirates Stadium of 60,000 Gooners. Cost of seating and the relative opposition were cited as excuses, but the general consensus was that the difference between styles of football was crucial. The elegant and orchestrated harmonies created by Arsène Wenger were indeed a world away from the crass 'delivery system' propagated by Mourinho. The Chelsea crowd are an advanced example of consumerist supporters. Their number includes a great horde of 'floating fans' who – as soon as the Blues fall on hard times or football takes a tumble down the fashion table, or, as on that September night, a match does not promise too much in terms of entertainment – may shift their allegiance to another club, or even another sport or entertainment.

In my view, the fragmented and stuttering 'Brown out' campaign, which has been perceived by many Hammers supporters as having much more impact than it actually had, is indicative of the fan response to the nature of the modern football business. It reflects the separation and antipathy that exists between those who market the game and those who consume it.

'Brown out' and 'Sack the board' are rallying cries against the way the football public has been reshaped by the necessary commercialism the sport must engage with to survive in the multi-dimensional market of which football is a part. It says a new chairman and/or a new board will be more humane, more just than what we have. This fabled regime will reincarnate legendary times and golden days when football did not bear the taint of filthy lucre. This is the hope invested in the Icelandic dawn that has risen over Upton Park of late. But this era has never really existed. The game has always been a reflection of the society it has existed in; how could it be separate from it? From the time when the Thames Ironworks effectively dumped the Corinthian ethics of its founding father Arnold Hills in favour of West Ham United's professionalism, profit – the effective exploitation of the supporter – has been the way of things. The 'Brown out' episode left the West Ham chairman looking stronger and more invulnerable than ever. As we have seen, this was not a first in Terry's tenure. This was because the 'Brown out' incidents were a concrete affirmation of the system. Unlike the dream of the bond campaign and later WHISTLE, it was, by virtue of its lack of any concrete impact, an acceptance that there will always be a chairman and that person will never be what we want them to be (*not* a chairman) and there will always be a board who we will always want to remove as this is the logical reaction of those who might feel exploited by them. This being the case, 'Brown out' is the future and limit of fan protest short of walking away; disapproval not revolution, more of a moan than the precursor of a 'people's coup'. Football coups will inevitably replace like with like and be based more on finance and market share than some arcane and imaginary model of community that exists only in the mind of the dying breed of traditional fans.

The person who is a football chairman will only come from a certain culture and will express that culture above and before anything else. You can't really expect anything more or less.

For Terry Brown to have got to where he was for the decade that overlapped the 20th and 21st centuries, he had to be of and in a particular social, spiritual and psychological milieu. His professional and mental framework separated him from the fan who had supported West Ham through thick and thin, from terrace to seat, through glory and failure. He might have had something of that in him – almost certainly he did and does – but first and foremost Brown is a dyed-in-the-wool entrepreneur. That was and is natural to him, an instinct he could not control, because to control it is not to have it. This is more than a belief system; for the Terry Browns of this world, it is also a faith that capitalism is in and of itself the most effective form of social betterment.

The accountant is the living spirit of Adam Smith and the embodiment of the protestant ethic that flourished in the 1600s, a time that gave rise to the phrase 'every man for himself, and the devil take the hindmost'.

Hence, 'Brown out' is a contextually correct expression of consumer dissatisfaction. But it also carries elements of a completely different set of values, the source of which is a simple democratic ethic that believes that the voice of the many will prevail over the will of the few. I think that is why that chant still has resonance to West Ham supporters in that it expresses – even if only in part – a worthy hope of a better world and a better way of doing things, and that the truth can still be found if we look for it. But, as long as we rely on football-club directors and an association with success to supply the building blocks of our own personal identities (the abomination of the 'Cockney Red' for instance), we will probably get the football clubs we deserve.

There is something about being all you can be which is more life enhancing than trying to be part of what everyone else is, because that seems better than you. We are made by adversity. Just *being* West Ham, beautifully, simply because that is what you are – or Orient, Aberdeen, Hartlepool or any signifier of region, place or history, detached from the forces of instruction, manipulation and deception – you can grow in a way that isn't possible by hanging your bobble-hat on the shiniest peg or becoming that dead leaf on the wind of fashion. 'You can't always get what you want, but if you try sometimes, you just might find ... you get what you need.'

CHAPTER 15
ARGENTINA TEL AND THE COCKNEY APACHE

Money can't buy friends, but you get a better class of enemy.
SPIKE MILLIGAN

In August 2006, as the transfer deadline approached, Carlos Tevez and Javier Mascherano came to Upton Park. Alan Pardew was pictured standing awkwardly between the exceptional Argentina stars who spoke hardly a word of English. The players had come to Upton Park as part of a plan the ultimate aim of which was a takeover of the club fronted by Kia Joorabchian.

Tevez and Mascherano arrived in a flurry of publicity, having been signed on the last day of the transfer window seemingly from Brazilian club Corinthians. Two top internationals joining the club was described at the time by the newspapers as 'a genuinely jaw-dropping coup' and 'catch of the day' that created a reason for 'Hammers supporters to dance on Green Street'.

But, at first, the Hammers imports were not well received. Pardew said at the time, 'You don't turn down the chance to sign two world-class players.' Hardly stirring stuff!

Reading between the lines, there was an acceptance that, even if they were sold within a year, the deal had to add short-term quality to the team and, in the longer stretch, buff up the sheen of the club's image.

Eventually, it came to be known that Tevez and Mascherano were part-owned by Media Sports Investment (MSI), formerly run by Kia Joorabchian; other owners included Just Sports Inc. and Global Soccer Agencies Ltd (GSA); Mystere Services Ltd was also involved.

Third-party ownership of players is common in South America, but variations of the practice are not unknown in Europe including England. The player, even if he is owned by a company or private businesspeople, still belongs to the club, because by FIFA regulations the 'federative rights', the registration, remain the legal property of the club. A single person or company can own only the economic rights. If a company buys the rights to a player, when they sell, a share of the payment will be transferred to the owner of the economic rights.

The advantage of this is that the club is sharing the financial risk with a partner, so it is easier for a club to buy a player who they are unsure about for, say, £10m. If the player makes the grade and is sold for £30m, then the club might feel they made a mistake by only owning half. But, if the player turns out to be mediocre and can't be sold, the club will feel vindicated in having shared the consequences.

As no actual transfer fees were involved in the Argentineans' move to Upton Park, the players' owner MSI could sell them to another club at the end of the season with only a relatively small profit to West Ham. Contrary to press-generated rumours, West Ham were not contractually obliged to play the Argentina internationals when they were fit and they were subject to the same selection process as every other player at the club; West Ham did not commit themselves to any limits on playing or not playing the Argentineans.

ARGENTINA TEL AND THE COCKNEY APACHE
JOORABCHIAN

Kiavash 'Kia' Joorabchian was born on 14 July 1971, in Tehran, Iran, the third son of Mohammed Joorabchian, who had studied economics and social administration in Tehran and in London, and worked as an economist for the Iran National Industrial Company in the 1960s and early 1970s.

Mohammed married Francis Anne Hawkins in 1963 in London. They had two sons, Alistair John and Siavash James, before they divorced in 1973. A few years later, Mo remarried in Iran and had two more children, Kia and his sister Tannaz. The family fled Iran for London following the fall of the Shah, and Mo ran car dealerships in Kent.

Kia was sent to Henley-on-Thames and Shiplake College in leafy Oxfordshire, an independent day and boarding school, before going on to study chemistry and business studies at Queen Mary, University of London, situated in the Mile End Road, very much Hammers territory.

He became a multi-millionaire from the sale of his equity company, American Capital. Kia founded Media Sports Investments (MSI) in 2004, which he used to take over the Brazilian football club Corinthians in a decade-long deal. After he purchased the 'Campeão dos Campeões' (Champion of Champions), he moved to Brazil and, in his first year in charge of the club, it achieved a 500 per cent increase in revenue.

TERRY, KIA AND PINI

Although West Ham had made it back to the Premiership, Brown knew that this would be a temporary situation unless new players that could compete with those being brought in by other rich club owners could be lured to Upton Park. He also believed that, if West Ham failed again in the near future, the fans would eventually resort to violence because he had experienced this before (see previous chapters) with all the possible consequences that would bring.

As it was, the Hammers Premiership status could be attributed to the sale of players via Pini Zahavi to Abramovich's Chelsea. But, of course, that well had dried up.

Pinhas 'Pini' Zahavi was born on 24 August 1943 in Ness Ziona, Israel, but in 2007 he was living in Tel Aviv and Marble Arch, London. He has been involved in some of the most expensive and controversial deals in football for more than a decade. Often described as a 'super agent' and 'transfer Svengali', he is registered with FIFA from his offices in Tel Aviv.

Zahavi's connection with the world of sport started when he was a journalist with the Israeli tabloid *Yedioth Ahronoth*. But, as an agent, he has been involved with at least two takeovers of English Premier League clubs and the transfers of top footballers including Rio Ferdinand and Juan Sebastián Verón. For his part in Yakubu Aiyegbeni's £7.5m move to Middlesbrough in July 2005, Zahavi was reported to have earned up to £3m, the biggest agent's fee ever disclosed in English football. That same year, the FA recommended that Pini be investigated after his involvement in the alleged 'tapping up' of Ashley Cole by Chelsea.

The players Pini continues to represent include Ferdinand, Eyal Berkovic, Yakubu, Kevin Campbell, Idan Tal and Giovanni dos Santos. Zahavi is also a co-owner of Charlton, a media company which holds the rights to cover many top football tournaments in Israel.

Brown's relationship with Kia started in August 2005. The West Ham chairman told Pini that West Ham was for sale for £70m. The club was a good investment, and had made a £6m profit the previous season. Sky would bring another £10m in 2007, and there was the potential to make £95m should Upton Park be made available for housing following the development of a new stadium.

ARGENTINA TEL AND THE COCKNEY APACHE

The Israeli agent had found a potential buyer fronted by Kia Joorabchian (a good pal of Pini). Joorabchian declared that he would make £200m available to West Ham, half of that sum to be used for buying players if his bid was successful.

Indulging in the coalhole shuffle (or the 'back basement two-step' as it is known across the pond), Joorabchian resigned as president of Media Sports Investments in June 2006. His father died on 13 August 2006 in London and, given the requirements of Islamic traditions, Kia was obliged to put his business plans on hold while mourning his father's passing. But, in September 2006, Joorabchian was back on the number 58 bus and once again hopped off in Green Street.

CRY FOR ME, ARGENTINA

Under Pardew's poor excuse for leadership, the Irons began to unravel. Things also looked ominous for Pardew as the board delivered the ritual vote of confidence in his capacities, although where this confidence came from is anybody's guess given his team's match–day performances.

Even when the early suspicions were raised about the involvement of MSI and the placement of the Argentineans at Upton Park was understood to be in lieu of a takeover bid, the worst anyone expected was that West Ham would not improve their standing from the previous season. But the loss of Dean Ashton after injury while on England duty followed by eight straight defeats (from 14 September to 24 October) – the club's poorest run for 74 years, going 11 matches without a win – was a nasty and unexpected consequence.

The most pathetic aspect of the whole affair for West Ham was that events tainted the club's reputation and, instead of increasing the Hammers' position as a top English club, the Irons looked like a little club that could only damage the careers of

Tevez and Mascherano. One tale that seemed to symbolise this was the reaction to Mascherano's request to wear Bobby Moore's number 6 shirt, which was initially granted, until Pardew stipulated that this honour had to be earned. George McCartney, who had arrived shortly before the Argentineans, was awarded it, and Mascherano was given the number 16 shirt.

In October 2006, it was reported that Joorabchian was negotiating to bring another South American, Carlos Alberto, to London E13 in the January transfer window. In that same month, the morning after Chesterfield dumped West Ham out of the League Cup, a number of season-ticket holders opened letters from the club banning them from the next two home fixtures at Upton Park because they had been caught standing up at recent matches. It was a stultifyingly stupid response. Just as the manager had been calling for vociferous support, the club was actively quelling that support. This said, the club had been obliged to act, as the London borough of Newham closed part of the Bobby Moore Stand because fans had been standing.

Reaction filled fan websites, outlining general outrage; one Hammer wrote, 'I hope I've been banned ... I could do with a break from that rubbish.'

By this time, West Ham's long-suffering supporters didn't know whether to laugh or cry as Upton Park's South Americans were being judged as failures in many quarters. But to judge the Argentineans on their performances after a few weeks was not only unfair, it was also ignorance in action. It is not unusual for managers like Sir Alex Ferguson and Arsène Wenger to give foreign players half-a-season at least to acclimatise, knowing it takes that long (and more) before a player can be accurately assessed in terms of their potential to succeed in the English game. Mascherano started only three Premiership matches and Tevez got just two outings before both were condemned as being unable to adapt to life in the Premiership. It was well known around Upton Park that Pardew was relying on 'existing club resources' to communicate with his multi-million-pound duo.

My good friend John Ballantyne (a regular columnist for West Ham fanzine *Over Land and Sea*), a former professional footballer who speaks perfect Argentinean Spanish (his lovely wife is a native of that fair land), told me of his previous experience with the club and West Ham's second Argentinean international in 2006 (the first had been Mauricio Taricco who got one game, against Millwall, for the Hammers in 2004): 'It really was a disgrace, the cultural level I mean. Lionel Scaloni had been brought on loan from Spanish club Deportivo. I was invited to attend one of the Fans Forums that had been set up – I think on Aldridge's initiative, this was the time of Joorabchian's first approach to the club to buy it out. I had already done my research on him in connection with the Brazilian club Corinthians. I put a few questions to Igoe, the financial director, and of course Aldridge. They were to say the least very nervy and thought I was some kind of journalist ...

'I approached them both at the interval and told them who I was ... A London bus driver, a season-ticket holder, and that I had a degree and Masters in Hispanic culture. I said that I understood that Scaloni needed help with translation and that was my language as I was married to an Argentine girl who happened to be a lecturer at the University of London.

'I gave them my details and they said they would be in touch, very positive, your Highness! ... Time went by and *OLAS* wanted an interview with Scaloni, still no response from the club.

'So little did they understand about Scaloni's cultural background that they made him a paella (a Spanish dish) at Chadwell Heath instead of a red-meat barbeque.'

(This is a bit like a player from the US going to Spain and being given pie and mash as a sort of signal that the hosts understand their player's cultural background.)

BROWN OUT

Back to Johnny B: 'It was embarrassing to say the least. I got asked by *OLAS* to go to the away game against Bolton ... Off we go! We went to the players' entrance after the game and I catch sight of Scaloni and shout to him in Argentine dialect. He immediately turns and comes straight over ... I say all the niceties and explain who we are and asked if he would be willing to do an interview for *OLAS* ... I mean the guy was gobsmacked and so pleased to hear his own language and it being spoken by a West Ham fan ... he had to be coaxed back on to the coach, he was so over the moon. Anton was eavesdropping, it was that engrossing. From that moment on, every time he saw us he would come over and talk as if we were mates ... and of course he was completely overwhelmed by the Irons. He always used to say to me that he never experienced anything like it before, and that West Ham fans were like Argentines in the sense that they were so passionate ... I asked him if they had an interpreter for him and he said that the physio spoke Italian with him and Yossi Benayoun used to help him out at times. Can you imagine it?'

To be honest, there were times when I barely knew what Pardew was talking about, so I didn't give people from half a world away much chance! But, the language barrier aside, it was clear to anyone with any kind of football background that Pards had little idea how to use players of the class of Tevez and Mascherano, preferring to play the former Crystal Palace midfielder Hayden Mullins rather than Argentina's World Cup and Olympic Games dynamo, 30-times-capped Javier Alejandro Mascherano, and Bobby Zamora (39 goals for West Ham in 139 matches, 11 goals in 2006/07) instead of the Hammer of the Year-to-be, the South American Player of the Year (2003, 2004), Argentinean Championship winner (2003), Copa Libertadores (2003) Intercontinental Cup (2003) Copa Sudamericana (2004) winner, South American Championship silver (2004) and Olympic gold medallist (2004) Tevez.

But, during the Hammers' disastrous run of results, Pardew managed to steer clear of all but minimal criticism. He had been given a bad time at the start of his reign at Upton Park and it seemed that a sort of guilt complex ran through the Boleyn Ground faithful, seeing he had been at the club when we climbed back into the Premiership and got the Hammers to a Cup Final. This appreciation overlooked the fact that West Ham's involvement in the play-offs was an indictment of a club that had every right to expect a place in the Premiership, and that Eagle Al had guided the team to squander a commanding two-goal advantage over a beaten Liverpool team that were in tactical chaos, structural confusion, with plummeting morale. Al's brigade gave away the lead not once but twice.

However, West Ham's troubles were not entirely influenced by the two new players or the takeover situation. The club's problems were more deeply set. The FA Cup loss and the pre-season injury suffered by Dean Ashton were compounded by what seemed like captain Nigel Reo-Coker's withdrawal of labour after he found out that Arsenal had made a bid for him during the summer that Pardew hadn't even mentioned to him. But there were bigger problems among the players.

Rumour piled on incident and this, together with the responses I got on mentioning Pardew when I interviewed players for my book *Black Hammers*, made it painfully clear to me that Al had lost the dressing room.

Something's rotten in the castle yard,
We know what it is and who did it,
But for God's sake tell us where it is!

In 2006, Brown was telling the world that he realised to compete in the Premier League the Hammers needed to change direction and that is why 'we looked far and wide to find the right people to invest in our club'.

As the word 'takeover' became synonymous with West Ham, Kia Joorabchian was back in the buyout frame and there were rumours of the involvement of a Georgian fugitive and a Russian oligarch, who had good cause to flee the wrath of Russian President Vladimir Putin.

Boris Berezovsky, friend and business associate of Neil Bush, the younger brother of US President George W. Bush (Berezovsky invested in an online educational company founded by the President's sibling), and once connected with Roman Abramovich via partnership in oil, was living in London.

Berezovsky, at one time said to be the richest man in Russia, had been the owner of *Kommersant* ('The Businessman'), part of a Russian media empire that he took over in the early days of the deregulated press in Russia. However, he had formed a partnership with a big-time Georgian fruit canner and television-station owner Badri Patarkatsishvili who, reportedly with Kia Joorabchian, acquired *Kommersant*, a move seen as a ploy to divert the Russian government's attention from Berezovsky's assets.

Patarkatsishvili, who was already chairman of the *Kommersant* board, was also a wanted man in Russia, suspected of organising an escape attempt of another of Berezovsky's companions, former first vice-president of Aeroflot airlines Nikolai Glushkov, who had attempted to flee from custody in 2001. Patarkatsishvili had Georgian citizenship and found refuge in his homeland as the Georgian General Prosecutor Office refused to hand him over to the Russian authorities.

Joorabchian denied rumours that Berezovsky and Patarkatsishvili were behind his takeover bid for West Ham, saying that his investors were from the Middle East and bigger than Roman Abramovich. But he had also told the *Sun* newspaper that, although he was a friend of Boris, 'I have never done business with Boris Berezovsky.'

This seemed a bit of a contradiction given his alleged involvement with *Kommersant*, and Berezovsky and Patarkatsishvili were also said to be behind the Joorabchian-fronted buyout of Corinthians. Patarkatsishvili was the end beneficiary of MSI Holdings, which owned MSI Brazil, and had very high percentage rights on Tevez and possibly up to 50 per cent of Mascherano.

This pair of 'colourful characters' liked their footie and it was rumoured that, alongside an 'anonymous Israeli' (the MSI 'main men'), a bit of dealing down in the old East End didn't seem to be out of the question.

Raf Shakirov was chief editor of *Kommersant* when Joorabchian was introduced as the newspaper's owner. He claimed he was certain then that the Iranian was 'an intermediary' for Patarkatsishvili, and that the Georgian was the man behind the Joorabchian bid. Patarkatsishvili, as the owner of Georgian club Dynamo Tbilisi, was barred under FIFA rules from owning another club, so he couldn't have taken on the bid himself.

In August 2006, Patarkatsishvili flogged his 100 per cent stake in the *Kommersant* to Alisher Usmanov, head of Gazprom's Gazprominvestholding subsidiary. Uzbekistan-born Usmanov had paid about $200m for the publishing house. However, although Patarkatsishvili had at one time expressed an interest in West Ham, Berezovsky never had any intention of being involved in a buyout of West Ham.

Joorabchian failed to progress his offer. So (as one story goes), Brown pounced on a suggestion passed on to him by David Dein, following West Ham's 1–0 win at Upton Park, to meet up with Eggert Magnússon again; Magnússon had a pal with a big portfolio of companies purchased with loans arranged by offshore hedge funds.

BROWN OUT

Joorabchian, who is thought to have a personal fortune in the region of £61m, was linked with a move for Fulham early in 2007. But he was issued with an international arrest warrant for money laundering at Corinthians on 13 July 2007, while MSI was still a majority investor in the club. Joorabchian denied any wrongdoing, insisting that all of his financial dealings were cleared by the Brazilian Central Bank.

I AM THE EGGMAN

Another version of the route to the Icelandic bid emerged, which told of how the FA, the English Premier League and the Minister of Sport had intervened in the West Ham takeover. It was said that the FA Premier League chairman, Sir David Richards, threw his weight behind the Iceland consortium led by Magnússon, and set up meetings between the group and the club. It was reported that Magnússon approached Sir David to help set up a meeting with Brown. However, the Icelandic bid was motivated by the interest of the chairman of Landsbanki, Iceland's second largest bank. The owner of the Landsbanki, 65-year-old dollar-billionaire Bjorgolfur Gudmundsson, employed Magnússon as his 'Coca-Cola sign' in his takeover of West Ham.

A takeover of West Ham was always likely to energise efforts for the Hammers to move to the new Olympic Stadium and Richard Caborn, the then Minister for Sport, supported this idea.

Joorabchian's bid was thought at this point to be backed by another of Kia's mates, billionaire Egyptian-Jewish immigrant to Israel property magnate Eli Papouchado, who had previously been interested in QPR. In October, Papouchado told the *Ma'ariv* newspaper, 'In these deals there is always a real-estate opportunity and that interests me.'

An unnamed associate of Papouchado told the *Sun* newspaper

how the 65-year-old had no special love of football and that 'Eli wouldn't know West Ham from West Brom … He really isn't interested in football.'

Papouchado owned a multi-national property company based in Israel, with interests in Britain, America, Africa and the Middle East. Joorabchian wanted to head the consortium and take active control of the club himself. His intention was that his investors would be silent partners; their interest in West Ham would have been purely financial.

During his time as MSI's director at Corinthians, Joorabchian failed to arrange for Berezovsky and Patarkatsishvili and the 'anonymous Israeli' (the investment trust's senior investors) to be part of his proposed buyout of West Ham. His resignation from MSI allowed him to look for alternative funding.

Joorabchian had claimed that his plans for West Ham could see them overhaul Chelsea as London's premier football club: 'In the near future West Ham can be bigger than Chelsea and maybe in seven years challenge Manchester United.'

Papouchado, or 'Papo' as he is known in the business world, established the Red Sea Group in the 1960s. Its operations involved hotel, medical, residential and retail property management in his native Israel, as well as in Europe, America and South Africa. Red Sea had a global workforce of more than 1,000. In 2002, the company bought a majority stake in the Irish business Gresham Hotels, restructuring the board before selling its shares.

Joorabchian's plan (which was no secret) was to import young South American talent to the Boleyn Ground, and develop them in the Premiership for sale and commercial profit.

TEL SELLS

That the Icelandic bid relied on borrowed money troubled Brown, so it looked like Joorabchian's crew had the advantage.

Magnússon hired strategic adviser Mike Lee, who had worked as a parliamentary campaigns officer with the Labour Party and then as special adviser to David Blunkett. Lee had also worked as the press chief for the English Premier League, and in 2000 was appointed director of communications and public affairs for UEFA, having responsibility for corporate communications and external relations, including links to governments, the EU and the international media.

In 2003, Lee was director of communications and public affairs at London 2012. He co-ordinated all external relations and campaigning elements of London's Olympic bid and co-chaired the creative team. Mike also led the international media and online campaign. Lee was involved in high-level political liaison and oversaw the work of the bid's sporting ambassadors. He was official bid spokesman and special adviser to Lord Sebastian Coe and was awarded an OBE in 2005.

Lee's contacts with the Labour party were seen as invaluable. Papouchado said that part of his takeover plan for West Ham included a move into the 2012 Olympic Stadium (this was also the ambition of the Icelandic consortium and part of Terry Brown's vision for West Ham's future, which also included making the stadium a central feature of the London Marathon). Caborn had been battling London Mayor Ken Livingstone about future uses of the Olympic Stadium. Livingstone wanted the stadium to seat 80,000 for the Olympics, and later reduce the capacity to 25,000 and make it the city's main athletics facility, replacing Crystal Palace. Caborn felt the stadium should follow the same route as the 2002 Commonwealth Games City of Manchester Stadium that was taken over after the Games by Manchester City.

It seemed Caborn lost this fight and by the time the Hammers visited Stamford Bridge on 18 November the deal was done. On 21 November 2006, West Ham announced that they had reached an agreement with a consortium fronted by Eggert

Magnússon for the sale of the club. The deal was worth £85m. Magnússon had been Brown's guest at the match against Chelsea the previous Saturday at Stamford Bridge, where it is believed the pair put an informal seal on the multi-million-pound takeover. Brown would make around £4m more than he had anticipated from the deal. He was to say, 'I didn't expect to make money when I bought the shares. I was a lifelong fan, and bought them to prevent a takeover by others.

'The Premier League took off with the help of Sky. When the club's shares increased in value, Charles Warner asked me if I foresaw it all happening, but I didn't. Nobody was more surprised than me.'

Born on 20 February 1947, Magnússon is an Icelandic businessman and former CEO of an import/export and bread- and biscuit-manufacturing company, a concern that employed around 40 people. Magnússon had been president of the Football Association of Iceland (KSÍ) since 1989, and served on the UEFA Executive Committee as a representative of one of UEFA's smaller member associations.

Magnússon was elected to the UEFA Executive Committee in April 2002, after previous membership of the Licensed Match Agents panel (1992–94), Fair Play Committee (1994–96) and Club Competitions Committee (1996–2002). He has contributed to the development of women's football as the Executive Committee's representative on the Women's Football Committee, and was a member of the Clubs and Leagues Working Group.

A former president of Valur Reykjavik (1984–89), one of Iceland's oldest football clubs, Magnússon has also served as a board member of Straumur-Burdaras, an Icelandic investment bank, and of the logistics firm Avion Group hf, both of which are listed on the Iceland Stock Exchange.

It was 65-year-old dollar-billionaire Bjorgolfur Gudmundsson who ploughed a generous lump of his considerable resources into buying the Hammers, but no one could have warned him that the rollercoaster ride he'd got on would be more Six Flags Magic Mountain than a sedate visit to Jorvik.

Gudmundsson, chairman of the non-executive board of Landsbanki, which has operations in a dozen countries, and an international investor with interests in various sectors – including financial services, international transportation, seafood processing and sales, real estate and publishing – may not have got involved with the Hammers had he known the palaver that would surround West Ham for much of what remained of the English football season, but, listening to Magnússon subsequently talking about his vision for the Hammers, it seemed as if he was in for the long term. This also seemed likely as, since Gudmundsson became Chairman of Landsbanki in 2003, the bank has taken a lead in sponsoring sport in Iceland, particularly football, where it has focused on the development of young players. However, in Iceland, a gate of 1,000 is seen as a respectable attendance for top games. The Premier League of course is quite a different prospect.

ALL'S WELL THAT ENDS WELL (OR IS IT?)

In the preamble to the takeover, Magnússon said, 'I am both delighted and honoured that Terry Brown and his colleagues wish to support our offer for West Ham. We can now end the uncertainty of recent weeks and move forward into the next phase of development of this great club, with Alan Pardew leading our efforts on the pitch.

'I fully appreciate the personal responsibility that will come with becoming chairman of West Ham and pledge to the staff, the players and the fans that I am here to serve and to do all that I can to deliver genuine success on and off the field.'

Brown commented, 'Since promotion back into the FA

Premier League, the club has invested funds wisely, strengthening the squad in key positions and moulding a young and exciting team faithful to the club's great traditions.'

WH Holding (a British-based organisation, whose current directors were identified as Bjorgolfur Gudmundsson, Eggert Magnússon, Thor Kristjansson, a member of the board of Landsbanki, and Gudmundur J. Oddsson, a partner at Icelandic law firm Logos Legal Services and head of the firm's London office) administered the takeover. It stated, 'Eggert Magnússon is fully committed to ensuring the club can continue its great tradition of success both on and off the field, to the benefit of supporters and the wider community.'

WH Holding went on to say that it 'strongly believes that an integrated approach is required to build West Ham's future and will be looking to develop West Ham's business both on and off the field, including investment in the training ground and facilities (including the Academy), stadium upgrades and player acquisitions, all of which will provide West Ham with the opportunity to build upon its existing strong foundations'.

It transpired that negotiations for the takeover had been going on since 1 September 2006.

In the documentation associated with the takeover, West Ham were described as 'one of the foremost professional football clubs in the FA Premier League, the richest football league in world football. The club has a history of achievement in English and European football. The club has won the FA Cup three times (in 1964, 1975 and 1980) and the UEFA Cup Winners Cup in 1965. The club has completed 40 seasons in the top flight of English football during the 48 seasons since 1958/59. Only five clubs have a better record in this regard. In the last nine years, the club has finished within the top 10 of the FA Premier League on five occasions, compared to the 11 top-10 positions achieved in the previous 72 seasons.

'West Ham also operates a very successful youth academy, with current and former members currently representing England and other international teams across all age groups.

'West Ham has sought to promote strong links with the local community. Its football in the community scheme is a registered charity which undertakes programmes which encourage social inclusion and integration using football as a vehicle to maximise personal development of young people.'

All this, of course, shows how far Terry Brown took the club during his years of involvement with West Ham. It has to be said that his detractors might be hard-pressed to name a West Ham chairman who has bettered his performance. Probably only William White, the chairman who guided the Hammers into the Football League after the First World War, could be said to have achieved more for the club.

The takeover documentation detailed the transition of West Ham to be the fifth Premiership club (after Chelsea, Manchester United, Portsmouth and Aston Villa) to be majority-owned by foreign interests: 'Following the Offer becoming or being declared unconditional in all respects, Terry Brown has agreed to step down from the Board of the holding company of West Ham, although he will remain a director and employee of the football club. Paul Aldridge will remain as Managing Director and Nick Igoe will remain as Finance Director.

'Upon the Offer becoming or being declared wholly unconditional, Eggert Magnússon will assume the position of Chairman of the Board of West Ham. Thor Kristjansson and Gudmundur J Oddsson will also be appointed to the Board of West Ham ...

'Terry Brown will be appointed as non-executive Deputy Vice Chairman. Each of Paul Aldridge, Nick Igoe and Scott Duxbury will remain as executive directors of West Ham United Football Club ... Sighvatur Bjarnason will be appointed to the board ...

Bjorgolfur Gudmundsson will assume the position of honorary life president of West Ham United Football Club and, in recognition of his service to the club, Terry Brown will be appointed as honorary life vice-president of West Ham United Football Club … Charles Warner, Martin Cearns and Christopher Manhire have agreed to resign from the boards of all West Ham Group companies. In order to ensure that the traditions of the club are preserved, Charles Warner and Martin Cearns (whose families founded the club) will become associate members of the club until their respective 75th birthdays … the existing employment rights of all management and employees of the West Ham Group will be honoured and pensions obligations complied with.'

In addition to Brown's profit on the sale of his 38 per cent stake, he retained his £592,000 chairman's salary until 2009. Brown also held on to eight seats in the directors' box and a further eight hospitality spots in the chairman's suite at Upton Park for life.

In the West Ham programme of Saturday, 25 November, Brown wrote a piece entitled 'It has been a privilege to serve you. Chairman Terry Brown reflects on a momentous 16 years at the helm of West Ham United.'

Terry told of how when he met Magnússon he was confident that he was the man to move the club forward. Control of the club was secured by the purchase of an initial 75 per cent stake, and Magnússon made it clear that he had no plans to replace the under-pressure Alan Pardew.

At that point, the club's debts had risen, following investment in new players and their salaries, to a total somewhere between £30m and £40m. But, with Gudmundsson's banking connections, the club could prepare to restructure their borrowings, which cost them £2.2m a year in interest, over a longer period.

Another sign of the new investors' long-term commitment

was their stated intention to pursue the move away from Upton Park to a new site in the London borough of Newham. There were negotiations for West Ham to take over the Olympic Stadium in Stratford, but, despite offers from the Icelanders that were rumoured to be between half and three-quarters of a billion pounds to subsidise the building of the stadium, the idea was blocked both at government level and the behest of London Mayor Ken Livingstone. A site for the new Hammers stadium was identified less than a mile from the Olympic site, but, for all the talk by state officials and Ken of being environmentally conscious, there seemed to be no problem with the building of two great stadiums so close together, potentially doubling the massive 'carbon footprint' over the East End.

Before November was out, Brown stepped down as chairman as part of the takeover of the club, but kept his title as honorary life vice-president and took on a role as a non-executive director. As part of Magnússon's takeover, it was agreed that Brown would be paid £492,000 a year for two years, and would receive his eight top complimentary seats at home games.

The following month, Pardew was finally put out of his misery and a seeming purgatory of embarrassment. On 13 December, West Ham boy (club and area) Llewellyn Charles Curbishley returned to Upton Park after a 27-year absence.

CHAPTER 16
IT DON'T MATTER

Football is nothing without fans.
JOCK STEIN

As the world entered 2007, the pain at West Ham continued. The end of January saw the Hammers' early departure from the FA Cup at the hands of fellow Premiership strugglers Watford at Upton Park.

Brown could not manage a second relegation and he understood that the Premier League was beyond him. He knew that survival among the big boys was going to require the same kind of financial muscle that was available to the likes of Chelsea, Manchester United and Liverpool and that pretty soon will probably come to clubs like Aston Villa, Newcastle and Arsenal. As I write, Bernie Ecclestone and Renault F1 boss Flavio Briatore have taken over QPR, and, if the likes of that club are going to rise like a phoenix from the ashes, how long will it be before Sunderland, Wolves and Spurs take their place on the football monopoly board of the billionaires' players? Why would Terry want to deal with what he very correctly predicted to be the possible consequences of fan discontent if he could hand West Ham over to big players and follow his innate drive to make money at the same time?

BROWN OUT
TA TA, JAVIER

During his time at Upton Park, Mascherano, not even playing for the reserves, quickly became frustrated with his non-selection, despite the team's predicament. In October, the Argentina national coach, Alfio Basile, had expressed his opinion that Mascherano should leave West Ham 'as soon as possible', and hoped, 'for God's sake, that Mascherano can go to Juventus'.

On 16 January 2007, Liverpool requested clearance from FIFA to bring Mascherano to Anfield on loan. FIFA's rules state that no player can play for more than two different clubs between 1 July and 30 June the following year, but Mascherano had already played for both Corinthians in Brazil and West Ham during this time.

FIFA cleared the deal on 31 January, but, although Liverpool submitted his registration details before the midnight transfer deadline, England's Premier League did not immediately announce that it would allow Mascherano to play for Liverpool, stating that it wanted to 'take time to satisfy itself with the proposed arrangements'.

On 10 February, Liverpool included Mascherano in their Champions League squad and gave him the number 20 shirt. Eventually, on 20 February, Mascherano's move to Liverpool was made official following the Premier League's acceptance of Liverpool's request to register the player at Anfield. The man who could not break into struggling West Ham's first team went on to be part of the Reds side that defeated Chelsea in the semi-final of the Champions League and was awarded a creditable runners-up medal in the competition.

Mascherano was in the Liverpool side that thumped Sheffield United 4–0 at Anfield. The year 2007 would not prove to be the best in terms of the Blades' relationship with Argentina.

IT DON'T MATTER
BYE, BYE, BROWN

On 28 February, around a month after Mascherano made his escape to Liverpool, Terry Brown resigned as a non-executive director of West Ham, but retained his title of honorary life vice-president. His seat in the Upton Park directors' box would also continue to be paid for over the final two years of his contract at the club.

A club spokesman said, 'The board have received Terry's resignation and can confirm he is no longer a director of the football club.'

Directors have responsibilities even when a company is controlled by a few individuals. One is to keep abreast of the company's financial affairs. Brown was unable to do so and his resignation became inevitable.

VALLEY OF DEATH

Brown sat with West Ham supporters during the 4–0 defeat away to Charlton Athletic, having not been given a seat in the directors' area. He had said publicly that Bjorgolfur Gudmundsson, the main financial backer for the takeover, was a 'world-class businessman' and, after the game at Charlton, it seemed he would need to be.

On 24 February 2007, I was at the Valley for what was seen as a critical match in terms of West Ham's future. As the Hammers fell apart, the support of the fans that had followed them from the other side of the river became more voluble. In the initial 10 minutes, the tension was palpable, but, when the home side netted and minutes later put themselves two goals ahead, it was pretty obvious to those of us educated in the 'culture of the Irons' that that was it. Just before the half-hour, the chant 'You're not fit to wear the shirt' went up, and as the half-time whistle blew great clutches of claret and blue support evacuated, unable to watch as their hopes faded in front of them on the pitch.

However, something happened during the break and we sort of went back in time. It was April 1991 again! Not for the first time in my experience of West Ham fandom, Cockney defiance slammed down in the face of adversity. And again, not for the first time, this courageous spontaneous protest brought a smile to my face and a tear to my eye. As our southern hosts hit us like a steel battering ram for the fourth time, the 'Appy 'Ammers had entered a noise-encased revelry; singing to the melody of Frankie Valley's 'You're Just Too Good to be True', we told the night:

Oh Christian Dailly,
You are the love of my life,
Oh Christian Dailly,
I'd let you shag my wife,
Oh Christian Dailly
I want your curly hair too.

Briefly, the home support applauded their rusty-coloured heroes; however, as their self-congratulation faded, in wide-eyed amazement they realised our singing had continued, undaunted by another goal.

The Charlton crowd seemed unable to understand what was happening. Awestruck is the term that comes to my mind; 'see the unbending Iron Will of the East – wonder and then despair. We are untouchable! We are by the definition "us" and as such are unbeatable!' This relentless attitude is rare and real, the Hammers thundered. Although for all intents and purposes beaten and destroyed, we rise! We really, really don't know when we are beaten. No matter if you become part of the manor by way of Bengal or Montego Bay, Lusaka or Lebanon, you kind of pick this up. It gets programmed into the spirit of all the Hammers.

The times I've learned the most about me and mine at the Boleyn Ground have not been those where we have triumphed. The moments when we have capitulated on the field are when the lessons about the soul start. These terrace teachings give rise to the heroics of support. It's not too hard to cheer victory, to 'sing when you're winning', but to be truly jubilant in the face of humiliating defeat – now that takes bollocks. It is 'we few, we happy few, we band of brothers'; 'I know I am … I'm sure I am … I'm West Ham till I die!'

Managing directors, chairman, shareholders, owners and consortiums come and go, but the fans are always there; always have been, always will be.

However, despite the show of support, by the time the Irons fans were making their way home under the Thames, the Hammers were nobody's favourite to stay in the Premiership. Relegation would have led to at least an £8m drop in television income via the loss of the share of the Premiership's new TV rights, which would earn even the bottom team £30m in the 2007/08 season. The Hammers would have got the new parachute payment of £12m, which would have softened the blow of dropping to just £600,000 a year in TV money from the Football League, but, with the backing of a wealthy and committed owner, the club would have been in better shape than they were in 2003 to withstand the financial pressures. Over the previous four years, West Ham had built relegation clauses into their players' contracts, which meant the value of the contracts would have changed if we had dropped.

The impact of that policy can be seen at the end of the 2003/04 financial year when wages dropped from £33.3m in the previous season to £23.2m. It went down by another £3m the following year until promotion in 2005 led to an increase, and the wage bill went up to £31.2m. These performance-related contracts are commonplace for teams at the bottom of the Premiership and applied to most of the squad inherited by Magnússon and manager Alan Curbishley. The club expected to make savings of £10m if they went down. But new signings, such as Lucas Neill, Luis Boa Morte, Matthew Upson and Nigel Quashie, who were bought for more than £9m by Curbishley in January 2007, were unlikely to all be on the same sort of deals.

The biggest difference from four years previously would have been that, while players like Joe Cole, David James, Glen Johnson and Jermain Defoe were sold for £27m but not replaced, Gudmundsson would almost certainly have given the manager the funds and backing to bring in reinforcements.

GAMBLING IT ALL AWAY

It all seemed to be happening in February when a culture of reckless high-stakes gambling among the West Ham players was exposed. It was said that it had caused divisions within the club and had destroyed morale to such an extent that the first-team squad, already ridden with cliques, was 'spiralling out of control'.

Players were said to be bleeding huge amounts of money to each other in card games – as much as £50,000 in one sitting. They had won and lost such staggering sums on the team coach to and from matches.

The training and dressing-room atmosphere was reported to be terrible with people refusing to talk to each other. It was alleged that one senior player, an established international, had recently won £38,000 from two team-mates in one afternoon. The losers had to pay up, and Alan Curbishley was no longer speaking to the player who won the money. Winger Matthew Etherington (who reportedly confided to a close Dagenham mate that the club was 'in pieces') and goalkeeper Roy Carroll had both sought help. A West Ham spokesman said, 'The club is aware of the fact that gambling is an area of concern and the manager has made it clear that it must stop. Steps have been taken to eradicate this in the team environment.'

It was rumoured that Curbishley had attempted to stop the card schools that had been going on since self-confessed gambler Harry Redknapp's time at the club; however, it seems that what had previously been camouflaged was now exposed. The new manager banned gambling in situations where he was responsible for the team, such as on journeys to and from matches. For all this, he had been unable to stop the poker sessions when training was over, and one recent session was said to have continued until 4 a.m.

Former England striker Teddy Sheringham spoke about gambling earlier in the season when promoting the online poker site 888.com: 'I can see why it becomes a problem, especially for young players who have so much money and time on their hands. I've always enjoyed a drink, but at the right times, and I play poker at the right times. Some people take it to extremes. You've got to keep it under control.'

Well said, Ted! One month from his 41st birthday, Sheringham was in talks with Australian side Sydney FC. However, in the end, Curbs wasn't able to get him quite so far from his squad. He toddled down the A12 to Colchester where he could practise his flop in the airy openness of the Essex marshland.

The gambling culture was one more headache for Curbishley. Since he had taken over in December 2006, West Ham had won only once.

Towards the end of February, Etherington admitted he was undergoing treatment for a gambling addiction, receiving counselling at the somewhat curiously named Sporting Chance Clinic in Hampshire. The 25-year-old, who had experienced a disappointing season, reportedly spent a week at the clinic in January. He commented, 'I have made a personal decision to take steps to tackle a gambling problem, which has developed in recent times … I would like to thank my family for their incredible support during this time, all of my team-mates at West Ham and manager Alan Curbishley for their understanding.'

Other problems also came to light, including alleged spats between rival cliques within the dressing room over 'territory' and wages. There was said to be growing tension between Curbishley and his players and doubts over the decision making of the new chairman. It was also reported that a recent signing was amazed when he was asked to a meeting to discuss club affairs with senior management in a lap-dancing club, though the club strongly denied that any such meeting took place.

At the same time, defender Anton Ferdinand was charged with assault and violent disorder following an alleged brawl outside a London nightclub in October 2006 (he was cleared of all charges on the grounds of self-defence in November 2007). But, with his court case pending, Ferdinand faced internal action against him after admitting that he lied to the club the previous month in order to celebrate his 22nd birthday with a party in the Knock Knock Club in South Carolina, USA. He had ludicrously pretended that he was visiting his sick granny in the Isle of Wight.

The manager had told his players not to go abroad, but Anton had disobeyed not just by a short trip to France or Germany but by trekking all the way to the southern states of America! That was absolutely ridiculous – a transatlantic flight through different time-zones with the prospect of returning to London and the build-up of what was a massive game with Charlton. He told the world the only thing it didn't really need to be told: 'I have made a stupid mistake.'

Curbishley said he would discipline Ferdinand, but he kept proceedings against his defender very discreet, which Anton might have appreciated.

IT DON'T MATTER
HAMMERS CHARGED

On 2 March, the Premier League announced that it was charging West Ham with breaking Rule B13, concerning clubs acting in good faith, and Rule U18 which states that: 'No club shall enter into a contract which enables any other party to that contract to acquire the ability materially to influence its policies or the performance of its teams.'

The Hammers were also suspected of contravening Rule U6 that reads: 'No person may, either directly or indirectly, be involved or have any power to determine or influence the management or administration of more than one club.'

The Premier League said in a statement, referring to the arrival of the two Argentineans at Upton Park, 'It is the board's complaint that there were agreements in relation to both these transfers that enabled third parties to acquire the ability materially to influence the club's policies and/or the performance of its teams in League matches and/or the competitions set out in Rule E10.

'The board's view is this constitutes a breach of Rule U18.

'Furthermore at the time of the transfer agreements for both Carlos Tevez and Javier Mascherano, and until 24 January 2007, West Ham failed to disclose the third-party agreements to the Premier League and/or deliberately withheld these agreements from the Premier League.

'The board's view is this constitutes a breach of Rule B13, which states "In all matters and transactions relating to the League each club shall behave towards each other club and the League with the utmost good faith".

'West Ham United has 14 days within which to respond to these charges.'

The League did not name the third parties referred to.

All Premiership clubs would be contacted in an effort to discover whether they had similar controversial signings (although the reasoning behind this was not made clear). The Premier League suspected that West Ham had agreements in place with the Argentineans' representatives, allowing them certain control, including how often the players featured for the first team. But in fact there were no such agreements.

In short, West Ham were accused of breaching ownership rules relating to third-party interference by signing the players who were owned by a collection of offshore companies. Again, Brown categorically denies this to have been the case. The club faced being docked six points and a massive fine over the Tevez/Mascherano player registrations. A League commission was appointed to investigate the entire affair.

Quite apart from the potential unprecedented disaster this would represent for West Ham, consigning the club to certain relegation, the Premiership's action also led to some interesting consequences. It was reported that Eggert Magnússon was considering suing Brown for non-disclosure of the problem, as relegation would have cost Magnússon big money. However, Brown insists that nothing was kept from Magnússon. Any legal action against Brown would be potentially crippling for Terry, as it could have involved a claim of loss of Premiership earnings that might have run into tens of millions. For all this, it may have been argued in court that Magnússon should have asked about or investigated the Tevez and Mascherano deal before he bought the club. Shouldn't he have conducted a due diligence – *caveat emptor*. Solid proof of the legality of the transfer should have been demanded before committing to buy the club. It seems unfeasible that Brown, or anyone else at Upton Park, was ignorant of the rules about bringing the players to the club.

West Ham released this statement on their official website: 'West Ham United FC is fully co-operating with the FA Premier League in response to their recent letter to all Premier League clubs on player registration.

'The club is in the process of providing the relevant documentation as requested and is confident that this matter will be settled in the very near future.'

West Ham argued that Pardew always had total control over team selection and, as such, the club intended to challenge the Premier League to prove that any agreements with Tevez and Mascherano's part-owners were significant enough to influence policy and performance of the team. The club claimed, 'In light of the legal advice received, the club will vigorously defend itself against the charge and provide a detailed response as requested by the Premier League within the time allowed.'

The first string of West Ham's defence would be based on the fact that, when the South American pair came to Upton Park, Joorabchian conducted transfer negotiations with Brown and West Ham's former managing director Paul Aldridge. Magnússon believed that his administration should not be punished for another regime's mistakes. He claimed that he would never have entered into the sort of agreement which had brought the Argentineans to the Boleyn Ground. But, if he was totally ignorant of how two very expensive players arrived at the club shortly before he took over as West Ham's chairman, that in itself is a bit of an indictment of him as a businessman. This apart, his consortium took over the club and, as the club's chairman, their problems were now his responsibility.

West Ham also intended to cite a precedent set in 1994 when Sir Alan Sugar, then the Tottenham chairman, saw a 12-point deduction rescinded after arguing that the club's offences – 35 financial irregularities – were committed by a previous administration, although this was not quite the same situation as existed at West Ham. The arrival of the Argentineans had hardly been kept under wraps.

If West Ham were found guilty, some precedent for points deduction certainly existed, although the cases were not exactly comparable. In 1999, goalkeeper John 'Teddy' Doig was brought into the Sunderland side that played West Bromwich Albion but he was unregistered and the Black Cats were deducted two points as a consequence. Bristol Rovers (1981/82) and Stockport County (1926/27) both had two points deducted for fielding ineligible players. Aldershot had one point deducted during the 1974/75 season for the same offence. More recently, AFC Wimbledon appealed against an 18-point deduction by the Ryman League. The Wombles had fielded an ineligible player, Jermaine Darlington, who did not have international clearance. Those 18 points had been accrued in the 11 games that the midfielder had played in, although Wimbledon's punishment was eventually slashed to three points. West Ham had only picked up five points in games featuring Tevez and/or Mascherano.

Although West Ham fiercely denied it, Brown and Aldridge indicated that they thought that the Magnússon regime was trying to ruin their reputations in an effort to distance the club from the decision to sign the Argentineans.

The predicament of the club could be discerned just by listening to the supporters at games: 'If you sit in row Z, and you're hit on the head, it's Zamora' (sung to the tune 'That's Amore', by Dean Martin, a melody that had been used to praise Bobby Zee in 2005) and 'We're shit and we're still beating you' (aimed at Tottenham fans in March). These ditties said more than all the media combined about the effects of West Ham's revolving door of managers, agents, chairmen and players, which had left the club with an ill-disciplined rabble of unmanageable proportions.

Of course, the £6m signing of Mathew Upson from Birmingham City (who had a long record of enforced lay-offs before coming to Upton Park and had played all of 29 minutes since his arrival in January due to injury) didn't help, but that seemed almost inconsequential against Tottenham on 4 March, after Anton Ferdinand gave away a ludicrous free-kick on the edge of his own penalty area, and Spurs equalised in the last throes of the game. Tottenham went on to win 4–3. That left West Ham 10 points adrift and many reports were suggesting that Alan Curbishley had not been able to gain control of the dressing room. It was rumoured that Whizz's (Curbishley was known as Whizz during his playing days at Upton Park, after *Beano* hero 'Billy Whizz') approach to his players might not have been helping the situation. Curbishley's relationship with the players was described by one pundit as 'very strange'. But he had been in post for just 10 weeks, and it was quite a lot to expect him to have built any kind of relationship following the club's recent history and the constant changing of personnel due to injuries, suspensions and lack of form. It was likely that he just hadn't had the chance to form any kind of bond or understanding with the playing staff.

Despite the seeming problems after the 4–3 defeat by Spurs, Magnússon described Curbishley as the 'first, second and third choice' to replace Alan Pardew. Magnússon was criticised for being impetuous when he dispensed with Pardew, but he had repeatedly stressed his long-term vision for the club. He explained, 'I want everyone to know that Alan Curbishley remains the man who we will build our future success on. Nothing has changed regarding our long-term plans and he still has my full support – 100 per cent. We will continue our fight to survive.'

But Julian Dicks, the former West Ham skipper left-back, saw the players as the root of the Hammers' problems: 'Some of the players just seem to go through the motions; there are three or four who, for me, don't seem to try.'

That was a view shared with many supporters.

However, Curbishley would have set his attitude and style of management well before he returned to the Boleyn Ground. Unlike Pardew, Curbs was never going to try to be 'one of the boys'. His first mentors were Ron Greenwood and John Lyall. John had told me at the time Redknapp left the club that Alan, even as a 12-year-old, showed 'an understanding of the game you don't usually come across in kids'. In 1997 (when I was writing *The First and Last Englishmen*), I talked to Greenwood about how Bobby Moore had a 'mind for the game'. I asked him about other players who he had seen at West Ham that showed the same type of intellect. He paused and said, 'As a young player, Alan Curbishley showed tremendous intelligence. He stuck in your mind because of that. I'm not sure his ability as a player matched what he had going on in his head, although he was a very good player. He was like some players you come across from time to time. You always think, "He might be a manager one day." Alan was like that. Always learning. Asking questions and able to concentrate.'

AL THE 'AMMER

Curbishley had been recommended to Ron Greenwood by his boyhood neighbour and West Ham's first black player John Charles, and, up to the time he left the club, Alan was open to such influences as Bobby Moore, Geoff Hurst, Billy Bonds, Ronnie Boyce and Trevor Brooking as well as international managers-to-be Clive Charles, Bobby Gould and Clyde Best.

An England Schoolboy International, Alan went on to represent his country at youth level, working with Pat Welton and former Hammer Johnny Cartwright (whose football inspiration was Ron Greenwood). He played for the Under-21 side managed by another ex-Hammer Dave Sexton, who had led Chelsea to FA Cup success in 1970 and the Cup Winners Cup a year later. Sexton took the Blues to the League Cup Final in 1972, but lost to Stoke City. At Queens Park Rangers, Sexton went within a point of the League title in 1975/76. Dave led

Manchester United to the FA Cup Final in 1979, but saw his side lose 3–2 to Arsenal in a dramatic match. In 1980, he guided United to runners-up spot in the League, when the Manchester Reds were only bettered by Liverpool.

Sexton was a very successful coach with England's Under-21 side and won the UEFA Under-21 Championship twice, in 1982 and 1984. After that, he went on to become the FA's first technical director at the FA's National School at Lilleshall in 1984.

Ron Greenwood selected Curbishley for the England B squad in 1981 but a fractured kneecap ended his involvement with his country.

When Curbishley moved from the Boleyn Ground to Birmingham City, he was managed by the hard-as-a-rock Ron Saunders and then former Hammer John Bond. Tony Barton, who had won international recognition as a schoolboy and youth player with England and was formerly Ron Saunders's assistant at Aston Villa, took Curbishley to Villa Park. Barton had presided over the Villains' European Cup-winning side in 1981/82. Lennie Lawrence brought Alan to Charlton. Lawrence is recognised as one of the most experienced and intelligent managers of his era. In 1986, he led the Valiants into the top flight of the game for the first time in 30 years and kept them there for four seasons. At Brighton, Curbishley's next port of call, he worked under Barry Lloyd. The former Fulham player took the Seagulls to promotion in 1988 and the Second Division play-off final in 1991. Lennie Lawrence brought Alan back to the Valley in 1990, where he served first as a player and then manager until he returned to West Ham in 2006.

As Charlton manager, Curbishley achieved two promotions (Division One play-off winners 1998 and Football League Champions 2000) and consolidated a place in the Premier League. Curbishley was named by the media among the favourites to succeed Sven-Göran Eriksson when it was announced in January 2006 that the Swede would step down as England manager after the 2006 FIFA World Cup. Several British Sunday newspapers reported in March 2006 that Curbishley had been interviewed for the job as his nation's manager by the FA.

Curbs managed 729 games for the Addicks, just one less than the record held by Jimmy Seed and is seen as arguably the best manager the club has ever had.

Like Martin O'Neill, Curbishley is a manager in the mould of Bill Shankly or Brian Clough in that he wouldn't see it as his job to make a massive effort to 'suck up' to players. He is a general rather than a corporal in his 'man-management', and as such tends to place emphasis on the realistic separation between playing and the managerial role. However, the man is anything but aloof. It is not unusual to see Alan travelling by public transport, and he is an approachable and affable man.

STRUGGLING

As winter turned to spring, an efficient self-destruct mechanism seemed to be killing off most of the remaining hope that the Hammers had. It was obvious to anyone who cared to look that Curbishley had inherited an adolescent dressing room that was symptomatic of what had gone wrong. The attitude among a group of players at West Ham was dominating play.

Fifteen years with Charlton as a manager, plus six as a player, had not prepared Curbishley for the shit-storm he encountered at Upton Park. But what could have prepared anyone for it? It is hard to think of any situation in modern football that even comes close to the madness Curbs walked into.

Apart from everything else, the expectations at West Ham were always going to exceed anything at Charlton, a club that cannot compete with the claret and blue traditions in terms of status, achievement or support. West Ham United have international recognition as *the* East End club and the home of Bobby Moore, Geoff Hurst and Martin Peters. They have broken ground with men like Clyde Best and Ron Greenwood. John Lyall remains probably one of the most popular managers in the history of the game among players and fans. Few people beyond the southern approach to Blackwall Tunnel have any idea of what Charlton have contributed to football or what they represent as a club.

Eggert Magnússon, who was showing himself to be a chairman who wears his heart on his sleeve, reiterated that he would keep faith with Curbishley. That was not terribly consoling when you consider he had said the same thing about Pardew before giving him the boot.

At a meeting with all the club's 150 staff, the Icelander asserted that there would be no redundancies even though the club were planning for relegation. But there were reports that Curbs would be given no more than a dozen games in the Championship and that, if West Ham were not leading the table, he would be the one out the door.

BACK FROM THE BRINK

West Ham were not relegated in 2007 (although Sheffield United and Charlton were!), but they will be relegated one day, sooner or later. We will face that and we will be better for it. In my granddad's words, 'It don't matter'.

As I write this, West Ham are due to play Everton this afternoon. If Dean Ashton scores a hat-trick or the Toffees bang in half-a-dozen, either way I'll be singing because we'll all be singing, but mainly because 'it don't matter'; give it 150 years and not one of the close to 40,000 present today at Upton Park will still be alive, but West Ham will still be around.

BROWN OUT

In the last third of the 2006/07 season, there was an idea mooted around Upton Park that, due to the poor play witnessed, the term the Hammer of the Year award should not be given. An interesting use of subtle sarcasm was the notion that Dean Ashton (who didn't play a game during that campaign because of injury) should have been given this. I was up for giving it to the supporters, but in the end was glad to see it going to the Apache (as Tevez became affectionately known at Upton Park) who kept us up. But, if it had been awarded to John Bond or Ade Coker (or both), that would have been just as good.

What was important was that the collective dream continued to be dreamed. The last time Everton came to Upton Park, they were smacked 1–0. That might not happen today, but it might and guess what … it don't matter.

CHAPTER 17
GREED

It is not from the benevolence of the butcher, the brewer, or the baker,
that we expect our dinner, but from their regard to their own interest. We
address ourselves, not to their humanity but to their self-love, and never
talk to them of our necessities but of their advantages.
ADAM SMITH 1723–90 (*THE WEALTH OF NATIONS,*
BOOK I CHAPTER II)

The goings on behind the resignation of 64-year-old Brown had been bizarre. When asked if he had favoured Joorabchian's bid over the Icelandic consortium, Brown said, 'No, didn't Kia come first? He had been around for a long time. The others came in late in the day.'

But an email and legal documents obtained by a newspaper claimed to prove that Brown and Paul Aldridge stood to benefit in the event of a takeover by the Iranian.

The email, allegedly sent by Brown to Joorabchian, suggested that the former MSI man raised his original offer of £70m by around £5m when it became clear that the first offer may have conflicted with Brown's position, as well as breaching takeover rules and stock-market regulations. It was also suggested that the increased bid would provide Brown with a package of £6m over three years. The email read, 'The new package was to be worth £6m – £1.5m signing on and £1.5m p.a. for 3 years. We have looked at alternative arrangements but none seem to meet the regulatory requirements. I would suggest therefore that I remain on my present terms and that we add the saving of £4.3m to the purchase price increasing that from £70,708,372 to £75,082,372.'

Brown denied that asking Joorabchian for a further £4.3m was a way of getting round the fact that he was unable to accept the original cash arrangement: 'If they are saving a cost, why not add it elsewhere? I did it for the benefit of the shareholders and the club and don't forget I was one of the major shareholders, so it wasn't necessarily to my disadvantage. Why give money away? It wasn't a way around anything.'

It should be remembered that Brown would have been liable for the highest possible rate of tax on any income.

It was claimed that, according to contracts drawn up by the club's lawyers Herbert Smith, Brown was offered the £1.5m bonus together with the yearly salary of £1.5m he had asked for to stay on as chairman indefinitely if the £100m takeover had been successful. He would also have become life president of the club and received eight directors' box tickets for every home game. The 'bunce' was rounded off with the promise of bonuses for youth-team success, car-park passes, hospitality in the chairman's suite and pension rights. It was further alleged that Brown would get £30m from the sale of his shares.

It was reported that Aldridge was offered a £1.1m bonus and a £1.1m annual salary for two years to continue to run the club after the Iranian businessman took control. This was said to amount to a 400 per cent increase on his wages at that time. Aldridge had been dismissed by Magnússon less than a fortnight after the takeover was due; it was said that this was connected to his close links with the Joorabchian bid.

Brown claimed the initial plan to pay him and Aldridge close to £10m was 'never going to happen … I'm an accountant and I wouldn't do anything like that. I don't need that, so it was never going to happen.'

He also said that he had turned down Joorabchian's offer

before the deal had fallen through because of fears that it might conflict with his position as a major shareholder in the club and fall foul of City takeover rules.

Although Brown and Aldridge claimed to have done nothing wrong in their dealings with the Iranian, Brown, while admitting that he had sent an email – amid accusations that he and Aldridge had been driven by greed – argued, 'I don't think it's greed. Remember this was not a secret deal. The whole board and all the shareholders knew about it. The offer was made to me but the board and shareholders felt it just didn't look right.

'It was something that came up but I rejected it very early on. It was never an issue because I didn't want the money. If I wanted that deal to happen, I would have had to put it to the shareholders and they would have voted. There is nothing irregular about it.

'I owned 40 per cent of the club – so one way or another I was going to benefit from adding on to the price and they accepted it. We have a duty to maximise the money for our shareholders and this was all legitimate … There is nothing irregular about it.'

Aldridge, who was not a major shareholder and did not have to reject Joorabchian's offer, added, 'At a very early stage the board and the shareholders were very well aware of the negotiations between the Joorabchian consortium, Terry and me. Yes, it is a lot of money but whether it is greedy is for other people to judge. But there was absolutely no wrongdoing in this.'

Brown explained, 'You've got to bear in mind that the Kia lot needed management. They needed Paul to stay on badly. When a company is taken over and you want to keep the management, you have to make them an offer. He'd have been a good investment and you know what people are earning in football.'

The leaked documents had been produced during an internal inquiry at West Ham. After they were used by the newspaper, they were rushed 'for investigation' to the Premier League. Brown and Aldridge were said to have attempted to persuade Eggert Magnússon to agree to an improved deal for Aldridge but the biscuit king refused and retained the pair only on their existing salaries. However, although Brown claims to have told the Icelander everything about the potential deal with Joorabchian, and indeed it would be surprising if the 'football man' did not know of Tevez and Mascherano, his financially sophisticated bankers were unable to carry out an effective 'due diligence'. Magnússon appeared to be upset when the internal West Ham inquiry discussed the draft contracts and email.

Mike Hanna, one of the members of the WHISTLE group sued by Brown in 2004 – following accusations of Brown's involvement in financial irregularities – took full advantage of the opportunity to get the boot in when he commented, 'At no time did Brown or Aldridge ever own up to being offered payments by Joorabchian … It shows again that Brown was somebody who wanted to maximise his bank account … He can never show his face at Upton Park again. He's a disgrace.' Quite how Hanna knew all this is unclear.

However, possibly to the disappointment of Hanna, Brown and Aldridge were not found guilty of any wrongdoing in their dealings with Joorabchian, and, of course, the perception of greed is relative.

Expecting football chairmen or any business person to take some sort of vow of poverty and sternly refuse potential windfalls when billionaires come along with acres of cash to splash is naive to say the least. When did Terry Brown ever say he would do that? Brown comes from a perspective that logically makes a case for profit as the driving force of all businesses and society in general, without which there would be no motivation for competition in trade and no incentive for investment in production. This philosophy depicts profit as a moral imperative, and, whether or not one agrees with this, it is a maxim of our capitalist society.

But of course, legal systems make attempts to temper excess even in the holy sphere of profit. Around a week after the uproar about the leaked documents, more 'revelations' exploded when it was claimed a 'secret payment' of £339,000 was transferred into a Swiss bank account to smooth the progress of the signing of Argentine midfielder Javier Mascherano. It was alleged that West Ham made the deposit (500,000 euros) into a Global Soccer Agencies account that was linked to agent Pini Zahavi. The money was transferred days after the deal was done. Despite Brown's insistence that the FA were told about this transaction, which was in effect payment for the loan of the Argentineans to West Ham, the FA promised a 'full probe'.

When questioned about the payment, Brown was nonplussed: 'Who paid it? Into where? You would have to ask the club; I am not going to comment on that. If it's wrong, it's the club that has done wrong but I very much doubt we have done anything that's wrong.'

According to Paul Aldridge, 'Legal advice was taken at the time and a payment was made strictly in accordance with all the relevant rules and regulations.'

Zahavi said he wasn't the owner of Global Soccer Agencies and denied that he had received a fee: 'I am the adviser, that's all; I don't own it. I have nothing to hide, I've done nothing wrong. I don't give a shit what rule West Ham broke. I am telling you, I am not GSA.'

Some you win, some you lose…

CHAPTER 18
FINE BY ME

Everything deep is also simple and can be reproduced
simply as long as its reference to the whole truth is maintained.
But what matters is not what is witty but what is true.
ALBERT SCHWEITZER

West Ham met the FA Premier League's charges full on during the first day of the hearing in London that lasted just a few hours.

The independent panel at the hearing was chaired by Simon Bourne-Arton, QC, and the other two members were Lord Herman Ouseley, the chairman of 'Let's Kick Racism Out of Football' and a former executive chairman of the Commission for Racial Equality, and David Dent, a former secretary of the Football League. Jim Sturman, QC, a specialist in criminal and sports law, was assigned to argue West Ham's case. He stated that the club were not influenced by Joorabchian and argued that he could have moved the players on whenever he wanted. But it was conceded that the club failed to provide relevant documentation for the transfers in August.

The club had told the Premier League that they had provided all the relevant documentation when the signings took place. This claim turned out to be incorrect. It was said that Nick Igoe, West Ham's financial director, presented some of the documents in January, when Mascherano was in discussions to leave Upton Park for Anfield.

The independent commission found West Ham guilty of agreeing contracts that allowed third parties – the businesses that owned the economic rights to Tevez and Mascherano – the potential to influence club and team matters, in violation of Premier League Rule U18.

The panel said that the allegations were 'exceedingly serious' because they amounted to a deliberate breach of Premier League rules. They found that West Ham were responsible 'for dishonesty and deceit'.

Bourne-Arton suggested that Paul Aldridge had lied to Richard Scudamore when the Premier League chief executive had asked how West Ham had secured the players at such low cost, and whether there were any documents that he had not seen. Aldridge explained that other documents existed but none that Scudamore needed to see. However, this was deemed to be untrue because there had been an agreement between West Ham and Joorabchian, who owned the rights of the Argentinean players. The panel declared, 'The chief executive [Aldridge] told Scudamore a direct lie; that there was no documentation in respect of the players that had not been seen.'

Both Aldridge and Brown disagree with this finding. But neither man was asked to speak or to give his side of the story. This being the case, it is questionable whether the 'finding' is anything more than an unsubstantiated allegation.

At the time the players signed, Brown had been in negotiations with Joorabchian to buy the club. West Ham paid Joorabchian £339,000 in agents' fees to sign the players on loan for the season. The panel stated, 'Messrs Brown, Aldridge and Scott Duxbury [then legal director] were anxious to complete the registration of these players by the deadline ... They knew that the only means by which they could acquire them would be by entering into third-party contracts. They were aware that the Premier League, in all probability, would not approve of such contracts. They determined to keep their existence from the Premier League.'

Duxbury, at the time of the hearing, was the deputy chief executive of West Ham. He was found to have misled the Premier League. He was said to have telephoned the League a few days prior to the transfers taking place to enquire if there could be a break clause in the contracts of the players, who were owned by offshore companies. It was said that he was informed that there could be no break and advised of the Premiership rules.

Duxbury believed that he was not obliged to disclose the agreement with Joorabchian and counselled Aldridge to say that all necessary information to register the players had been provided. After it became apparent that the players were going to sign for West Ham, the Premier League asked Duxbury whether a third-party agreement was in place. According to the Premier League, Duxbury had said there wasn't (although he denied that he gave an answer to such a question).

The panel stated, 'Jim Sturman [West Ham QC] submits that all Duxbury is guilty of is an error in judgement. We do not for one moment accept those propositions.'

The ownership of Tevez was divided between two companies – 65 per cent was controlled by Just Sport and 35 per cent by Media Sports Investments. These companies could have chosen to end his four-year contract with West Ham in January in exchange for £2m, and West Ham would not have been able to challenge the sale. But the players were signed on a one-year loan deal, which meant West Ham could insist that they stayed at Upton Park for least one year.

Mascherano had a similar five-year contract. Equal shares in his ownership were held by MSI and Global Soccer Agencies

(GSA), a Gibraltar-registered organisation with offices in Israel. Mascherano could be moved on for £150,000.

West Ham were fined £3m for not providing all the documentation and for being untruthful to the Premier League. They were fined £2.5m for the agreement that allowed for Joorabchian to influence club policy. The panel said that the £5.5m penalty reflected the club's guilty plea (this in spite of the club's claim that they would defend themselves against the allegations), rather than the £8m estimated punishment had the matter proceeded to a hearing. The huge fine was meant to reflect the points deduction that the panel was permitted to impose.

The verdict cleared Magnússon of any wrongdoing, and he believed this opened the door to compensation from the previous regime – Brown, Aldridge, Scott Duxbury and the rest of the West Ham board under Brown's chairmanship. Duxbury remained the executive director responsible for legal affairs at West Ham, who were found to have been 'anxious to complete the registration of the players by the deadline of August 31'.

As a result, Duxbury was said to have been put 'under considerable pressure from his superiors'. But, according to Terry Brown, this was incorrect.

Duxbury, who 'surprised' the panel with his assertion that he was not aware of the content of Rule U18, breached by the transfers, was found to have misled the company secretary of the Football Association Premier League (FAPL) Jane Purdon, in conversations and correspondence leading up to and following the transfer. Duxbury maintained that Purdon did not tell him on the telephone that a deal which involved a third party having the ability to exercise a break clause in a player's contract was an infringement of Rule U18. Purdon said she did. However, in the last analysis, is it more likely that there had been an error in paperwork, a failure to produce one piece of paper, than all the convolution that was implied?

But it was hard to believe that Duxbury, who graduated from Manchester University in 1994 with a law degree and who had worked as assistant solicitor to Maurice Watkins, a Manchester United director, the legal director of the club – responsible for the protection in law of West Ham United, a multi-million-pound concern – did not know about or acquaint himself with Rule U18, particularly given the fact that he was dealing with a highly complex transfer.

But Duxbury claimed that he checked the rules and counselled Aldridge that it was acceptable not to disclose *all* the details of the arrangement that brought the Argentinean pair to Upton Park.

West Ham had said that they believed that the contracts were valid and never suggested anything to the contrary to the inquiry. That was why the club was obliged to admit guilt to a prima facie breach of Rule U18 which prevents a third party from influencing club policies or the performance of players. But it is highly questionable if the deal was much different from any other loan arrangement. The crucial point in terms of the whole outcome was Magnússon's decision to plead guilty to what was a highly defensible position.

In effect, this meant that West Ham were adjudged to have readily agreed to a situation where a third party could sell two players apparently without considering if this would be in the footballing interests of the club. This appeared to suggest that the two players were exempt from any authority within the club as West Ham were unable to sell the players or cancel their contracts. This seemed to translate to the club's influence over the Argentineans being waived. However, what needs to be remembered is that this was not meant to be a permanent situation; this was made obvious at the hearing when Sturman made the point that the contracts for Carlos and Javier were not worth the paper they were written on as they translated to a restraint of trade, unenforceable in British courts. The Argentineans were at Upton Park in what could be understood as a loan deal not unlike many others. Players on loan can be recalled, and not allowed to play for the club to which they are loaned. Isn't that 'influencing' another club?

The gamble of bringing the two players to Upton Park was reliant on the club being taken over by the man from Iran. If that had happened, it could have altered the entire situation, and the Hammers might have had two of South America's best players on their books for the 2007/08 season.

FINE BY ME

The record fine (that was paid into a Premier League charity account), plus legal costs that West Ham were liable for, amounted to a massive financial slap for the club. But the Premiership had thrown the Hammers a lifeline that would have been worth as much as £40m. With £1.7 billion of television-rights money to spend, Premier League officials were able to send its constituent clubs a huge cheque the following season.

The panel did not dock points from West Ham because, at that late stage in the season, it would have meant consigning 'the club to certain relegation' and that the players and fans who were not to blame were being punished as much as, if not more than, West Ham's administration. The panel also acknowledged that West Ham had pleaded guilty; there had been a change in ownership of the club and the finance director had brought the problems to the attention of the FAPL when Liverpool wanted to sign Javier Mascherano in January.

It is important to note Terry Brown approached West Ham and offered to give evidence to the independent commission and that offer was not taken up. He did not offer and was not asked to give evidence to the Premier League. The parties involved did not put any evidence from Brown to the commission, and the commission was not in a position to obtain evidence from Terry. The commission's decision does not identify the evidence upon which it based its conclusions about Brown's involvement in relevant events. Paul Aldridge was in much the same position.

According to Brown, he was not directly involved in the negotiations for the transfer of Javier Mascherano and Carlos Tevez, and he was at all times guided by the advice of those within the club charged with dealing with the transfers and, in particular, by the advice they gave regarding the application of the Premier League rules and any necessary disclosure of documents to the Premier League in accordance with those rules.

Terry Brown has maintained throughout that he did not apply any undue pressure on others to conclude the transactions in the form they were concluded, and did not seek to secure the transfers to safeguard his own personal gain.

In the last analysis, Eggert Magnússon pleaded guilty to a breach of the rules and it was that plea that sealed West Ham's fate. Faced with the possibility of months of ongoing doubt about what club would be relegated from the Premiership, the panel opted to decide against a points deduction; it would not be a 'proportionate punishment' on seven grounds, including West Ham's guilty plea, the fact the club was under new ownership and that they were fighting relegation (as actually docking the Hammers points would have all but confirmed their relegation from the Premiership).

Though the panel's judgment stated that, 'The registration of Tevez can be terminated by the Premier League', in the short term, the club were told that they needed a new agreement with Joorabchian if Tevez was to play any further part in the Irons' fight against relegation, the independent panel finding that Tevez's third-party contract with West Ham was 'unenforceable by law'. It thought that a new deal was possible, given that Joorabchian did that with Liverpool when they signed Mascherano in January, an arrangement that was approved by the Premier League.

On the Friday before the away game at the JJB Stadium (28 April), Magnússon and his advisers met representatives of the offshore companies who had controlled the transfer rights to Tevez, the MSI Group and Just Sports Inc. and managed to secure a loan agreement similar to that drawn up by Global Soccer Agencies and Mystere Services which permitted Mascherano to move to Liverpool in January. By the evening, the new contract was lodged with the Premier League and the Irons were boosted by Premiership clearance for Tevez to play for the rest of the season. Dave 'Wigan Man' Whelan, chairman of the also relegation-threatened Lancastrian club, was livid.

CHAPTER 19
FALL OUT

The range of what we think and do is limited by
what we fail to notice. And, because we fail to notice that we
fail to notice, there is little we can do to change; until we notice
how failing to notice shapes our thoughts and deeds.
R. D. LAING

While the fine imposed on West Ham was the most severe punishment in British football history, there was widespread disbelief in the game that West Ham did not have points deducted. What had initially been seen as a pragmatic interim measure was scuppered by the deal with Joorabchian falling through, by which time the two players at the centre of events were wearing claret and blue shirts and smiling at the cameras.

Even if West Ham had been docked points, it would have been hard to make this stick in court because Tottenham Hotspur, having made illegal payments to their players, successfully appealed against an FA ruling to deduct points from Spurs in 1994. This appeared to be a guiding precedent in West Ham's eventual punishment. Just as Sir Alan Sugar could not be held to account for the actions of a previous administration, nor could Magnússon. But this felt more like a convenient excuse for what happened rather than a reason.

Before West Ham's fine, the £1.5m (increased from £600,000

before the points deduction was rescinded) that Tottenham were ordered to pay in December 1994 had been the biggest ever paid.

However, three directors had remained on the West Ham board after the takeover: Brown, Nick Igoe, finance director, and Scott Duxbury, the legal director when the Argentinean players were signed, remained involved with the club as deputy chief executive.

West Ham had said that they would appeal if they had been punished by a points deduction and thought was given to appealing against the fine, but the risk of the penalty being increased probably discouraged this.

West Ham started to consider taking legal action against Brown on the grounds that he did not act in good faith. Magnússon was reportedly ready to withhold his predecessor's privileges and more than £1m in payments to the former chairman, refusing to pay him the two-year salary of £600,000 agreed during the takeover.

Joorabchian continued to protest his innocence, arguing that the deal with West Ham was no different to any loan arrangement. He cited Alex Song's move to Charlton, Everton's dealings with Tim Howard and Glen Johnson's sojourn at Portsmouth. He argued, 'We used top lawyers, top accountants. We made sure everything was done. We've been involved in many other deals and didn't have a single problem … It wasn't a shady transfer. It wasn't a controversial transfer. It wasn't a strange transfer.'

For me, and not a few other Hammers fans who had bothered to look at the facts of the case and the state of football in general, including Terry Brown, the overriding impression, particularly after the 'Argie Irons' made their way to Liverpool and Old Trafford, was that West Ham were 'not allowed' to have players of that class.

Kia claimed that the 'proof is in the pudding', as the Premier League had not required him to provide the panel with evidence, because it was understood that he had done no wrong.

FALL OUT

Joorabchian admitted no knowledge of claims that the Brown administration at Upton Park had not presented the appropriate documents to the Premier League, but believed that, whatever the situation, it could have been addressed in a way that would have avoided the ensuing furore. This was likely. Given the circumstances, a chairman with more experience of the way English football works might well have nipped the situation in the bud.

The latter point is probably correct. Mascherano went to Anfield with a contract not altogether different from his contract with the Hammers, which was approved by the FAPL. Much the same could be said about Tevez's move to Old Trafford. There is no reason to believe that the same could not have been done by and with West Ham in August 2006.

Tevez continued to play for the Hammers after the allegations were made about West Ham breaking rules. The FAPL had the authority to have terminated his registration without any delays. For logical reasons, that didn't happen. But, again, West Ham and the FAPL could have settled on a situation not unlike that pertaining to Liverpool and Mascherano.

Joorabchian insisted that Tevez's future at West Ham was something that needed to be decided by the player and the club, not MSI. He stated, 'West Ham's board have to decide what their intentions are. Maybe they will think they want Carlos and build around him. Or maybe they will think that, for the money, they can buy four or five great players.'

The Iranian maintained that, despite reports that there had been no negotiations about Tevez with West Ham, the player had 'great affection for the club and the supporters' and that he had been 'very happy' at the Boleyn Ground. But there were rumours of possible deals worth tens of millions of pounds to take Tevez to Inter Milan and Real Madrid for £30m.

At the start of May, Paul Aldridge was threatening to sue the

Premier League following critical comments from the inquiry. But Aldridge was not called to the two-day hearing, a fact that he found baffling and improper given the judgment. He claimed, 'I made myself available [to attend] – but no one's asked me.'

The inquiry found that 'Aldridge ... told a direct lie, namely there was no documentation of whatever kind in respect of these players which the FAPL had not seen.'

Once again, this 'finding' seems rather hollow when neither Aldridge nor Brown was given the opportunity to give evidence.

Aldridge commented, 'Naturally, my sympathies lie with the club that I was chief executive of for 10 years in respect of what seems a very harsh sanction. However, my own personal and professional reputations have been besmirched. The findings accuse me of acting dishonestly and lying. This is hardly natural justice in my view. Until the publication of these findings, my integrity had never been questioned during my career. Accordingly, I have placed the matter in the hands of my lawyer who will be taking the matter further on my behalf.'

A press statement released by the inquiry panel following the hearing concluded, 'Mr Aldridge was not a witness to be called by either party. He has not made a statement.

'We do not know what he may have said ... he has thus not been here to answer for himself, and we can only proceed upon such evidence as we have.'

The kernel of the whole episode was that Tevez and Mascherano scarcely made any impact on the club's results at the start of the season.

GOALS

Before the panel sat, two of Tevez's four goals came in defeats, while he added the second in the 2–0 home win over Middlesbrough.

His most important contribution came in the 2–1 win at

Blackburn where, without his penalty, the Hammers would have drawn. This was the only one of his four strikes (prior to the hearing) that was significant, gaining West Ham an extra two points. At a cost of about £40,000 a week, West Ham had spent £1.3m in wages on Tevez. In terms of goals, he had little effect, and, given that his four goals came from 23 appearances, perhaps West Ham's rivals could have consoled themselves with the thought that Alan Curbishley's team may have been no worse off without Tevez.

On 5 May, Carlos Tevez scored twice and West Ham defeated Bolton Wanderers 3–1 at Upton Park. The result pulled the Hammers out of the bottom three of the Premiership for the first time since December. But no sooner had the last bubbles floated out into the sky above London's Docklands than it was reported that a third of the Premiership's clubs were revving up to go to court and prepare to bankrupt the Hammers if they managed to avoid relegation. This of course made great headlines, but for Terry Brown this was not a probability. Watching events late in the season, it seemed that clubs entered the fray in a full-blooded manner only when it seemed there was a real threat of their own relegation.

Initially principal among the protestors was Wigan chairman Dave Whelan, who, as Curbishley said, 'had his say and then had it again'. Other angry executives from Sheffield United, Fulham and Charlton – and there was said to be at least two others – would join in according to results (Watford were not in the shake-up as their fate had been settled regardless of what happened to the Irons). It was reported that this fluctuating collective swore to take legal action over what they considered to be 'a matter of principle'. However, there appeared to be no avenue open to challenge the panel's ruling. A leading sports lawyer, Gerard Elias, declared in the press, 'They cannot appeal the decision because they weren't a party to it.'

But, as the panel had found that West Ham had misled League officials about player contracts, breaking Rule B13, this seemed to allow any clubs who saw that their interests would be damaged to sue West Ham privately, as they could argue that, by lying to and misleading the League, West Ham, in effect, had lied to rival clubs.

According to Elias, 'A club might have a claim if they could establish that, as a result of West Ham playing players they should not have done, the club was subsequently relegated, and if it could show, as a result of that, that they have lost financially because they are in the Championship.'

If a club were to win an action directly against West Ham, it would have dealt a huge financial blow to the Hammers. Loss of Premiership status for any club could translate to a cost of around £60m.

The Premier League's chief executive, Richard Scudamore, visited the clubs baying for the Irons' blood in an attempt to ease the situation, but he met a furious response. One of the reasons given by the panel for not deducting points – despite finding West Ham guilty of dishonesty and deceit – was that the timing, so late in the season, would have meant 'West Ham would have certainly been relegated'.

Scudamore was repetitively informed by the executives of the clubs concerned that this was 'nonsensical'. Wigan chairman Dave Whelan said, 'There has been a large element of dishonesty here. The Premier League is in a bit of turmoil on rules, regulations and honesty.'

Stuart Benson, a director at Fulham, claimed, 'All the clubs should have their points reinstated [from games wherein Tevez was involved]. Every point lost is worth millions.'

Sheffield United pointed to their 1–0 defeat by West Ham on 25 November, in which Tevez started, as a clear example of the Hammers' unfair advantage. Middlesbrough, who lost 2–0 on 31

March, with Tevez netting the second goal, were another club who might have felt they had directly suffered. West Ham had gained 23 points from games in which Tevez played a part (more than half of their total of 38).

Tevez gained 84.5 per cent of supporter votes to become Hammer of the Year, 17 times more than Bobby Zamora who finished second in the poll, which clearly shows his huge impact in the last part of the season.

Sheffield United's chairman Kevin McCabe fumed, 'We started looking into this as soon as the announcement came … the tribunal did not take into any account the effect of playing those illegal players on the other clubs in the relegation battle. It seems only to have considered a breach of the rules and not the implications. It is also very odd that there was a very clear admission [by Magnússon who wasn't even at the club at the time] that West Ham had told lies … one-third of the Premier League is together; it may have an effect on the League in terms of asking for a review of the decision-making process from the tribunal. That could lead to a different ruling. It seemed obtuse.

'West Ham have admitted that they fielded players illegally. Tevez is a brilliant player and that gives them an advantage.'

However, according to West Ham, the offending part of Tevez's contract had been changed after the offences were discovered. Mascherano, who hardly played for the club, had moved to Liverpool on an acceptable contract. There was also the fact that Liverpool, with the Champions League in mind, on 5 May had seriously impacted on relegation matters by fielding what was more or less a reserve team against Fulham at Craven Cottage (this is against Premier League rules!). The home side's 1–0 victory gave them 39 points and a -20 goal difference. That meant that only Charlton could overtake them if they won both of their remaining games (Spurs at the Valley, Liverpool at Anfield), and Fulham lost their last match against Middlesbrough (a side that had been struggling in the last part of the season). Was anyone going to sue Liverpool? Certainly not Fulham – a club that went strangely silent on matters – looking pretty much safe with one game of the season to play.

When Alan Curbishley kept West Ham up, the press was buzzing with insistence that the club should have been relegated weeks before with a large points deduction. Meanwhile, when Sheffield United's relegation was confirmed, the Blades manager Neil Warnock and his chairman McCabe were vocal but now seemingly alone.

Blame was being fired everywhere. It was the FAPL's fault for not docking West Ham points. Rafa Benitez and Sir Alex Ferguson were made liable for failing to field full-strength teams and referee Rob Styles was also put up for shame. It was everyone's responsibility except Warnock, McCabe and Sheffield United, as Warnock confirmed when he claimed, 'You can blame everyone really, can't you?'

In the last part of their Premiership campaign of 2006/07, West Ham had won seven out of nine games and, although Tevez had been instrumental in that end-of-season run, other players were also involved as were all the other relegated clubs.

When matters were settled, it was remarkable how quickly Whelan went quiet. It was then the turn of Kevin McCabe and his temporary sidekick Sean Bean to threaten to sue more or less everyone, although the Blades during the course of the season had pulled together less points than 17 other Premiership clubs.

McCabe's problem was that the punishment that was given to West Ham was in accordance with Premier League rules under a procedure approved by all Premier League members, including the 'gang of four' (the clubs that had been said to have threatened to band together to try to make sure that the Hammers were deducted points).

FALL OUT

Sheffield United's second difficulty in terms of bunking out of relegation was that, while there has been a history of clubs being deducted points, there existed no directly correlating precedent for a points deduction as a punishment for West Ham's offence and no evidence that the Blades or the Latics would have been treated any differently if they had been guilty of a similar offence.

In fact, the club that was most damaged by the chaos that followed the signing of the Argentineans were the East Londoners themselves, who for the initial seven months of the season buckled into an incompetent, lethargic shambles. The team that got to the FA Cup Final in 2006, that had finished on the verge of a place in Europe (as of right) the previous season, a side that were tipped to be hitting the top slots of the table, had certainly been spooked by something (and that wasn't just Sheffield United).

Tevez and Javier Mascherano's arrival at Upton Park coincided with West Ham's nine-game run without a win. The newcomers were said to have negatively affected player morale and were widely blamed for the Hammers' troubles. West Ham might not have been involved in the relegation scrap if the Argentineans hadn't happened along; as such, it is almost unbelievable to see Tevez as single-handedly keeping the Hammers up.

However, Apache, with whom the Irons fans fell in love for his bare-chested dives into their arms, scored the only goal in West Ham's final game of the season, defeating the Premiership Champions Manchester United at Old Trafford. That win meant that West Ham finished the season three points above the Blades, who were relegated in 18th position. Had West Ham finished the season level on points with Sheffield United, the Hammers would have gone down because of inferior goal difference.

West Ham's players and management turned things around

in the last few weeks of the season and this says much for everyone concerned, chiefly Alan Curbishley, the players and fans, who decided to get up and fight unlike their new chairman who said he would fight but then gave in – throwing his hands up to plead guilty for an offence that had allegedly been committed when he didn't even have anything to do with the club. As such, to portray the Hammers' 'great escape' as a product of an unfair advantage gained from contractual irregularities amounts at best to sporting sour grapes of astronomical proportions.

Any further penalty handed out to West Ham United as a result of legal action from Sheffield United or even the mooted exclusion from the 2007/08 FA Cup, as the Hammers had fielded an ineligible player in the third round in 2007, would have been no less than a punishment of the current West Ham management, players and supporters for what were seen as the sins of the Brown and Pardew era.

A Premier League arbitration panel met on 18 June to hear Sheffield United's claim against the failure to dock points from West Ham. This came to nothing and, while still seeking redress via the European courts, the Blades and McCabe have markedly failed to dominate the Championship.

Following his capitulation, the new West Ham chairman, soon after paying the huge fine imposed on his club, declared, 'Terry Brown is not welcome at Upton Park at the moment, although I have nothing personally against either him or Kia Joorabchian.'

But Scott Duxbury is now a chief executive at the club, while Nick Igoe continues in his role as finance director.

In mid-September 2007, following a boardroom reshuffle a couple of days earlier, Magnússon gave an interview to the Icelandic newspaper *Morgunblaðið*, entitled 'I needed time to breathe – Eggert Magnússon quits as managing director but remains chairman'.

He said he 'just needed time to breathe. A lot has been going on and taking up my time but now I can focus on bringing West Ham into the future.'

He told how Duxbury would no longer have responsibility for day-to-day running of the club, but said, 'There is no drama in this. We are strengthening the foundation of the club.'

Magnússon claimed that the changes made were logical and said that he would continue in his role as chairman. He confessed that doing two jobs at the same time resulted in having to deal with heavy pressure. He told how he hadn't planned on being a managing director and chairman, but had been obliged to when Aldridge was dismissed, a man who had been in post for decade. He went on, 'I'm first and foremost a football fan and I will follow the team wherever it goes despite these changes.'

According to Magnússon, the future of West Ham had not been fully planned: 'We are set to relocate to a new ground … the new West Ham Stadium will fare well … and would be part of a commercial and housing area.'

This feels very much like a retreat. It may well be that Magnússon is feeling how he looks during West Ham games, mostly very tense.

CHAPTER 20
DRAWING BACK THE VEIL

Slander cannot destroy an honest man –
when the flood recedes the rock is there.
CHINESE PROVERB

It feels like I'm stating the obvious as I write that there has been a deal of confusion about the Argentinean players that came to West Ham what feels like quite a long time ago. But looking at what evidence is available it is hard not to conclude that their contracts were and are still owned by Kia Joorabchian.

If this is the case, it is information that the Premier League must have, although they do not seem inclined to volunteer it. It would also be understood by West Ham; however, it is something the club might not be able to readily acknowledge. This would also not constitute news to Manchester United or Liverpool, although they may, perhaps understandably, not protest the fact.

The problems started in terms of Tevez and Mascherano when an attempt was made to implement the rules; at that point something akin to chaos ensued.

It seems difficult to see how the careers of Carlos and Javier are not influenced by a third party, but, in England, they may not be (and may never have been) isolated cases. It has been alleged that, for years, the Premier League has had the role of creating conduits between registration and ownership.

The more I look at the issue of third-party ownership, the more it seems that it has quite an assortment of incarnations. However, according to Martin Samuel (*News of the World*, 8 July 2007), the cash for the majority of players currently plying their trade at Leeds United can be traced back to City investors. Those largely nameless but doubtless colourful characters will have to be 'recompensed' on the sale of their 'investment'.

If a process works, it is not long before everyone adopts it in one way or another. Sir Alex Ferguson has said that he did not sign Tevez in 2005/06 as he was uncertain about the conditions the transfer might carry with it. But, of course, Sir Alex managed to get over his doubts, seemingly regardless of the legal battles that continued to rage as Carlos pulled on the red jersey. So confident was the Old Trafford manager that he went to the extraordinary lengths of sending representatives to Venezuela where Carlos was playing for his country in the Copa America to make sure Tevez would be conscripted to the cause of United. But of course, all dealings, on that occasion, were 'watertight'.

However, there was not a word uttered about a transfer fee for arguably one of the finest strikers on the face of the planet, who would rake in something like £4m per annum. At the same time, he was not a permanent signing. In fact, it is quite unclear what happens to Carlos after a couple of years appearing on the stage of the Theatre of Dreams.

All this begs the question: Does Tevez continue to have contractual forces exerted on him by Joorabchian? If not, why not? It appears that no one has 'bought' Carlos's contract outright.

What seems certain is that Manchester United have Tevez's registration for 2007/08, but so did West Ham. However, this does not negate Kia's stake in the player.

Liverpool's arrangements in respect of Javier Mascherano throw up the same issues and unavoidable conclusions. The evidence we have suggests that Javier is a Liverpool player by way of a kind of fixed-term loan deal and as such the contract used to take him to Anfield is seen to conform to the regulations of the Premier League. But Mascherano's connections prior to his move to Liverpool continue to exist and presumably have the potential to impact on his future career.

The above situations represent part of the facts of life for modern football and there is nothing illegal about them. Manchester United seemed to be Joorabchian's 'club of first choice' in terms of leasing his players, but for reasons that might be guessed at – not least a reluctance to take on a couple of unproven (in the Premier League) South Americans (a mistake United have made before) – Sir Alex stood off and poor old West Ham became the proving ground. But, if the right deal came along, the 'goods' could be shipped out and it was this practice that was labelled as breaking Rule U18.

With Mascherano and Tevez looking set to stay with their 'big' clubs, the problems associated with moving on do not appear to be an issue for the time being. However, this does not mean that the third-party owners will just let the clubs and players do 'their own thing'. Put starkly, these players seem to be on fixed loans that carry an option to buy when their loan period expires. It is at the point of expiry that a new auction begins (and this will be dictated by the success or otherwise of the players).

If everything is as it seems, Tevez does not belong outright to Manchester United in the same way as he was never the property of West Ham. He did not sign on loan from Corinthians or West Ham; he is loaned to Manchester United by an agency whose business it is to purchase the rights to South American players and trade against these rights throughout Europe.

BROWN OUT

At the moment, English football, principally by way of its focus on West Ham, seems to be in denial about the situation that the game abhors third-party agreements. But this is just the tip of the proverbial iceberg and, although potential examples of this practice could be produced, it takes us nowhere by pointing to possible or actual incidents because, by way of Javier and Carlos, it seems as plain as the big red nose on football's face.

SEATS, ETC.

Terry Brown's service contract included seats in the directors' box for life. However, Eggert Magnússon chose to terminate that contract in connection with the signings of Tevez and Mascherano, although throughout Terry relied on the advice of the company's managing director, legal director (who is still on the West Ham board) and four other experienced lawyers as well as the advice and approval of his board of directors.

According to Brown, Magnússon refused to discuss the Premier League's action against the club with him or Aldridge and would not allow either of them to appear before the Premier League commission to help defend the club's position. But press coverage seems to have blamed Brown for the problems arising from Tevez and Mascherano coming to Upton Park and this has not been helped by statements emanating from the club.

Magnússon, having said that West Ham would defend their position, changed the plea to guilty of both the charge of not acting in the 'utmost good faith' and the charge of breaching Rule U18 at the last minute, although there seemed to be an opportunity to challenge this charge. This being the case, it might be understood that West Ham were not 'found guilty' (as has been reported seemingly on a blanket basis) because the club *pleaded* guilty and as such any 'judgment' became superfluous.

During the summer of 2007, clubs would not approve the banning of so-called 'third-party ownership' at their AGM, but introduced a rule that required the future submission of the paper that West Ham had not submitted at registration. This indicates the strength of West Ham's case and yet the club simply pleaded guilty to both charges, which stands in contrast to the approach of Liverpool and Manchester United, both of whom refused to accept the League's arguments, and eventually signed Tevez and Mascherano on terms that, for the interested observer, were hard to differentiate from those West Ham had deployed.

Following Paul Aldridge's threat of legal action, the Premier League released a statement confirming that Aldridge had tried to address the commission (as did Brown), but had been refused permission to do so. At the time of writing, Aldridge is seeking redress from Mr Bourne-Arton QC (chairman of the commission) through the Bar Council.

Brown had a trouble-free career as an accountant and businessman and, shortly before the takeover, West Ham were one of the few clubs to receive a clean bill of health from Lord Stevens after his investigation into the financial dealings in football. Terry's conduct during his 14 years as chairman of West Ham, despite any mistakes he might be accused of making, has been beyond reproach.

Brown is a rich man in his own right, and has been so since his late twenties. He has never needed West Ham as a financial entity. The profit he made from his sale of shares after many years would probably have been bettered if he had invested the time, effort and money he sank into West Ham elsewhere. The idea that he was motivated by money to stay on (or otherwise) is ridiculous when taken in the context of his business life. In reality, although he was always focused on the ambition of making West Ham a viable financial concern, he had hoped to continue to be involved with the club he loves and has spent a lifetime supporting in one way or another. Along with Aldridge, it is hard to see how this well of experience could be spurned so needlessly. However, according to Terry, Magnússon made it clear to both him and Aldridge that they had no future at West Ham and never asked for advice. Just from a business perspective, where all information is deemed desirable, this makes no logical sense.

Brown and Aldridge, with their combined decades of experience of the Hammers, might have saved West Ham substantial amounts of money in transfer fees and salaries had their expertise and contacts been used by the new board.

Despite all that has happened, all the needless hatred and disproportionate abuse he has suffered, Brown remains a huge supporter of West Ham United.

According to the accountants Deloitte & Touche, West Ham are the 19th largest club in the world based on turnover. In their *Football Money League Report* (2005/06), the Hammers were lodged between the mighty Glasgow Rangers and the legendary 'Eagles of Lisbon' Benfica. Among English clubs, West Ham had the eighth biggest turnover:

1 Man United
2 Chelsea
3 Arsenal
4 Liverpool
5 Newcastle
6 Tottenham
7 Man City
8 West Ham

This is a remarkable achievement for a team not playing in Europe and recently subject to relegation. If European competition could be coupled with the probability of moving to a new modern stadium with a much improved capacity, West

Ham United have the potential to push on to even greater heights and can be seen to be an extremely valuable 'trophy asset'. In the middle of Europe's largest regeneration area, with sell-out gates for every match and one million dedicated supporters throughout the south-east of England and fan clubs across the world, the Hammers have blue-chip power in football. That is the legacy of Terry Brown. I think he should have his seats.

CONCLUSION

A dream you dream alone is only a dream.
A dream you dream together is reality.
JOHN LENNON

I am not a journalist. I have written this book as a lifelong fan of West Ham United. I have tried to do this in an authentic way by explaining what I think and how I see things. This has not been for ego's sake, but to simply provide a view of a supporter, a perspective that is more and more forgotten in today's game. I know Terry Brown has also experienced things from my side, but I have not been where he has in terms of running the club, and I don't think I would want to be. It is easy to criticise but much harder to respond to that criticism. I am also aware of that. But this book has been a search for truth and very much to Terry's credit he has helped me in this cause.

Terry Brown, a man of striking professional intelligence and personal affability, has had a chequered and colourful career at West Ham; Upton Park has not been a dull place during his watch. Brown has presided over a whole ocean of sentiments and thus made watching the Hammers a life-enhancing activity. But he is a man that seems to be unable to help making things happen. He has been in command during a time of great change wherein West Ham stood on the cusp of a wave from which they could have fallen into the depths of mediocrity or begun a rise to a new level of excellence. But Brown is also a man suited for such a situation. In his life, he has journeyed far on a personal level.

Despite the assertion that the club wouldn't sell its crown jewels, one by one the likes of Ferdinand, Lampard, Defoe, Cole and Carrick left Upton Park under Brown's stewardship, making over £45m profit from their sales between 2000 and 2004. With the exception of Defoe, who was initially pinched from Charlton, these players were nurtured from the start of their football lives by the club, all went on to represent England at international level and all have reached the potential that was obvious in them from an early age.

Defoe is rumoured to have caught the interest of Sir Alex Ferguson, and if the move goes ahead then it would mean all five ex-Hammers would be plying their trade at Chelsea and Manchester United – the top two clubs in the country and arguably Europe and the world.

While there are still those among the Hammers supporters who hanker after the return of Harry Redknapp, and more who still view the man as the epitome of what the Irons are about, few fans will forgive Brown for the loss of so many world-class players. However, the club is a Premiership outfit and Upton Park is a ground fit for that status. Even after the initial modernisation of the Boleyn Ground, the restricted capacity – just over 26,000 following the £11.5m construction of the 7,600-seat Bobby Moore Stand (opened in February 1994 to replace the South Bank) and 5,900-seat Centenary Stand (opened in January 1995 to replace the North Bank), plus the installation of seats in the lower East Stand in the summer of 1994 – meant that Brown had to compete against the likes of Manchester United, Arsenal,

CONCLUSION

Liverpool, Newcastle United and Chelsea under a handicap almost from the word go.

But during Brown's time West Ham twice pushed themselves into European competition and completed a further close to £40m development that produced a near-40,000-capacity stadium. While this isn't rip-roaring success, it certainly doesn't constitute failure, especially given the disadvantage of what seemed like endless years of Harry Redknapp.

Taking a step back, one could also make the case that during Brown's tenure as a board member there has been a general improvement in the standard of play. While West Ham's 2006/07 season was poor, the club's performance over the first six years of the 21st century has produced some of the best results for many years. Terry has told of his pride in the way West Ham regenerated the Academy which had been more or less in stasis at the time of his appointment as chairman.

Other milestones were the purchase of the Boleyn Ground's freehold (which made way for the ongoing development of Upton Park) and the redevelopment of the training ground. With the exception of just a few seasons, during Brown's time as chairman, West Ham have played in the top flight of world club football and that has made everything else possible.

However, Brown has always understood that the two relegations that took place during his time as a board member cast shadows of anxiety that have not helped the club's development. He felt that these downturns also did much to divert the public perception away from the progress West Ham have made over the years. In retrospect, his major mistake, losing Billy Bonds in favour of Harry Redknapp, was costly. His management style, which allowed people to get on with the jobs they were employed to do, was often abused. But on the whole it probably had as many advantages as disadvantages. In truth, in modern football, it is unlikely that any real alternatives to this stance are possible; running a Premiership club is not a one-man-band option.

It has been said that Brown and several other board members have been overpaid, particularly following the team's slides out of the Premiership and the resultant financial losses. He has pointed out that, when the club finished seventh in the Premier League, there were at least nine football administrators elsewhere earning more than him and that many of those also benefited from share-option agreements at their clubs. Unlike many other Premier League clubs, West Ham had not had a tradition of paying dividends while in the Premier League. Aston Villa, a similar club to West Ham in financial terms (while both teams were in the Premier League), paid dividends of around £1m per annum, but the West Ham board, some of whom were the major shareholders, chose not to pay dividends. Brown has argued that supporters who complain about the remuneration of board members need to bear that in mind, and the fact that, following relegation in 2003, salaries were halved. He also expressed the view that fans are perhaps not as conscious as they might be that everyone in football tends to be very well paid.

For Brown, the most important aspect of his chairmanship is the growth in the attendance at home games. In West Ham's best ever League campaign, 1985/86, the home gates average for the season at that time was 21,179. Brown has pointed out that the Irons played in the First Division the season before he was appointed chairman and the average gate was 21,342. His first home game as chairman was against Charlton Athletic at Upton Park; the match produced what was considered a reasonable gate of 17,000 (as Charlton were ground-sharing with West Ham at that time). Terry's second home game as chairman, on 5 September 1992, saw Watford come to the Boleyn Ground. The match attracted 11,921. One of West Ham's next home games, against Sunderland, pulled in 10,000. In the winter of 2004, after being relegated, West Ham had home gates of 35,000 (an increase of almost 70 per cent over the 1985/86 season) including the 92 executive boxes and first-class executive facilities, for matches against Wigan Athletic and Ipswich Town.

These figures are impressive, but they do not really provide a fair comparison. When Brown first rose to the chairmanship, West Ham were suffering in the aftermath of the bond scheme in a period – before the Premiership – when football was comparatively in the doldrums. It must also be remembered that, in the second half of Brown's time as chairman, Britain, and East London/West Essex in particular, was riding on an economic high, with the UK generating the fourth largest economy in the world. Almost full employment, low interest rates and low inflation meant that, for many, things had never been better. At the start of his time at the helm, the country was suffering in a relative slump, conditioned by high unemployment, interest rates and inflation.

But Brown has presided over the improvement of the amenities provided to supporters, online facilities and enhanced ticket-sales services. Open days have taken place during school holidays for young supporters. West Ham in the Community and the Learning Zone have also played their parts in developing the Hammers' fan base. This said, most other clubs of West Ham's status have developed in a similar way.

Terry has confessed that his biggest disappointment as chairman, apart from the obvious issues surrounding relegation, was the way West Ham bought and sold so many players in the transfer market and gradually allowed player salaries to escalate to such a level that, when the time came when the club did need to urgently strengthen the squad, it was a financial impossibility. Most of this recklessness went on under the management of Harry Redknapp. It still amazes me that every time a manager has come under scrutiny in the last few years – Glenn Roeder,

BROWN OUT

Alan Pardew and Alan Curbishley – an appreciable number of fans have called for the return of Harry. H achieved little during his time as a player and a manager at Upton Park, but he did generate a long list of poor buys, some of which were reputed to have been guided by agent reports alone.

Brown once told Harry, 'I'm an accountant and I'm very suspicious of everyone in football.'

For Terry, there is no friendship among and between football executives, and, as was shown towards the end of the 2006/07 season, all are fierce rivals.

But Brown was a long-time admirer of Richard Murray, his counterpart at Charlton Athletic, and Rupert Lowe, who up to July 2006 was the chairman at Southampton. He also had high regard for the chairman of Ipswich Town, David Sheepshanks, who was particularly helpful advising Brown following relegation in 2003.

One of the constant criticisms levelled by Hammers fans is that Brown and his fellow board members failed to invest their own money in the club. But Terry has pointed out that very few directors invest their own money in their clubs, and when they do there are often financial reasons beyond mere altruism. For example, among other reasons, some large investments in football clubs have attracted substantial tax benefits for the investor. According to Brown, in his experience, the chairmen who made serious investments in their clubs purely from an emotional point of view can be counted in single figures and it has hardly ever paid off in terms of finance or results. But the money required now to make a serious impact in the Premier League is simply beyond the scope of most businesspeople.

Throughout Brown's time as chairman of West Ham, there was a sustained stream of criticism from fans, but he has claimed that neither he nor his wife Jean was affected by this. Jean, having grown up with the club, working in the docks and for the

270

CONCLUSION

Football Association, as well as handling the more difficult complaints about Brown's holiday villages, was acclimatised to such responses, while Terry accepted it as an occupational hazard of a football chairman's life.

For Brown, too much power has shifted the way of the players and agents but he believes that this was probably inevitable. However, the one issue, above all others, that Terry would like to see tackled in football for the long-term good of the game is, as Sepp Blatter said, the damaging effects of the Bosman ruling which means that clubs such as West Ham struggle to retain outstanding young players, some of whom have taken 10 years to develop.

In the West Ham programme of Saturday, 25 November 2006, saying his farewell to the Hammers, Brown wrote, 'We concentrated on developing the ground at Upton Park, then building the club. I accept I made some mistakes and was intensely disliked by fans at the end, but I tried to do my duty, and leave the club in good hands.'

In that same programme, he said that he wanted to better his record of watching the Irons play by not missing a single match over the coming 16 years, although that would prove difficult as he was quickly made very aware that he was no longer welcome at Upton Park so soon after the damaging experience of West Ham's £5.5m fine at the end of the 2006/07 season. Sadly, he was probably right about the sentiments of the Hammers supporters. Brown has become the scapegoat for most of West Ham's ills, although, as I think this book has shown, this is not wholly justified. Indeed, it is likely that history will view Terry much more kindly than might be assumed from current opinion. Essentially a modest man, he has kept his many generosities mostly to himself. There are those who profess to hate Brown who have little idea of what he is like as a person, merely following red-top headlines to reach their conclusions. Such, sadly, is life.

BROWN OUT

Brown's departure from Upton Park marked the moment when West Ham United, one of the last major clubs in Europe to remain in the control of its founding families, succumbed to the expedience of modern football finance.

On 6 May 2007, Duncan Revie, the businessman son of legendary and infamous Leeds United boss Don Revie, was reported to be trying to raise £40m in the hope of buying the Peacocks. Brown was said to be among the other interested parties.

As a chairman, Brown matched his peers and bettered many, and, while West Ham fans cannot love such a figure, in his realm he commanded respect and admiration. You can be sure there will not be another Terry Brown. His time has passed. But he bridged the gap between what was and what is, and this alone makes him a figure of social and historical interest in our game.

Terry loved – and I would want him to continue to love – football as a game and he cared – and I hope continues to care – about West Ham. However, he was what he was. First and foremost, driven by classical and pragmatic financial theory, Brown was a formidable foe – for the fans that chose to run up against him, managers, players and in particular other chairmen. His mistakes were relatively few in number given the length of his reign, but he matched each one with at times a frisson of genius, but usually his actions were tinged with the flair associated with a master of his craft. His last performance was perhaps his best.

The Hammers could have ended up in the hands of the lowest common denominator in football finance, a fate that would have led to utter oblivion. As it is, we may not have Albert Schweitzer at the head of the boardroom table, and the future might be devoted to little more than a kind of growth that will threaten to extinguish what remains of the soul of West Ham (that resides in the club's support, nowhere else), but we can deal with this, if we can hold to that spirit which is 'us'. I for one think we can. Why? Because we are good enough to.

CONCLUSION

In a time before there was a West Ham, when East London ended just west of Aldgate, the people that lived in the area from where the Hammers have traditionally drawn their support by a Thames whose shores spread far beyond the banks that now restrict it had no collective name. But a few decades after William built his tower alongside London's main highway, that flowing, rushing, tidal road whereon Rome founded a city, the tiny groups that made a living downstream, fanning out from the prehistoric stronghold of Uphall Camp (Apollo's Camp) in Barking, became known, male and female, as accomplished estuary sailors and fisher folk, whose petite daughters bore a hardy beauty while their sons were tough and belligerent little warriors. Collectively, they were referred to as 'The water people, North of the River, East of the Tower'.

In the early 1880s, Rudyard Kipling mentions the ancient lands east of London in his first novel *The Light That Failed* and in the poem 'The River's Tale'; he writes of the area where Terry Brown was born: 'And Norseman and Negro and Gaul and Greek Drank with the Britons in Barking Creek'.

This vision celebrates a history that has made the area a rich and vibrant genetic rainbow for its population. The people of the world have met and still meet, meld and merge in East London. That has been our lucky heritage, our pride and our honour. Nothing has hit us that we have not overcome; no challenge has been too much. People are everything: perennial, wonderful and infinitely beautiful in their wisdom and inner power. West Ham is people, water people. North of the River, East of the Tower.

TERRY'S TIMELINE

1982 – Terry Brown becomes executive club member at Upton Park

January 1983 – West Ham reach League Cup quarter-final

February 1987 – West Ham reach League Cup quarter-final

March 1989 – West Ham reach League Cup semi-final

May 1989 – West Ham relegated

Monday, 5 June 1989 – John Lyall, West Ham manager, sacked

July 1989 – Lou Macari becomes West Ham manager

February 1990 – Lou Macari resigns as West Ham manager. Billy Bonds takes over

March 1990 – West Ham reach League Cup semi-final

May 1990 – West Ham finish seventh in Barclays Second Division

November 1990 – Terry Brown and Peter Storrie join the West Ham board

April 1991 – West Ham reach FA Cup semi-final

May 1991 – West Ham finish runners-up in Barclays Second Division and are promoted to Division One

September 1991 – Peter Storrie becomes managing director of West Ham

November 1991 – West Ham announce plans to initiate a bond scheme

May 1992 – West Ham finish bottom of Barclays First Division and are relegated. Terry Brown becomes West Ham chairman. Harry Redknapp made assistant manager

May 1993 – West Ham Barclays League Division One Champions and promoted to the Premier League

August 1994 – Billy Bonds leaves West Ham after turning down Terry Brown's offer of a director of football role. Harry Redknapp becomes West Ham manager

1996 – Terry Brown becomes the full-time paid executive chairman of West Ham

January 1998 – West Ham reach League Cup quarter-final

October 1998 – The Professional Footballers' Association demand that West Ham make John Hartson's punishment for kicking Eyal Berkovic in the head at the Hammers' Chadwell Heath training ground public

December 1998 – Neil Ruddock and midfielder Trevor Sinclair appear at Havering Magistrates Court in Romford. Ruddock is charged under the Public Order Act with affray having allegedly thrown a glass bottle at a Mini. Sinclair is charged with criminal damage to the car

August 1999 – West Ham win Intertoto Cup and qualify for the UEFA Cup

December 1999 – West Ham win League Cup quarter-final tie, but forced to replay having fielded an ineligible player

January 2000 – West Ham are defeated in League Cup quarter-final replay

May 2001 – Harry Redknapp sacked as West Ham manager. Glenn Roeder takes his place

June 2001 – Glenn Roeder becomes manager of West Ham

February 2002 – Glenn Roeder given a three-year contract

April 2003 – Glenn Roeder suffers from a brain tumour.
Trevor Brooking stands in as manager

May 2003 – West Ham relegated to Nationwide League
Division One

July 2003 – Glenn Roeder returns to work

August 2003 – 'Brown out' campaign. Glenn Roeder sacked.
Trevor Brooking stands in as manager

October 2003 – Alan Pardew becomes West Ham manager

8 December 2003 – WHISTLE bring their campaign to oust
Terry Brown from the board to the club's AGM

April 2004 – WHISTLE publish a dossier raising concerns
about Terry Brown's financial management of West Ham

6 May 2004 – West Ham threaten to sue WHISTLE that
results in a public apology by WHISTLE

May 2004 – West Ham reveal that, for the year ending May
2004, the club made pre-tax profits of £11.8m; the previous
year there had been a deficit of £5.3m

May 2005 – West Ham win Coca-Cola Championship play-off
final and promoted to the Premiership

October 2005 – Terry Brown re-elected

May 2006 – West Ham lose FA Cup Final but qualify for
UEFA Cup place

July 2006 – It is announced that West Ham winger Shaun
Newton has been banned for seven months by the Football
Association after testing positive for cocaine

31 August 2006 – West Ham United pull off what is seen as a
transfer coup by signing Javier Mascherano and Carlos Tevez

1 September 2006 – West Ham admit to be in 'exploratory
discussions' about a potential takeover. Kia Joorabchian, who
crafted the transfer of the Argentinean players, is involved

4 September 2006 – West Ham deny they are contractually
obliged to play Tevez and Mascherano in every game

10 September 2006 – West Ham draw 1–1 with Aston Villa,
Tevez making his debut off the bench

22 September 2006 – Eli Papouchado is reportedly interested
in investing with Joorabchian

26 September 2006 – West Ham manager Alan Pardew says
talk of a takeover may be having an adverse effect on the team

October 2006 – Anton Ferdinand charged with assault and
violent disorder following an alleged brawl outside a London
nightclub

21 November 2006 – West Ham accept £85m takeover bid by
Eggert Magnússon

1 December 2006 – Paul Aldridge stands down as chief
executive

3 December 2006 – Mascherano makes his final appearance
for West Ham in 2–0 defeat by Everton

11 December 2006 – West Ham manager Alan Pardew is sacked

13 December 2006 – Alan Curbishley becomes manager of
West Ham

31 January 2007 – Mascherano signs for Liverpool

February 2007 – Culture of gambling exposed at Upton Park.
Anton Ferdinand admits to lying about visiting his sick
grandmother in the Isle of Wight in January and confesses he
had been celebrating his 22nd birthday at the Knock Knock
Club in South Carolina, USA

20 February 2007 – Mascherano is cleared to play for
Liverpool as the FA Premier League accepts his registration

24 February 2007 – Mascherano makes debut for Liverpool v
Sheffield United. The Blades are beaten

28 February 2007 – Terry Brown resigns as a non-executive
director of West Ham

2 March 2007 – West Ham are charged by the Premier League
for breaching its rules in relation to the signings of Tevez and
Mascherano

TERRY'S TIMELINE

4 March 2007 – Tevez scores first goal for West Ham in 4–3 defeat by Tottenham Hotspur. Nigel Reo-Coker and Shaun Newton accuse West Ham fans of racist abuse

4 April 2007 – A three-man panel is appointed to investigate the signings of Tevez and Mascherano

26 April 2007 – The hearing into the transfer of Tevez and Mascherano starts

27 April 2007 – West Ham fined £5.5m. A points deduction is ruled out after the club pleads guilty. Magnússon considers suing Brown and Aldridge and by implication the rest of the board who served with them

18 June 2007 – Sheffield United unsuccessfully appeal against West Ham's punishment

BIBLIOGRAPHY

Belton, B. (1997) *Bubbles, Hammers and Dreams*, Derby: Breedon Books

Belton, B. (1998) *The First and Last Englishmen*, Derby: Breedon Books

Belton, B. (1999) *Days of Iron*, Derby: Breedon Books

Belton, B. (2002) *When West Ham Went to the Dogs*, Derby: Breedon Books

Belton, B. (2003a) *Founded on Iron*, Gloucestershire: Tempus

Belton, B. (2003b) *Johnnie the One: The John Charles Story*, Gloucestershire: Tempus

Belton, B. (2004) *Burn Johnny Byrne – Football Inferno*, Derby: Breedon Books

Belton, B. (2005) *The Men of 64: West Ham and Preston North End in the FA Cup*, Gloucestershire: Tempus

Belton, B. (2006a) *Black Hammers*, London: Pennant Books Ltd

Belton, B. (2006b) *West Ham United Miscellany*, London: Pennant Books Ltd

Belton, B. (2006c) *The Lads of '23: Bolton Wanderers, West Ham United and the 1923 FA Cup Final*, Nottingham: Soccerdata

Belton, B. (2007a) *War Hammers*, Gloucestershire: Tempus

Belton, B. (2007b) *Black Routes: Legacy of African Diaspora*, London: Hansib Publishing

Belton, B. (2008) *East End Heroes, Stateside Kings*, London: John Blake

Blows, K. and Hogg, T. (2000) *West Ham. The Essential History*, Swindon: Headline

Bower, T. (2007) *Broken Dreams*, London, Sydney, New York, Toronto: Pocket Books

Bragg, B. (2007) *The Progressive Patriot. A Search for Belonging*, London: Bantam Press

Fenton, T. (1960) *At Home with the Hammers*, London: Nicholas Kaye

Greenwood, R. (1984) *Yours Sincerely Ron Greenwood*, St Agnes: Willow Books

Groves, R. (1948) *West Ham United*, London: Cassel & Co.

Helliar, J. and Leatherdale, C. (2005) *West Ham United, The Elite Era*, 2nd ed., Essex: Desert Island

Hogg, T (2005) *West Ham United Who's Who*, London: Independent UK Sports Publications

Hogg, T. and McDonald, T. (1995) *1895–1995 Hammers 100 Years of Football*, London: Independent UK Sports Publications

BIBLIOGRAPHY

Hutchenson, J. (1982)
The Football Industry, Glasgow:
R. Drew

Irving, D. (1968) *The West
Ham United Football Book*,
London: Stanley Paul

Irving, D. (1969) *The West
Ham United Football Book
No. 2*, London: Stanley Paul

Korr, C. (1986) *West Ham
United*, London: Duckworth

Lyall, J. (1989)
Just Like My Dreams,
Harmondsworth: Penguin

Moynihan, J. (1984)
The West Ham Story, London:
Arthur Baker Ltd.

Northcutt, J. and Shoesmith,
R. (1993) *West Ham United.
A Complete Record*, Derby:
Breedon Books.

Northcutt, J. and Shoesmith,
R. (1994) *West Ham United.
An Illustrated History*, Derby:
Breedon Books

Oliver, G. (1995) *World Soccer*,
2nd ed., Bath: Guinness

Redknapp, H. with
McGovern, D. (1998) *Arry*,
London: CollinsWillow

Ward, A. (1999)
West Ham United 1895–1999,
London: Octopus

283

BROWN OUT

Journals, Newspapers, Magazines, Websites

East London Advertiser
Ex-Magazine
Express
Guardian
Independent
Independent on Sunday
Mail
Mail On Sunday
Metro
Mirror
Newham Recorder
News Of The World
Observer
Soccer History
Star
Stratford Express
Sun
Sunday Express
Sunday Mirror
Sunday People
Sunday Telegraph
Sunday Times
Telegraph
Times

http://www.eufootball.biz/Clubs/201006-Politics-entering-West-Ham-takeover.html